THE BEGINNINGS OF
MODERN COLONIZATION

THE BEGINNINGS OF MODERN COLONIZATION

Eleven Essays with an Introduction

CHARLES VERLINDEN

Professor in the University of Ghent
Director of the Belgian Academy, Rome

Translated by
YVONNE FRECCERO

CORNELL UNIVERSITY PRESS

ITHACA AND LONDON

International Standard Book Number 0-8014-0588-2
Library of Congress Catalog Card Number 78-124727

PRINTED IN THE UNITED STATES OF AMERICA
BY VAIL-BALLOU PRESS, INC.

Preface

This book relates to a vast new field of research: the transition from medieval colonization to the colonization of modern times, the importance of which for the understanding of some of the more permanent characteristics of Atlantic civilization has been emphasized in the introduction and in the first section. I express my desire that it may help to stimulate research in this direction. (I provided a sketch for colonial America as a whole in my article "Modernità e medioevalismo nell' economia e nella società coloniale Americana," Università di Napoli, Instituto di Storia Economica e Sociale, *Annali*, IV [1965], 1–60.)

I am grateful to Cornell University Press for providing me with the opportunity of making accessible in English this series of articles already published in various languages other than English and in scientific reviews which are sometimes difficult to find outside the countries in which they are published.

C. VERLINDEN

Rome
October 1970

Contents

Introduction

This book is a collection of historical essays on the beginnings of "modern" colonization by European man. It does not deal with colonies that existed during Antiquity or during the period generally called contemporary by Western historians, which, so far as America is concerned, begins with the independence of the United States, and in Europe with the French Revolution. Between the end of Antiquity and the beginnings of the contemporary epoch there extends a long period of thirteen centuries which is generally divided into ten medieval centuries (fifth to fifteenth) and three "modern" centuries (sixteenth to eighteenth). During this long stretch of time colonization evolved, without interruption and with a remarkable continuity, in a pattern that is steady and easily discernible, provided one keeps to the most general characteristics of this social and economic phenomenon.

What in fact is the original meaning of "colonization"? The word derives from the Latin *colere* meaning "to cultivate," "to put to use," "to make of value." Therefore it is not surprising that the first meaning of "colonization" and of "to colonize" should be agricultural. In this sense it might be said that the progressive populating of the earth was a vast enterprise of colonization, for man continually appropriated new lands to his needs and made them productive, put them to use in various ways. This process has not come to an end and it has kept changing in accordance with the development of technology.

In Europe, colonization in this sense was essentially a medieval phenomenon. During Antiquity there had arisen in Mediterranean Europe an urban civilization with an already considerable commercial and industrial development. Initially the point of departure had been Greece, whose various peoples had founded, in Italy, in the south of France, and in Spain, a number of urban colonies surrounded by an agricultural hinterland that was small in extent. Then Rome, during its centuries of strife, had gradually extended its authority as far as the Rhine and Danube and simultaneously into Great Britain. Its civilization was urban to the point that the people who had created it bore the name of the city which became its capital. Even the Roman Empire was an assembly of *civitates,* of cities, surrounded by agricultural regions intended to feed them and under their authority. Vast expanses were still covered by forests or moors crossed by the Roman roads that linked the urban centers, but everywhere the forests and moors had been penetrated by agricultural colonization, had been put to use for the profit of the urban population. At the end of the Roman Empire a considerable number of the men charged with this task formed the judicial and social category of the *coloni,* obvious proof that "to colonize" had always been understood in its original meaning.

The extent of the control exerted by the Romans over nature diminished as the distance from the Mediterranean increased until the Rhine and Danube were reached; past these borders urban civilization had not penetrated, and colonization, the putting to use of the soil, was little in evidence. For this reason, beyond the frontiers of the Empire the slightest increase in population was enough to cause famine and misery. As long as the Roman Empire remained powerful, the barbarians, that is, the non-Romans, tried to gain admittance to it by offering the only sort of capital for exchange that they possessed—their bodies—for the Romans to put to use either as soldiers or in the agricultural colonization of the regions bordering the frontiers. These two forms of employment of barbarians, moreover, were frequently confused or combined; the Germanic laeti, for example, were soldiers and laborers at the same time. When the Empire lost its strength, the relationship between Romans and barbarians changed character [1] and, instead of placing themselves at the Romans' service, the tribes at the time of the great invasions pressed toward the Mediterranean world in order to enjoy an easier life and the more abundant resources which had accumulated from centuries of good use, that is, from agricultural colonization. The peoples of the forests and moors, in flight from famine and afraid of overpopulation, threw themselves into the care of the world of towns. This world was naturally much more heavily populated than the forests, but its riches had so grown through careful use that they seemed inexhaustible to all the peoples coming from the Europe of the forests or from the Asia of the steppes, who launched successive attacks on the towns during several centuries of confusion and recession.

Some degree of order was gradually restored in the eighth and ninth centuries, and the monasteries and seigneurial manors became centers from which a new effort to put the land to use, i.e. colonization, would begin. The forests and uncultivated lands had absorbed a lot of territory within the

[1] One example is provided by the occupation of the northwest of the Empire by the Franks, which I treated in my book *Les origines de la frontière linguistique en Belgique et la colonisation franque* (Brussels, 1955) and, later, in my article "Kritische beschouwingen over de aanwending van toponymisch materiaal bij de studie van het ontstaan der taalgrens in België," *Bijdragen en Mededelingen der Naamkunde-Commissie van de Koninklijke Nederlandse Akademie van Wetenschappen te Amsterdam*, XI (1957), 9–20. My conclusions have been discussed but not modified since. On this subject see R. Grand, *Recherches sur les origines des Francs* (Paris, 1965), and A. Joris, "On the Edge of Two Worlds in the Heart of the New Empire: The Romance Regions of Northern Gaul during the Merovingian Period," *Studies in Medieval and Renaissance History*, III (1966), 3–52, esp. p. 19.

boundaries of what had been the Roman Empire, and beyond this ancient political frontier—which was also the frontier of civilization—everything or nearly everything remained to be done. It was then that the Carolingian Empire and the states that succeeded it in France and western Germany took up the task abandoned some centuries before by the Roman Empire. Embryons of cities were born. The forest and moor were once more tamed to fields, and again they became a tempting prey to new hordes of barbarians whose lack of technological development and of persistence of effort constantly exposed them to the danger of famine, as a result of overpopulation —a point easily reached in the regions in which they originated, since their resources had not been developed by agricultural exploitation. Hence came the new invasions, of which the most important were those of the Scandinavians or Norsemen and of the Hungarians. Both stopped when these peoples settled in areas that had been colonized previously, i.e. put to use for agriculture.

Meanwhile the demographic increase in "urban" Europe, the Europe of both the old and new town, was great enough so that not only was that Europe put to more and more use, but it also could consider extending beyond its frontier a part of the energies it had accumulated within. The exploitation of Europe, its internal colonization, continued, but external colonization was about to begin at the close of the eleventh century.

It was at this time that the term "colonization" began to assume the meaning which it still carries today—that is, conquest followed by exploitation—together with the resulting unfavorable moral connotations which those two terms evoke in the minds of contemporaries. It was at the end of the First Crusade that the European colonies in the Holy Land were founded. These colonies were the result of the conquest of Moslem Palestine by the Christians of western and southern Europe, and they were exploited, i.e. put to use from an economic viewpoint, by the conquerors. Already this is a phenomenon that is entirely comparable to that which would be produced in the New World after Columbus' discovery. An initial reflection occurs here. It has become the custom, in a certain kind of historiography, to see in the colonization of America a manifestation of the beginnings of capitalism. But it would be difficult to see the eleventh century in Europe, when the colonies of the Holy Land were created, as a capitalist era. Capitalism and colonization are therefore two distinct historical, economic, and social phenomena, and the emotional values that might be assigned to one have nothing to do with the other. Admittedly, this in no way excludes the possibility that the historical phenomenon "colonization" and the historical phenomenon "capitalism" could in certain phases of human development have followed intersecting trajectories or followed parallel courses. These are phenomena that can be observed historically and scientifically, but they do not bear sentimental appreciation.

This is even more valid if one considers that similar appreciations vary by necessity according to the historico-political or historico-religious background of those who express them. Thus, taking again the example of the Christian colonies in the Holy Land, their creation is an instance of violent conquest and exploitation to the profit of foreigners in the eyes of a Moslem nationalist, who, nevertheless, would not hesitate to speak of a "holy war" when considering the vast undertaking of conquest and exploitation which contributed to the expansion of Islam. Conversely the Crusades, and therefore the Palestinian colonies or later the Latin Empire of Constantinople and the colonial kingdom of the Lusignan on Cyprus, would appear to Western Christians not forewarned by the historian's critical sense to be the reward of unreproachable warriors whose epic exploits were aimed at snatching from the infidel the tomb of the founder of their faith. Similar statements could be made about all the colonization of every era, even in relation to the primarily agricultural colonization discussed earlier. In fact, when the Greeks founded their Mediterranean colonies they fought and subdued the native populations of the places where these colonies were created. Rome did the same in order to found and colonize its Empire, and it has always been this way even when the Germans from the Rhine Valley moved toward the valleys of the Elbe or the Oder in order to conquer and colonize them, when the Spanish or the Portuguese pushed Islam back to the south in the course of the Iberian Reconquest,[2] when later they conquered and colonized Spanish America and Brazil, when the Cossacks brought under the subjection of the empire of the Muscovite tzars the endless stretches of the Siberian plains, or when the frontier of the United States was constantly pushed toward the west by intrepid pioneers who finally extended it to the shores of the Pacific. Everywhere colonization was a process by which the frontier of a less technologically developed or less organized civilization—and organization is also a technique—yielded before a civilization whose technological equipment was superior. That this process was accompanied by violence and forms of exploitation which certainly could be described as abuses is evident everywhere, but what is even more evident is that in every case colonization constituted a process of acceleration of technological development. This alone is sufficient to justify the extraordinary importance it has assumed, everywhere and in all forms, in historical development. It can be stated, without fear of error, that no historical phenomenon has contributed as much as colonization to extending man's control over nature, to which in the last analysis all human effort has been dedicated since the origin of our species. In fact it is owing to colonization that technological progress did not re-

[2] See my studies "Le grand domaine dans les états ibériques chrétiens au moyen âge," *Recueil de la Société Jean Bodin,* IV (1949), 177–208; "Quelques aspects de l'histoire de la tenure au Portugal," *ibid.,* III (1938), 231–243; "La condition des populations rurales dans l'Espagne médiévale," *idid.,* II, 2d ed. (1959), 169–200.

main limited to areas where it first arose. For this reason, the "colonized" were able to assimilate all or part of the technology of the "colonizers" and to induce the latter, by force or by reason, to recognize their right to independence.

Having considered the continuity of colonization in its broadest sense, we must now examine it in a more limited aspect, in the sense in which the term is generally used: the creation and putting to use by a metropolis with an advanced technology of overseas settlements in zones where economic and particularly technological development has been slower. Let us note immediately that such a limitation of the meaning of "colony" and "colonization" is for the most part arbitrary, for it excludes to the detriment of the history of colonization the putting to use and exploitation of zones touching directly on the metropolis and forming a single continental block with it. It cannot be denied that there was a period, and a fairly long period, in which the West of the United States seemed to be a sort of colonial territory in its relationship with the Atlantic states of the Union; it was only the progressive increase in the human occupation of these zones and in their technological level which enabled them to be assimilated with the eastern zones and even to outstrip some of them. On the other hand, Soviet Siberia is far from having reached the level of technological development which would earn for it equality with the more advanced European territories of the Russian Communist empire. In this case it is clear that one can still speak of Russian colonies or even of Russian colonialism, whereas, practically speaking, this is impossible to do with respect to the United States. A similar statement can be made concerning territories that have been occupied and developed much earlier than the two contemporary superpowers, especially certain European countries. Thus the lower technological development of considerable parts of southern Italy in no way excludes the idea of colonization on the part of the more industrial North after the achievement of national unity. Another example, different in nature and chronology, might be the greater influence of Castile in Spain since the end of the Reconquest and precisely at the time of colonial expansion, in the strict sense, across the Atlantic. It would be easy to add to this list examples taken from the most diverse parts of the world.

However that may be, in this volume we are concerned exclusively with certain phenomena which prepared and initially brought about "modern" overseas colonization.

It has been customary to think of colonial history in the strict or narrow sense as beginning immediately after the great discoveries. Sometimes allusion is made to medieval precedents but most often this is done very briefly and, what is more serious, superficially. One of the principal aims of this book is to point out that the concept of continuity, or in other words the absence of a gap, between the Middle Ages and modern times can be applied to colonial history in the strict sense.

Following what we said earlier concerning colonization in the broad sense, this question might be asked: Why be concerned solely with the continuity between medieval colonization and colonization in modern times? Did not the peoples of Antiquity also found colonies overseas? Did not the Phoenicians and the Greeks also create colonial settlements on all the shores of the Mediterranean, the center of maritime life at that time, and for a long time to come? Such an objection can easily be met. There are indeed analogies between ancient colonization in overseas territories and the colonization that followed the great discoveries, but there was no continuity in time. In fact, as we have already said, medieval overseas colonization—although it, like colonization in Antiquity, had the Mediterranean as its framework—did not begin until the Crusades. A dozen centuries are thus missing in the chronological chain. This hiatus suffices to make the overseas colonies of Antiquity a completely separate and distinct entity.

On the contrary, medieval colonization—primarily Italian —in the Mediterranean was still in existence when modern colonization resulting from the great Atlantic discoveries began. Obviously, then, there is continuity here, at least as far as chronological succession is concerned.

At first glance it would seem possible to make the same statement about colonization in the modern era (the fifteenth through the eighteenth centuries) on the one hand and colonization during the contemporary era on the other. It is clear, however, that the overseas colonial empires that were created after the liberation of the United States and Latin America cannot be considered a simple extension of those of the previous era. The reason for this is not only geographic changes but technological transformations. This statement requires some explanation. In fact, though some colonizing countries continued to possess until quite recently most of the colonies they held during the so-called modern era—Holland is one striking example—there are others, like England, France, Spain, and Portugal, who lost almost all their colonial possessions or acquired other new ones. From this perspective, however, there is no greater gap between modern and contemporary colonies than there was between the medieval colonies in the Mediterranean and modern colonies in the Atlantic zone. After the great discoveries the geographic distribution of the colonies was also completely changed.

The real break between modern and contemporary colonization is to be found in the techniques of exploitation. Overseas colonization during the nineteenth and twentieth centuries originated solely as a result of the industrial revolution. Without the enormously increased demand for raw materials and commercial outlets, without the enormous build-up of military fleets and maritime transportation, overseas colonization would never have developed as it did during the nineteenth and twentieth centuries. Moreover, this is also true of internal colonization, like that of Siberia or the West of America, and here again the scope of the phenomenon can be measured by the degree of technological or industrial development of the area that acted as the point of departure for expansion. It is this unprecedented breadth of scope, whatever the local variations may be, that rules out continuity with the so-called modern era. On the other hand there are no essential differences between the colonial techniques of the Middle Ages and those of modern times, and it is my aim in this book to prove this contention.

The book consists of three parts, the first of which, "Europe and America," treats the problems involved in trying to deal with the continuity between overseas colonization in medieval and modern times within the framework of the evolution of Western, or more precisely Atlantic, civilization.

The first chapter, "The Transfer of Colonial Techniques from the Mediterranean to the Atlantic," is the English translation of Chapter IX of my book *The Origins of Atlantic Civilization,* which has appeared in French, Italian, and Dutch.[3] It gives evidence to support the thesis formulated above concerning the continuity between medieval overseas colonization in the Mediterranean and colonization of the modern era in the Atlantic. I have devoted to this subject a series of other articles, which do not appear in this collection.[4] The second chapter studies the continuity and the differences between medieval slavery[5] in Europe and

[3] *Les origines de la civilisation atlantique* (Paris and Neuchâtel, 1966); *Het ontstaan van de Atlantische beschaving: Van Renaissance tot Verlichting* (Ghent, 1965); *Le origini della civiltà atlantica* (Rome, 1968).

[4] See in particular my article "Les origines coloniales de la civilisation atlantique: Antécédents et types de structure," *Journal of World History,* I (1953), 378–398, and my short book *Précédents médiévaux de la colonie en Amérique* (Mexico City, 1954).

[5] I have published many articles on medieval slavery. For Spain, Portugal, and the South of France see my book *L'esclavage dans l'Europe médiévale,* I: *Péninsule Ibérique—France,* University of Ghent, Werken uitgegeven door de Faculteit van de Letteren en Wijsbegeerte, vol. 119 (Bruges, 1955); for these countries, as well as Italy and the Mediterranean area, see my articles "Traite et esclavage dans la vallée de la Meuse," *Mélanges Félix Rousseau* (Brussels, 1958), pp. 673–686;

colonial slavery in America. It has been published in Spanish by the University of Córdoba in Argentina and in French by the Institut des Hautes Etudes de l'Amérique Latine of the Sorbonne.[6] And finally the last chapter of this first section defines the relationships between Western and Atlantic civilizations, taking into particular account colonial history. It has appeared in Dutch in the *Tijdschrift voor Geschiedenis* of Groningen and in Spanish in the review *Atlantida* of Madrid.[7]

Medieval colonization was primarily the work of the

"Esclaves alains en Italie et dans les colonies italiennes au XIVe siècle," *Revue belge de philologie et d'histoire*, XXXVI (1958), 451–457; "La Crète, débouché et plaque tournante de la traite des esclaves aux XIVe et XVe siècles," *Studi in onore di Amintore Fanfani* (Milan, 1962), III, 593–669; "L'esclavage en Sicile au bas moyen âge," *Bulletin de l'Institut Historique Belge de Rome*, XXXV (1963), 13–113; "Traite des esclaves et traitants italiens à Constantinople (XIIIe–XVe siècles)," *Le Moyen Age*, LXIX (1963), 791–804; "Orthodoxie et esclavage au bas moyen âge," *Mélanges E. Tisserant*, V, *Studi e testi*, CCXXXV (Vatican City, 1964), 427–456; "L'esclavage en Sicile sous Frédéric II d'Aragon (1296–1337)," *Homenaje à Jaime Vicens Vives* (Barcelona, 1965), I, 675–690; "Esclavage noir en France méridionale et courants de traite en Afrique," *Annales du Midi*, LXXVIII (1966), 335–443; "Patarins ou Bogomiles réduits en esclavage," *Studi e materiali di storia delle religioni*, XXXVIII (1967), 683–700; "Les débuts de la traite portugaise en Afrique (1433–1448)," *Miscellanea mediaevalia in memoriam J. F. Niermeyer* (Groningen, 1967), pp. 365–377; "L'esclavage dans le royaume de Naples à la fin du moyen âge et la participation des marchands espagnols à la traite," *Anuario de historia economica y social*, I (1968), 345–401; "Le recrutement des esclaves à Venise aux XIVe et XVe siècles," *Bulletin de l'Institut Historique Belge de Rome*, XXXIX (1968), 83–202.

[6] "Esclavitud medieval en Europa y esclavitud colonial en America," *Revista de la Universidad Nacional de Córdoba: Homenaje jubilar a Monseñor Dr. Pablo Cabrera* (Córdoba, Argentina, 1961), 177–191; "Esclavage médiéval en Europe et esclavage colonial en Amérique," *Cahiers de l'Institut des Hautes Etudes de l'Amérique Latine*, VI (1961), 29–45.

[7] "Civilización occidental y civilización atlantica," *Atlantida*, IV (1966), 278–297; "Westerse beschaving en Atlantische beschaving: Een theoretische beschouwing," *Tijdschrift voor geschiedenis*, LXXX (1967), 6–22.

Italian city republics, which created colonies first in the Holy Land and then on the remains of the Byzantine Empire along the shores of the Aegean, the Ionian, and even the Black seas. These colonies used a slave economy like that used later, but with increased breadth, in the colonies founded in America by the various colonizing powers. This aspect of medieval colonial economy is studied in the first chapter of the second section, which appeared first in French in the *mélanges* dedicated to the French historian Lucien Febvre.[8] The other three chapters in this second section deal with the influence of Italians in Portugal and Spain at the beginning of the modern colonial era as well as in the first Portuguese and Spanish colonies. The second appeared in French in the *mélanges* in honor of the Italian historian Armando Sapori; [9] the third, also in French, in the works of the Fifth Congress of History of the States of the Crown of Aragon at Saragossa; [10] the fourth, in Italian, in the review *Economia e storia* directed by the former First Minister of Italy, Amintore Fanfani, Professor of Economic History at the University of Rome.[11] All these chapters deal with the role played by Italians as agents of transition from medieval colonization to that of modern times.

The third section, entitled "Early Western European Colonization," also contains four chapters. The first deals with the career of the Genoese Antonio da Noli as colonizer of the Islands of Cape Verde in the service of Portugal,

[8] "Aspects de l'esclavage dans les colonies médiévales italiennes," *Hommage à Lucien Febvre* (Paris, 1954), II, 91–103.

[9] "La colonie italienne de Lisbonne et le développement de l'économie métropolitaine et coloniale portugaise," *Studi in onore di Armando Sapori* (Milan, 1957), pp. 617–628.

[10] "Les influences italiennes dans l'économie et dans la colonisation espagnoles à l'époque de Ferdinand le Catholique," *Fernando el Catolico e Italia*, V° Congreso de Historia de la Corona de Aragón, *Estudios*, III (Saragossa, 1954), 269–283.

[11] "Gli italiani nell' economia delle Canarie all' inizio della colonizzazione spagnola," *Economia e storia*, VII (1960), 149–172.

and, briefly, of Spain.[12] The second concerns a Flemish precursor of Columbus in 1487, captain by deed of gift in the Azores, in the service of Portugal.[13] The third deals with Columbus himself and with the medieval character of his rights and privileges.[14] The last and most extensive chapter is an institutional study of the various forms of land concessions in the Portuguese colonies from the fourteenth century to the beginning of the sixteenth.[15]

[12] "Antonio da Noli et la colonisation des Iles du Cap Vert," *Miscellanea storica ligure,* III (1963), 129–144; "Antonio da Noli e a colonização das Ilhas de Cabo Verde," *Revista da Faculdade de Letras,* 3d ser., VII (1963), 28–45.

[13] "Een Vlaamse voorloper van Columbus: Ferdinand van Olmen (1487)," *Tijdschrift voor geschiedenis,* LXXIV (1961), 506–516; "Un précurseur de Colomb: Le Flamand Ferdinand van Olmen (1487)," *Revista portuguesa de história,* X (1962), 453–466.

[14] This is a chapter in my book on Columbus, which first appeared in German: *Kolumbus: Vision und Ausdauer* (Göttingen, 1962), then in Dutch: *Columbus* (The Hague, 1962), and then in an amplified version in Spanish in collaboration with F. Perez Embid: *Cristóbal Colón y el descubrimiento de América* (Madrid, Mexico City, Buenos Aires, and Pamplona, 1967).

[15] "Formes féodales et domaniales de la colonisation portugaise dans la zone atlantique aux XIVe et XVe siècles et spécialement sous Henri le Navigateur," *Revista portuguesa de história,* IX (1960), 1–44.

PART I
Europe and America

1. The Transfer of Colonial Techniques from the Mediterranean to the Atlantic*

The colonization of the Atlantic world is generally considered to be an unprecedented and completely original phenomenon. This view is erroneous, however, since colonies existed in the eastern Mediterranean or Levant at the end of the Middle Ages. It was there that the technique of colonization which spread across the Atlantic world originated. The study of medieval influences on colonization in the Atlantic zone, i.e. America and Africa, opens up a new field of historical research and modifies the traditional perspectives from which we are accustomed to examine relations between the Old and New Worlds. Such a study, moreover, implies a conception of colonial history different from the old "external" conception. This point requires some explanation.

During the colonial era historians were interested almost exclusively in the colonies as a function of the metropolises. They studied the colonies founded by a particular nation from a nationalist perspective. The study of the medieval precedents of Atlantic colonization requires, on the contrary, knowledge of reciprocal influences in a very large area and cannot be accomplished unless one deals with the American continent, the Atlantic archipelagoes, and a large part of Africa on the one hand, and western and southern Europe on the other, as well as Italian, Catalan, and French medieval colonies in the

* Translated, with revisions, from "Le transfert des techniques coloniales: De la Méditerranée à l'Atlantique," ch. 9 of *Les origines de la civilisation atlantique,* by C. Verlinden (Neuchâtel: Editions de la Baconnière, 1966), pp. 157–178.

3

Mediterranean. Reciprocal contacts and influences, in both administrative and economic terms, are so important that we must consider the various colonies and metropolises as forming part of one large historical area. Instead of merely examining the external diplomatic and commercial history of the colonies, we must study and compare their internal economic, social, and institutional development. By doing this, we find that certain phenomena are continuous, and we are thus able to understand the transfer of colonial techniques.

I am not suggesting that Spain, Portugal, France, England, the Netherlands, and the Scandinavian countries introduced identical economic and social institutions and structures into their Atlantic colonies. The obvious differences in the development of the metropolises, in the eras in which the colonies were founded, and in the geographical and anthropological environment prevented such similarities. Their common atmosphere, characterized by phenomena of filiation or continuity, is undeniable, however. If we adhere constantly to the influence exercised over the various Atlantic colonies by the economic, social, and administrative institutions of the colonies in the later Middle Ages, and of the metropolises, if we combine this study with an analysis of the influence and transformations of the indigenous populations, it becomes possible to follow the development of colonial history in a way that will be useful not only to those interested in the past, but equally to those who are studying the contribution of the West to the countries now in the process of developing.

We have too often lost sight of the fact that from the early twelfth century the eastern Mediterranean countries provided an outlet for the European desire to colonize, and this situation continued not only after Columbus but, for the Venetians at least, long after the beginning of English colonization in America.

Colonization in the Mediterranean began immediately

after the First Crusade in the Holy Land with the Crusade principalities and the Italian establishments—Genoese, Pisan, and Venetian—which were founded there. These establishments were even more truly colonial than the Crusade seigneuries, since politically they were more closely connected with their various Italian metropolises than the French barons of Palestine and the Peloponnesus were with the king of France, whose feudal ascendancy rapidly became purely theoretic. Besides, the Italians far more than the barons pursued specific economic objectives. The Venetians, for example, became immediately involved in the sugarcane plantations with the object of exporting. We shall see later in this chapter that it is possible to establish continuity from their activity as planters in the Holy Land in the twelfth century to the introduction of sugar cane to the French and English Antilles in the seventeenth century.

Colonial activity in the eastern Mediterranean spread from the Holy Land to the islands, archipelagoes, and mainland of southeastern Europe. At the end of the twelfth century, Cyprus became a Franco-Italian possession and remained so until the beginning of modern times. A large part of Palestine was conquered by the Turks in the thirteenth century, but the colonies in existence there were replaced by more valuable colonies, in Crete by the Venetians after the Fourth Crusade, and by the French and Italians on the islands of the Aegean and Ionian seas as well as along the coast of the Balkan Peninsula.

After the fall of the Latin Empire of Constantinople, held under the protection of the Venetians, in 1261, the Genoese, allies of the Byzantine emperors who had just reconquered their throne, were able to penetrate as far as the Black Sea, where they began to colonize the Crimea. With this as their starting point, they proceeded to occupy various well-situated spots further east. This whole region later became known as the Khazarian empire, from the name of the Khazars or Chazars, who had once dominated the South of Russia. It is evident that even the idea of a maritime and colonial empire, whatever its dimension, was familiar to the later Middle Ages.

While the colonies in the eastern Mediterranean were still in their early stages of development, Europeans, and especially Italians, were beginning to explore, map, and populate the Atlantic archipelagoes. As early as a generation before 1300, the Genoese had begun regularly sending their galleys beyond the straits of Gibraltar. Together with other Italians and sailors from the coastal regions of western Europe they pushed further and further to the southwest of the Atlantic, and even to the northwest, though to a lesser extent. It is interesting to discover, in the course of this expansion, scientists, captains, sailors, and merchants who had already been involved in the colonies in the eastern Mediterranean. Methods and techniques passed from one colonial zone to another. Inhabitants of the Iberian Peninsula, with the strong support of Italians, began to colonize the Canary Islands in the second half of the fourteenth century; some years later, it was the turn of the Madeiras and the Azores, where lands were distributed by methods very similar to those followed by the Italians in their colonies in the Levant. The settlement of the Atlantic archipelagoes, where a plantation economy was already in operation before the middle of the fifteenth century, attracted colonists from the Iberian Peninsula, and also from Italy, Normandy, and later from Flanders. On the other hand, the Iberian colonies in the Balkans, especially those developed by concerns like the Catalan and Navarrese companies in the duchies of Athens and Nauplia, assumed, beginning in the first half of the fourteenth century, a form very similar to that introduced two centuries later into Mexico and Peru by Cortez and Pizarro. With no break in continuity, Iberian colonization, assisted by Italian admirals, pilots, sailors, merchants, and scientists who were charged with the important technical tasks, extended along the African shores and reached the

Far East as well as the Caribbean and the rest of America. Almost immediately, English, Breton, Norman, and even Danish sea expeditions followed in the wake of the Italo-Iberian explorers and colonizers. Until the end of the sixteenth century, however, the French, Dutch, and English could not be considered serious rivals by those who until that time had had the monopoly of colonial activity. These nations, too, had made an early bid for the collaboration of technicians from Venice, Genoa, Seville, and Lisbon. English colonial ambitions were aimed simultaneously at three objectives: the colonial absorption of Ireland, penetration of the zones previously monopolized by the Iberians, and the gaining of a foothold in regions of the Western Hemisphere that the latter had not yet penetrated. To achieve these ends they could not in the beginning do without the aid of Italian and Iberian specialists. Only later were the English, French, and Dutch colonists able to manage without those who had learned the secrets of colonization in the Italo-Iberian world.

During the centuries following the Crusades the attractiveness of overseas expansion and the profits to be made from overseas colonies contributed greatly to the development of European commercial methods. There is a direct line of development between the *compere* or companies that administered the municipal finances of Genoa, the *mahona*s or colonial Genoese companies of the fourteenth century, the Bank of St. George (also Genoese) which played a role of prime importance in the administration of the colonies in the Crimea and the Levant, and the Spanish and Portuguese organizations for the control of commerce and colonial settlement on the one hand, and the Dutch, French, and English companies which directed the colonial expansion of those nations on the other. Even in medieval Genoa close ties existed between the colonial *mahona*s and the national debt; regarded from this angle, the famous Mississippi and South Sea companies are only a link in a long tradition.

Individual connections can be similarly traced. A good example of this is provided by Sebastian Cabot, a Genoese who belonged to a merchant family originally from Venice and held a very high position in Spanish colonial administration; he became the chief promoter of the English Muscovy Company for whose organization he was responsible. The fact that the Muscovy Company was a joint-stock company was certainly attributable to the experience acquired by Cabot in Italy and Spain, since this type of organization was new in England, even though it had existed for some time in southern Europe.

Another individual example of the continuity between medieval colonization and colonial activity in the Atlantic—in this case up to the beginning of the seventeenth century—is a man named Pallavicino, one of the most important shareholders of the Virginia Company. He belonged to a family mentioned since the thirteenth century in hundreds of documents concerning overseas trade in the archives of Genoa. His ancestors had possessed and governed a colonial marquisate in Greece since the fourteenth century.

If we turn to institutional aspects we can establish, during the whole period that concerns us in this volume, a real continuity in the organization of colonial societies and in the methods of internal administration of the colonies. Frequently earlier institutional forms served as models for new. Here is an example originating in medieval England. Shortly after 1066 the Normans founded what was to become the Palatinate of Durham; though its organization and function were modified in the course of succeeding generations, the institutional framework could still be used for the proprietor's colonies in Ireland and for those in Maryland and other American possessions in the seventeenth century.

But generally the connections are neither so direct nor so simple. Colonial organization in the Mediterranean in the Middle Ages and in the Atlantic area at the beginning of the modern era can be divided into three main types. First,

there is the feudal type of colonial landowning that existed
in the Crusade colonies in Palestine, Cyprus, and medieval
Greece, and on an even vaster scale in the Spanish, Portuguese, Dutch, and English colonies in the Atlantic. A second
type of colony involved the formation, in the metropolis,
of a company which received a charter from the government
and thus enjoyed almost complete administrative autonomy.
These company-controlled colonies were as much in existence in the Middle Ages as during the early modern period.
Genoa, for example, administered the Aegean island of
Chios by means of a *mahona* similar to the English companies in Virginia or Massachusetts and the French or Dutch
companies in the East and West Indies. A third type of
colony was based on an agreement between free citizens. In
the Middle Ages the most striking examples of such agreements concerned communal or military groups. The consti-
tutions of some of these communes served as models in
certain colonial areas. Genoa, for example, used its own
communal constitution in the colonies of Pera on the
Bosporus and Caffa in the Crimea. So-called free companies
fought in nearly all the European wars in the later Middle
Ages, and their members were bound together by an agreement. In some cases these companies were transplanted overseas, and a new agreement was established with the object
of regulating not only their internal government but also the
control of the conquered country. This was done by the
Catalan and Navarrese companies in their colonies in Greece
in the fourteenth century. When the English colonists in the
New World reached lands that had not previously been
controlled by the government or by a company, they drew
up agreements or covenants. In this way the English
separatists put into effect the Mayflower Agreement when
they arrived in New England instead of disembarking in
Virginia, where they had received permission to land. Roger
Williams' followers established the Providence Agreement,
which covered civil government, when they were banished

from Massachusetts; the Connecticut colonists did the same in their Fundamental Orders. One of the origins of these agreements was the idea of covenant so dear to the English Calvinists and Nonconformists, but there was a precedent for them which goes back to the Mediterranean colonies at the end of the Middle Ages, long before the appearance of Protestantism.

The connections are simpler as far as maintaining colonial politics under the control of the metropolitan government is concerned. The Casa de Contratación, which administered Spanish colonial commerce, was derived largely from Genoese colonial administration, as can be seen from the statutes drawn up by the Genoese Pinelli in 1503. The Spanish and Portuguese administrative bodies in charge of the colonies exercised an influence on the institutions created for the same purposes by England, France, and Holland. Men like Usselinx, the founder of the Dutch West Indies Company, or Linschoten, who did the groundwork for Dutch expansion in the East Indies, to mention only two, had learned the principles of colonial administration while working in the Portuguese colonial service. Even the main provisions of the Navigation Acts, which were so important, had been applied in the Mediterranean several centuries before Cromwell.

All this does not mean that the institutions established in the Atlantic colonies were merely copies of those in western Europe and the Levant at the end of the Middle Ages. In the Atlantic colonies there was a gradual and active adaptation to the new milieu. But from the Atlantic point of view, the common origin is much more important than the adaptation which is an inevitable law of life. This common origin is European and goes back to the Middle Ages. That is why, from the beginning of the colonial era, the direction followed by history has been identical on both sides of the great interior ocean of the Western world.

Land Concessions in the Mediterranean Colonies and in the Atlantic Zone

The study of land concessions made in the Atlantic colonies reveals both a direct descent from medieval colonization and an adaptation of medieval metropolitan institutions to the new colonial milieu.

Forms of landowning that originated in the western and southern European feudal systems were transplanted, particularly in their French and Italian versions, to the Levant during the later Middle Ages. The colonial lords, like those in the metropolis, would possess domains inhabited by a half-free class who owed them fairly heavy work dues. Moreover the manpower they employed—and this is an essentially colonial characteristic—also included slaves captured during the continual frontier wars against the infidels of Palestine or bought in the slave markets of other colonies in the Levant. The seigneury was held from the King of Jerusalem, the Latin Emperor of Constantinople or the King of Cyprus, all of whom came from western Europe like their barons; and even in the colonial regions, where there was no king or emperor, the landowners were always vassals of a suzerain of western origin. To be invested with a fief one had to provide the suzerain with a knight's service and as large a following as possible.

Crete was the most important Italian colony in the Levant. From the beginning of the thirteenth century Venetians possessed *casalia* or rural domains in that island and cultivated them by means of the work imposed on the *parici* (Greek serfs). They often employed slaves as well. These landowners owed military service to the Venetian government, just as did the Greek nobles who had joined the colonial regime.

The Genoese colonies in Palestine were much less extensive than the huge Venetian colony of Crete but they had been acquired more than a hundred years earlier. The first

land concession received by the Genoese in the Holy Land
was granted on July 14, 1098, by Bohemond of Antioch, a
Christian lord and Crusader. Bohemond thus created, within
the framework of his own colonial principality, a con-
dominium administered by himself and the Genoese state. It
was not a question in this case of an agricultural domain
given to a nobleman in exchange for a knight's service but of
the concession of an urban district to an allied state. Later
other Crusaders in Palestine granted similar possessions to
the Genoese, for, like Bohemond, they wished to show their
gratitude for the help they had received in their struggle
against the Moslems. Such concessions always included a
warehouse, or fonduk, and exemption from taxes. The Venetians and Pisans obtained similar benefits for the same
reasons, but the former sometimes managed to have important rural zones included. In the seigneury of Tyre they
received 21 entire villages and a third part of 51 others, out
of a total of 114.

After obtaining a series of concessions along the Palestinian shore the state of Genoa began to enfeoff a portion to
members of its nobility. This explains how the powerful
Embriaci family held from Genoa, for a theoretically limited
time, a series of urban areas in Palestine. For the state
of Genoa it was a means of paying the debts it had contracted
with the Embriaci for maritime expeditions that they had
undertaken. This is the first example of the connection between national debt and colonial concession: the state wished
to discharge what it owed or at least to postpone its liquida-
tion.

Similarly, Genoa granted concessions to companies; here is
proof that colonial companies were not the creation of
northern European countries in modern times, as is often
believed, but that their origin goes back to the Middle Ages
and that they existed first among the Mediterranean nations.
This is true of almost all the commercial techniques in
general and colonial techniques in particular.

Within the Genoese colonial system these companies were called *mahonas*, which signifies reimbursement, indemnification, thereby emphasizing their connection with the national debt. The first example was the *mahona* of Chios. Twenty-nine galleys had been equipped for the state at private expense, and since the government was not in a position to reimburse these citizens, their leader was authorized, in 1346, to conquer the Greek island of Chios, which possessed at that time nearly all available vegetable mastic. The creditors would hold the island from the doge of Genoa with the right to administer and exploit it economically and fiscally for twenty years, after which the state would pay the 203,000 pounds that it owed. In fact, the Republic was never in a position to keep to its agreement, and the colony remained in the hands of the company formed by the mahonists, i.e. by those who should have been indemnified and their descendants or successors. This company later acquired other islands and continued to increase its constituted capital by stocks, a procedure repeated later by colonial companies in the Atlantic zone and in the Indies.

The various types of colonial concessions that existed in the Genoese possessions in the Levant were handed on to the Iberian nations and merged with the feudal forms inherited from the medieval past of those countries. This is particularly evident in the colonization of the Canary Islands, begun by the Portuguese in the middle of the fourteenth century. Lanzarotto Malocello, one of the Genoese captains serving the king of Portugal, discovered a part of the Canary Islands, took possession of it in the name of the king, and held by his authority two of these islands for several years. In this way Mediterranean colonial practices were transplanted to the Atlantic zone. About the same time, Catalans and Castilians also became interested in the Canary Islands. The discoverers and colonists sent there by those nations had to pay their own expenses and were reimbursed by means of feudal concessions. This system was applied throughout the Atlantic archipelagoes that were colonized as much by the Portuguese as by the Castilians. Since these concessions were granted by the kings of Portugal and Castile, their institutional characteristics derived from feudal law as elaborated in those two countries during the Middle Ages. The process, however, was the same as in the Levant; moreover, the beneficiaries were sometimes Italians.

Land concessions in the Madeiras and the Azores were granted first by Henry the Navigator, and then by the king of Portugal to hereditary captains who held public authority. At Porto Santo, in the Madeira Islands, the captaincy was given, in 1446, to Bartolomeo Perestrello, a knight of Italian origin, whose daughter later married Christopher Columbus. He had the right to will the captaincy to his male heirs and their descendants. He administered justice in the name of Henry the Navigator, who himself held the island from the king. He could levy special taxes on the mills and machines used in the sugar plantations and he was allowed to subenfeoff lands.

There were also examples of gifts to groups. In 1496 the Castilian Alonso de Lugo set up a company for the conquest and settlement of the island of Palma, in the Canaries. Several Italian capitalists were members and received territorial concessions in reimbursement of their expenses. This is how the Genoese Cristóbal de Ponte came to hold from the Crown of Castile a castle surrounded by lands, a part of which he subenfeoffed to a third party.

It would be wrong, however, to believe that the feudal type of colonial concessions was the only system employed by the Iberian governments. They also created colonies by settlement and, as soon as the colonists were numerous enough, created municipalities which had a development parallel to that of the seigneuries of the first colonists. In the course of the sixteenth century, when the central power succeeded in exercising a more effective control over the colonies, it tried to suppress the feudal privileges of the first discoverers and colonists. In behaving this way the kings were only following the normal tendencies of absolute states at the beginning of modern times. Functionaries then began to replace the feudal lords, and they strove to make the common law of the monarchy prevail over the privileges of the first colonists; but, everywhere, the state had left the first risks to private initiative, since its fiscal system was still too primitive to provide the necessary funds.

In America this system was maintained as long as the central authority was not strong enough to take over the complete control of the colonies. The Spanish conquerors went to America with the intention of acquiring lands and free manpower. They were prepared to risk their lives to become lords, with all the powers and possessions that would involve; but, when the king wished to diminish their privileges, bloody revolts broke out, especially in Peru, when the Crown suppressed the privileges of Pizarro's and Almagro's companions.

The Portuguese in Brazil had recourse first to the system of hereditary captaincies, as in their Atlantic archipelagoes. But in the middle of the seventeenth century the government succeeded in strengthening its control, thus putting an end to the golden age of Brazilian feudalism while at the same time maintaining the system of demesnes. This was also true of the Spanish possessions. The Spanish *hacendados* and the Portuguese *fazendeiros* were from then on powerful lords who, even if they had lost a great part of their political power, remained masters of the land and people from an economic and social point of view, like European nobles of the same period.

The situations were analogous in the majority of American possessions belonging to the colonial powers of northern Europe, even though those states had not founded colonies before the seventeenth century. Though it is true that the colonists of Massachusetts and Connecticut concluded agreements among small landowners, it must also be noted that the feudal type of land concession was by far the most numerous and extensive among the English colonies of North America. Moreover the companies held their territories equally from the king and played the role of a sort of collective lord. In French Canada the seigneurial system formed the basis of colonization, and what is even more surprising at first sight, in the American possessions of the Republic of the United Provinces, where no prince could be considered the keystone of a feudal hierarchy, the colonial concessions still maintained the traditional form.

The Dutch example is so striking that it is worth closer examination. The Dutch state was born of the revolt against the despotism of Philip II; it was a product of the Reformation and of the emancipation of the middle class resulting from the development of commerce and industry. The politics of the West India Company, was no less feudal so far as land concessions were concerned. It was a chartered company exercising public authority, which it held from the Dutch Estates General in the same way as a vassal held land and powers from his lord. The company's very position was feudal, so it is not surprising that its method of land distribution should be so. The people to whom the company gave seigneuries in fief were "patrons," and the land tenure involved military obligations as well as agricultural prestations. Default in one of these obligations could mean seizure, as a European fief could be seized.

Here is a concrete example of a colonial Dutch fief. As late as 1669 the company directors signed an agreement with a German nobleman, the Count of Hanau, establishing a fief on the coast of Cayenne, in South America. It was understood that the Count owed homage for the land granted him and that the fief would owe the company a special tax on the death of the vassal. The fief in question was quite large; it covered thirty miles of coast and might stretch as much as a

hundred miles into the interior if the Count could find
enough people to occupy it. The coastal region had to be
cultivated within twelve years or the noncultivated lands
would revert back to the company. The Count of Hanau
also received every sort of public power including jurisdiction over lesser crimes (whenever bloodshed was not involved), which he wielded in the name of the Estates General. He owed a knight's service for his fief, and he was
guaranteed the right of inheritance and the right to subenfeoff. The company would act as the feudal court if the
Count should encounter difficulties with his own vassals, who
owed him homage just as he owed it to the company.

The Dutch granted fiefs not only on the South American
continent but also in the Antilles. In the whole of this zone
the "patron" would receive land together with seigneurial rights. In New Holland, the valley of the Hudson, on the
other hand, the soil became the property of the grantee and
only the seigneurial rights that went with it were held in
fief. Certain seigneuries carried with them the right of jurisdiction over more serious crimes involving the death sentence, others involved only jurisdiction over lesser crimes.
Certain patrons could levy tithes and rents, others could
tax only the fishing and hunting preserves. When the Dutch
extended their dominion to northeastern Brazil, it was
decided, by a decree of 1634, that the colonial municipalities would receive lands in hereditary fief, as well as the right
to elect a governor to be assisted by regents or magistrates.
This was indeed a strange mixture of European municipal
and feudal law, handed down directly from the Middle
Ages but transplanted into this new Atlantic milieu.

The Transfer of Sugar Production from the Mediterranean to the Atlantic

Historians of colonization often believe that the medieval
colonies in the Levant were solely commercial centers which
served as ports of call on the routes leading to the interior

of Africa or Asia. From a commercial standpoint this view would be exact, but it overlooks certain aspects of medieval Mediterranean colonization which foreshadowed Atlantic colonization in modern times, especially the agricultural and industrial activities.

A combination of agriculture and industry characterized the sugar-cane production in which the Italian republics became interested when they acquired possessions in Palestine after the First Crusade. Sugar cane had been introduced into the Holy Land by the Arabs, who thus became the liaison for sugar between the Asiatic East and the Mediterranean world as they were for paper, the compass, and Arab numerals. In the course of the wearisome marches in Palestine during the First Crusade the warriors of the West came to know the sweetness of what one chronicler called "this unsuspected and inestimable present from Heaven." We have seen that Palestine after its conquest was divided into seigneuries according to the rules of Western feudalism. Tyre, conquered in 1123, was the first of these to manufacture sugar. A series of villages was conceded to the Venetians, who immediately drew profit from the fields of sugar cane and the sugar presses that they found there. The dues on the lands were often paid in sugar, and certain Crusaders received the right to send their sugar duty-free to the port of Acre, where it was bought by exporters, some of whom were equally exempt from paying duty. The knights of the Teutonic order and the Hospitalers possessed sugar-cane fields near the Palestinian towns of Tripoli and Tiberias. Thus it was not surprising that the Assize of Jerusalem should contain a large number of provisions concerning sugar.

During the thirteenth century sugar production increased in Syria and in Palestine, especially around Sidon, Tripoli, Galgala, and Jericho. A castle near Mamistra, in the interior of Palestine, was even called "Canamella," which means sugar cane, obvious proof that this crop was harvested in its fields. Even in 1300, when there was hardly anything left of the colonial economy in Palestine, the domain of Krak, near the Dead Sea, and Jericho and Beirut were producing sugar to be exported to western Europe.

After the fall of the last Christian bastions and their conquest by the Turks at the end of the thirteenth century, Syria, which had provided Europe with sugar during the Crusades, relinquished its role to Cyprus. This did not mean that the sugar industry disappeared from Palestine but that henceforth the sale of sugar was oriented toward the Moslem world. The French dynasty of the Lusignan had established a prosperous colonial kingdom in Cyprus. Here, too, the cultivation of sugar cane had been introduced by the Arabs who had conquered the island in the seventh century, but it was not until the fourteenth century, after the collapse of Christian Palestine, that Cyprus became a truly important center of production.

The richest plantations were found on the southern coast of the island, where the sugar-producing royal domains of Lemva, Paphos, Aschelia, and Kuklia were situated, as well as the lands of the Venetian Cornaro family, near Piscopi, the Bishop of Limassol, the Catalan Ferrer family, and the Hospitalers' monastery near Kolossi.

The Cornaros managed their plantations according to capitalist methods. The agricultural work was done by slaves of Arab or Syrian origin, by local serfs, and by emigrants from the Holy Land. Arguments over the use of water often involved the landowners in conflict with their neighbors, and more than once they were faced with problems of canalization or handling. Hydraulic mills were used to press the sugar cane, but the Cornaros' industrial activity was not limited to this first step in the transformation of the product. In the seventeenth and eighteenth centuries sugar cane grown in America was not refined on the spot but was processed in specialized European factories, whereas Cyprus in the fifteenth century supplied the finished product in the shape of sugar loaves or powdered sugar. For this purpose the Cornaros used huge copper boilers manufactured in Italy; every year they invested large sums of money in the enterprise and assigned a special budget to its maintenance and administration.

The kings of Cyprus themselves produced great quantities of sugar which were sent to the warehouses in Nicosia where they were taken over by exporters. Often this sugar was used to pay royal debts, and in the fifteenth century the king gave his plantations as securities to private capitalists, to the state of Venice and to the famous Bank of St. George in Genoa.

The Venetian colony of Crete, like Cyprus, played a part in sugar production, but much more sugar was produced by Sicily in the central Mediterranean. The Arabs had first introduced it there too at some time during their possession of the island up to the middle of the eleventh century. When the Normans conquered Sicily, the sugar industry continued to prosper in the Palermo area, and in the twelfth century the king and the great monastery of Monreale owned sugar presses. About 1200 a crisis arose which Frederick II later tried to remedy by sending for master sugar-makers from the oldest production centers in Palestine. He had very little success, and in the fourteenth century the cultivation of sugar cane decreased. But in 1449 a new press was invented which restored prosperity. Production increased immediately in the coastal regions, and the Sicilian refineries became more numerous than before.

In the western Mediterranean, Moslem Spain was also familiar with sugar-cane cultivation. About 1300, the sugar of Málaga was sold as far away as Bruges, and a large commercial company in Ravensburg, in southern Germany, which had previously been engaged in the sugar trade in Valencia, began to produce the product there about 1460. This company used the new Sicilian press, another proof of the transfer of techniques from one end of the Mediterranean to the other. In Portugal sugar cultivation began in 1404, when the Genoese Giovanni della Palma was the first to produce it in Algarve, the southernmost province of the country.

By the early fifteenth century, then, the production of sugar had spread from the eastern basin of the Mediterranean to the shores of the Atlantic. Three colonial regions —Palestine, Cyprus, and Crete—had played a part in this development; three noncolonial zones—Sicily, Spain, and Portugal—had participated in it. Spain and Portugal produced less than Sicily, but all three contributed to the expansion of sugar-cane production across the Atlantic zone.

Again it was the Genoese who served as the liaison between the Mediterranean and the Atlantic, and it was their capital that stimulated production in the Madeiras, a Portuguese colony, as well as in the Canary Islands, a Spanish possession. The Genoese had already been involved in the cultivation of sugar cane in Sicily, and from there the plant and the indispensable agricultural techniques were carried to Madeira. Production had begun there in 1455, but it was only after 1472, when sugar from Madeira was exported directly to Antwerp without first going through Lisbon, and when, as a result, northern Europe absorbed the product in ever increasing quantities, that the island experienced a real boom in industry. Already in 1480 some seventy vessels sailed to and from Madeira with full loads of sugar, and the output, which consisted of six thousand arrobas in 1455, rose to eighty thousand in 1493. At that time there were eighty master sugar-manufacturers on the island, which meant that there were eighty different establishments. Soon exportation had to be controlled to avoid a fall in price, and in 1498 quotas were fixed for the different ports of destination. But this system was soon suspended; demand grew to such an extent that Madeira supplied Italian markets and even Constantinople and the Aegean island of Chios, both areas close to the former centers of production in the Levant which had at one time provided sugar for the whole of Christian Europe.

The boom in the sugar industry in the new Atlantic colonies was due, in the first place, to the fact that as Turkish dominion extended over the eastern Mediterranean, it caused a general setback in trade and industry and, in particular, the complete suppression of sugar exportation. This was the cause of the development of sugar-cane production in the Portuguese empire, from the Madeiras first to the Azores, later reaching São Tomé, in the Gulf of Guinea on the coast of West Africa, and finally Brazil, while in the Spanish empire it spread from the Canary Islands to Santo Domingo, Puerto Rico, Mexico, Peru, and finally Cuba. European demand increased more rapidly than the production in the colonies; this is what enabled Barbados, Jamaica, and the other English Antilles, and Guadeloupe and Martinique in the French Antilles to enjoy a late prosperity.

In the Spanish Canary Islands as in the Portuguese Madeiras the Genoese again played a large part in initiating sugar production. In 1526 there were no less than twelve Italian and Spanish plantations on Grand Canary Island, eleven on Tenerife and one on Gomera; the majority were always held by the Spanish. Other foreigners were equally interested and the powerful German firm of the Welsers, from Augsburg, even tried at one time to produce sugar on the island of Palma.

Columbus had come from the Canary Islands on his second voyage in 1493 when he introduced sugar cane into Haiti, which was called at that time Española. In addition to the small establishments which employed only Indian slave manpower, larger establishments soon appeared which used horses or hydraulic power for the mills. The increase in production augmented the need for slaves on the big plantations, and since the supply of Indians was rapidly exhausted, Negroes were brought from Africa in ever increasing quantities. The first technicians came from the Canary Islands, but the boilers were at first imported from the metropolis. Soon they were manufactured on the island itself thanks to the credit granted by the Crown. The Welsers of Augsburg, who engaged in much colonial speculation, invested capital both in the sugar plantations and in the slave trade.

The first hydraulic press was built in Puerto Rico in 1527. The beginnings were not easy, but in 1547 production began to increase. Here, too, the influence of the Canary Islands can be seen, and in 1569 the Canary authorities were still sending to Puerto Rico master sugar-manufacturers and other technicians.

The first *ingenio de azúcar* (plantation) appeared in Jamaica in 1527. Production was aided by Portuguese immigration from the Atlantic archipelagoes, but it never assumed great importance during the period the island was held by the Spaniards. In Cuba, where the sugar industry enjoyed a spectacular rise during a relatively recent epoch, the beginnings were slow and not very promising. Although sugar cane was introduced as early as 1511, production only became important after 1600, and even then the returns were poor.

Cortez brought sugar cane from the Antilles into Mexico during the years immediately following his conquest, and he himself owned plantations in the valley of Oaxaca. Pizarro introduced it into Peru in 1533, a year after his arrival.

Such were the beginnings of sugar production in the Spanish possessions in America. In the Portuguese empire we have seen it spread from the Madeiras to the Azores, and to São Tomé in the Gulf of Guinea, where in 1554 there were some sixty sugar-making establishments. Sugar cane had been introduced there in 1520, at the same time as it had been brought to the archipelago of Cape Verde, from where it spread to Brazil.

During the years following 1530, the Portuguese began to grant portions of the Brazilian coast to hereditary captains, and they alone had the right to possess mills or hydraulic machines for sugar pressing. Nevertheless in 1570 there were sixty *engenhos* or plantations between Itamaracá and São

Vicente, but none as yet in the region of Rio de Janeiro, although there were twenty-three in the North of the country around Recife and eighteen in the region around Bahia. Genoese in association with merchants from Antwerp again played a part in this expansion by creating plantations and supplying capital. In 1628 there were as many as 235 plantations in Brazil, and at that time Portugal was supplying the refineries of England, Flanders, and Germany. The old centers of production in the Mediterranean had completely given up competing, and the Atlantic zone had achieved complete supremacy. Despite the ever increasing Brazilian sugar production, Madeira sugar was still the most valuable during the sixteenth century. It was only in the seventeenth century, as a result of the constant shift in production toward the west, that Brazilian sugar took first place. The Azores and São Tomé stopped planting sugar cane at that time, and even Madeira lost much of her importance. The slave trade thrived as the sugar production increased, so it is possible to say that sugar was the principal cause of the development of slavery in the colonies. The big establishments where mills and melting-pots were used employed between 150 and 200 Negroes, and we know how greatly the numbers of Negroes increased in the population of Brazil beginning with the seventeenth century.

Although Brazil continued until the early eighteenth century to play the main role in production, the French and English Antilles began in the seventeenth century to send increasing quantities of sugar to the European market. In 1625 parts of the island of Saint Christopher had been occupied at almost the same time by the English and the French, and twenty years later both nations began to sell the sugar of this island in the metropolitan markets. By the Treaty of Utrecht in 1713 the English became sole masters of the island, and the sugar industry began to be quite important.

In 1627 the English settled on Barbados. Like Madeira

at the beginning of the Portuguese colonization, this island was too thickly wooded for the settlers to establish significant plantations right away, but exportation began in 1646. However, only after 1655 and the immigration of the Dutch, who had been chased out of Brazil by the Portuguese reconquest, did sugar production become wholly satisfactory, especially after the adoption of the *tayche,* a boiler of Portuguese origin. Manpower was supplied by white prisoners—mainly Scottish and Irish—during the Protectorate of Cromwell, and later by imported Negroes. Under Charles II, thirteen planters were raised to the rank of baron, obvious proof of the wealth they had acquired. The Negroes on Barbados at this time numbered about twenty-five to thirty thousand.

In 1656 the Spaniards lost Jamaica to the English, who in 1664 introduced, or to be precise reintroduced, sugar cane from Barbados. In 1675 there were seventy-five mills, and around 1700 sugar became the principal export. Production continued to grow throughout the eighteenth century, as it did in the other English islands of the Lesser Antilles: Nevis, Antigua, Saint Vincent, Dominica, and Granada.

The French set out from their base on Saint Christopher in 1635 and occupied Guadeloupe and Martinique. The sugar technique in these islands followed the Brazilian methods used by the Dutch and the Jews in Recife before the Portuguese reconquest. On these islands too there was a large increase in production during the eighteenth century. Even before this time the French had added an important portion of Santo Domingo to their possessions in the Caribbean and had restored prosperity to its sugar industry, which had been badly neglected by the Spaniards after 1600. Under the French regime production greatly increased and remained very substantial until the great slave revolt of 1791, which ended in the independence of Haiti.

This revolt was a catastrophe for the planters of the island, but Jamaica, Brazil, and particularly Cuba benefited from it.

The latter island, a Spanish possession, did not assume any importance in sugar production until the middle of the eighteenth century: the circumstances were then favorable and Cuba was ready to profit from them. This was not the case for the other Spanish possessions, but the Danish possessions of Saint Thomas and Saint Croix had for some time been enjoying a truly advantageous situation.

At about this time, as a result of Napoleon's continental blockade, sugar cane began to suffer from competition with the sugar beet. The details of sugar production, its localization, and its international market changed completely. There is no need here to go into these new characteristics or their repercussions on prices and consumption. We simply want to show that the history of sugar-cane production presents a particularly striking example of the passage from the medieval economy of the Mediterranean to the colonial economy of modern times in the Atlantic area. The methods invented in the Middle Ages in the Mediterranean zone made possible the expansion of sugar production across the Atlantic world, where, in the beginning, both capital and technical personnel came from the Mediterranean region. In this particular area of economy the continuity is evident. There has been a gradual shift to the West, from the Palestinian sugar plantations in the twelfth century to those in Cuba in the eighteenth century. This is certainly very convincing evidence of the filiation which bound medieval colonial economy with that of modern times.

From Roman to Colonial Slavery

Everyone knows that in the modern era slavery reached an impressive stage of development in the colonies, particularly in the American colonies. On a superficial level the relationships between colonial slavery and medieval European social history are not obvious since slavery is generally believed to have disappeared from most European countries at the end of Antiquity. In actual fact, although serfdom was a structure much more characteristic of medieval society than was slavery, nevertheless the latter did exist in many European countries during the period between the fall of the Western Roman Empire and the time of the great discoveries. It even continued to exist up to the beginning of the nineteenth century, for there were still some slaves in Sicily in 1812, in Spain in 1820, and in Portugal in 1836.

Christianity had an extremely important influence upon slavery but, being centered on spiritual values, the Gospel did not aim at suppressing this social condition. Christ, according to one text, did not come to change the condition of men but their minds. The changes brought about by Christianity had more influence on the progressive transformation of slavery than did the often contradictory teachings of the Church Fathers, but they did not bring about its disappearance. In fact the Church allowed believers and even its dignitaries to possess slaves but recommended that they should be treated humanely. Emancipation was a pious work; it was neither obligatory nor even expressly recommended.

It is not surprising, then, that slavery existed in the German states at the beginning of the Middle Ages. The source of slaves, just as under the Roman Empire, was, above all, war, and even war among Christians. The slave trade was equally important. The biography of a seventh-century saint relates that whenever the hero heard that slaves were going to be sold he hastened to redeem them. Sometimes, according to this account, one ship alone would transport more than a hundred of these unfortunate creatures, among them Welshmen, Bretons, North Africans, and especially Saxons, great numbers of whom were thrown onto the market at that time. The slave boats which our seventh-century saint met were thus no less laden than the Portuguese sailing ships of the middle of the fifteenth century which plied the seas between the western coasts of Africa and Lisbon with their holds full of Negroes.

In the eighth or ninth century, slavery was replaced by serf-dom in almost all of western Europe, but slave trade across the sea continued. Pagan Slavs were captured along the banks of the Elbe and sold in Moslem Spain. They were brought through Germany and France and shipped from the ports of Provence to the Caliphate of Córdoba. In Great Britain pris-oners taken in the wars between Anglo-Saxons, Welsh, Irish, and Scots were often enslaved. As late as 1102, a council held in London forbade everyone "henceforward to follow the guilty practices which until that time in England had permit-ted the sale of men like wild animals." Actually by that time slavery had become rare in Great Britain; it was only the condition of a small fraction of British society in the border regions. When political unity was achieved slavery disappeared as it did in other states populated by diverse races but con-trolled by one central authority.

The slave trade between the Slavic regions and Moslem Spain decreased in the tenth century and disappeared com-pletely after the fall of the Caliphate of Córdoba. The Chris-tians of southern Europe, instead of selling slaves to the Mos-lems, strove to deprive the latter of their liberty, and in this way slavery continued in Mediterranean Europe.

As a result of the war against the infidels slavery was a mat-ter of course in the Iberian Peninsula as long as Christian king-doms were at war with Moslem states. In central Spain the struggle continued until the conquest of Granada in 1492, the same year as the discovery of America. But even later, Moslems captured at sea were regularly sent to the slave markets in Spain, just as Spaniards and other Christians were sent to slave markets in Moslem North Africa.

In Catalonia, in the Roussillon—French today but belong-ing to Aragon in the Middle Ages—in the kingdom of Valen-cia, more slaves came from the slave trade than from war. Generally the deeds of sale guaranteed that they were not Christian, not stolen, and not protected by the King's Peace. The first of these clauses disappeared in the fourteenth century, and many Greeks and Christian Slavs were sold at that time in Spain, Italy, and the South of France.

In Spain female slaves were generally cheaper than males, although the opposite was true in most of Italy. This was because much of the slave manpower in Spain was used in agriculture and in industry, whereas in Italy the domestic slave predominated in the cities and therefore more female workers were required.

During the fourteenth and fifteenth centuries a great number of slaves were imported into eastern Spain and other Mediterranean regions. Most of the trade was carried on by Italians, and the slaves came from the Italian colonies on the Black Sea and the Balkan Peninsula. These Tartars, Russians, and Caucasians, both men and women, were sold all over the Mediterranean world by Genoese and Venetians who bought them from the men who hunted them.

In Portugal and in Castile slaves were still captured in frontier raids until the middle of the thirteenth century. About this time the Portuguese *Reconquista* came to an end, and no independent Moslems were left in the country. From then on slaves could be acquired only outside the kingdom. During the fourteenth and fifteenth centuries, when a series of African islands were discovered, the slave hunt began immediately. Castilians and Portuguese hunted the Guanches of the Canaries—a race that is now extinct—but they bought even more slaves from the interior of the African continent.

These black slaves had for a long time been imported into southern Europe through the Moslem countries of Africa. The demand during the fourteenth century had increased to such proportions that a special caravan route had been created from the Sudan across the Sahara to the peninsula of Barca in Cyrenaica. The Portuguese under Henry the Navigator created a direct sea route for the black slaves like the one they would establish for the spice trade at the time of Vasco da Gama. There was no longer any need for intermediaries along the caravan routes and in the Moslem ports of North Africa. The Portuguese themselves loaded their holds full of slaves directly in the Senegal or in Guinea. After the death of Henry the Navigator, Diogo Cão went as far as the Congo, and from there, as well as from Angola, increasing quantities of slaves were sent first to Portugal and later to America when the sugar plantations began to grow in number and size.

Since the fifteenth century *asientos* or concessions for the slave trade were granted by the Portuguese government. Thus the Florentine firm of Bartolomeo Marchionni bought the monopoly of slave trade on the Slave Coast, just as later monopolies were sold for buying in Africa and selling in America. The control of this ignominious traffic was in the hands of a special administration, the Casa dos Escravos, or Slave Bureau, a subdivision of the Casa da India, the Portuguese colonial ministry. This traffic along the African coast at the end of the Middle Ages was a transition toward colonial slavery in America. Since the American aborigines, enslaved at the beginning of Spanish colonization in the Antilles, became extinct with frightening rapidity, they were replaced by Negroes imported according to the rules of the *asientos* at the end of the Middle Ages. The passage of medieval slavery in the Mediterranean and southern Europe to colonial slavery in America was thus scarcely noticeable; it was a phenomenon of simple continuity.

When we turn, however, to the study of medieval precedents in the use of slaves in the colonial economy it becomes a question of derivation. Slavery as a sad aspect of colonial technique in its early stages first appeared in the Italian colonies of the eastern Mediterranean. The Italians, accustomed to slavery at home, found the institution flourishing in the regions of the Byzantine Empire or Moslem states where they settled. Slaves were already present in their first possessions in Palestine, either on the plantations or as domestics.

Some of them were to be found on ships as merchandise or as servants. Later, in the smaller Italian colonies that served mainly as markets or ports, slaves were used primarily as servants, whereas in the larger colonies they were used both in agriculture and in industry. There could often be found for sale in the Italian colonial markets women taken in raids in the Caucasus, Tartar children sold by their own parents, and Greeks and other orthodox Christians. Some of them assisted the merchants in their trades, others worked in the fields, still others were domestic servants. When Salveto Pessagno, a member of the Genoese family that supplied Portugal with six admirals, died at Famagusta, Cyprus, early in the fourteenth century, he left two Greek slaves of mixed blood and two other captives, all four of them his personal servants.

The Venetians had for some time played a part in the slave trade in these regions, and Tana, at the mouth of the Don, was their most important market. Crete was also a prosperous slave market, and many Catalans did business there in the fourteenth century. They sold entire herds of slaves taken in raids in Greece or in the numerous islands in the Aegean. Such quantities were not absorbed by the island alone, for Crete was also an important transit market on the sea routes of the slave trade; but some of the slaves were employed in the *casalia* or agricultural settlements in the interior of the island, and the Venetian government was careful to import them for this purpose. The Genoese did the same for their sugar plantations in Cyprus and mastic plantations on Chios. Sometimes slaves were also used in mines, as in the alum mines in Phocaea, a Genoese colony on the coast of Asia Minor. This variety of uses to which slaves were put illustrates clearly the degree to which medieval colonial slavery served as a model for Atlantic colonial slavery. Slave manpower had been employed in the Italian colonies in the Mediterranean for all the kinds of work it would be burdened with in the Atlantic colonies. The only important change was that the white victims of slavery were replaced by a much greater number of African Negroes, captured in raids or bought by traders.

   This chapter has shown that the majority of the techniques of colonization that developed in the Atlantic area in modern times had their origin in the later Middle Ages in the colonies of the eastern Mediterranean. It is clear that there was a general movement from east to west, from the time of the Crusades until the seventeenth and eighteenth centuries. This movement was a complicated process of reciprocal influences among European colonies in the Levant and the European metropolises on the one hand, and the colonies of the Atlantic archipelagoes, the African continent, and the American continents on the other. In the course of this evolution all the geographical and cultural elements of the Western world appeared to be parts of one great historical area. What was true of early colonial techniques also became true in the course of time for the whole of Western civilization, since it spread across the immensity of the Atlantic zone precisely by the techniques whose transplantation from east to west has been described in the preceding pages. Continuity provides a living identity, that is to say of the same essence on both sides of the ocean, despite the indispensable adaptation to different environments. The basis of the various civilizations in the Atlantic zone, is found to be of common origin, however diverse the nuances may be. From the very beginning, history follows the same direction on the two shores of the Atlantic. Nowhere is there a simple copying of precedents, but all parts of this immense zone appear to have a single, fundamental identity when compared with the situations which characterize non-Atlantic civilizations.

2. Medieval Slavery in Europe and Colonial Slavery in America *

In a lecture I gave in 1950 to the International Congress of Historical Sciences in Paris,[1] which dealt with medieval influences on colonization in America, I felt it essential to emphasize the historical continuity that exists between medieval societies, including their too often ignored colonial aspects, and American colonial societies. I indicated that in institutional matters this continuity implied a kind of colonial "acceptance" of feudal law. Just as the Roman law that was accepted in Europe during the last centuries of the Middle Ages was not an exact copy of that of the jurisconsults of ancient Rome but the fruit of evolution and adaptation, so also feudal law or the law of the domain or any other kind of law which could be introduced from Europe into America was made to adapt to the new milieu. The same process of adaptation can be found in other aspects of social and economic structures. There remains nevertheless a common origin, and American colonial societies, in their essential structure, just like the European societies themselves, are branches growing from the one common trunk of the Middle Ages. This is particularly true of the Ibero-American societies, born at the very beginning of the colonial epoch, when the Spanish and Portuguese societies which gave birth to them had

* Translated from "Esclavage médiéval en Europe et esclavage colonial en Amérique," *Cahiers de l'Institut des Hautes Etudes de l'Amérique Latine,* VI (1961), 29–45.
[1] The lecture was published as "Les influences médiévales dans la colonisation de l'Amérique," *Revista de historia de America,* XXX (1950), pp. 440–450.

scarcely themselves emerged from their medieval form. However important and original the indigenous foundation was, what was superimposed, or even imposed, was the heritage of the Middle Ages. And what has emerged, despite the indigenous element, or rather together with the indigenous element, forming one culture, transformed by enforced contact with the conquerors, is a society of the *ancien régime,* as the European societies of that same period were also societies of the *ancien régime,* in which the medieval heritage remained essential. Contrary to current terminology, there was no longer any Old or New World. Centered around the Atlantic, there was only one world, in which history moved in one direction. That direction was determined by the common point of departure, the Western Middle Ages. Just as the lingering traces of the Middle Ages in Europe were terminated by the revolutionary abolition of the *ancien régime,* so in America the end of the same heritage as an essential element in the sociopolitical complex was brought about by the emancipation and independence of the old colonies. The break took place at the same time on both shores of the Atlantic.

In order to study the continuity which I think is to be found between the Middle Ages and modern times where American colonial history is concerned, it seems to me we must distinguish between two kinds of preparatory phenomena, those of connection and those of adaptation. One of the most important of the preparatory phenomena was medieval European slavery; colonial slavery especially was a phenomenon of adaptation, and I will attempt to distinguish its characteristics by comparing them with those of medieval slavery.

I have devoted and will continue to devote a series of articles to slavery in medieval Europe, and I have published the first volume of a complete work on this subject; [2] a major

---

[2] *L'esclavage dans l'Europe médiévale,* I: *Péninsule Ibérique—France,* University of Ghent, Werken uitgegeven door de Faculteit van de Let-

part of that volume is devoted to Spain and Portugal, with which we shall be concerned here as far as they relate to Latin America.

Medieval slavery was not an exclusively Iberian phenomenon. All the countries of Europe were familiar with slavery for a considerable part of the Middle Ages, and even in the countries whose social evolution was rapid, slavery did not disappear before the tenth century. But by that time the evolution toward what I can only call serfdom, for lack of a more adequate and generally valid term, had begun everywhere, even in the countries in which slavery survived until the end of the Middle Ages and long after, as well as in the others.[3]

The Latin word *sclavus,* the common source of the words *esclave, esclavo, escravo, schiavo, Sklave,* and *slave,* did not take root during that initial period when slavery was common to the whole of Europe.[4] This early slavery was inherited without a gap from ancient slavery. The slave at that time was the *servus,* the *mancipium* of Rome. It was only when slaves were recruited from entirely new sources that other terms appeared to indicate the nonfree, and among these was *sclavus,* derived from the ethnic name of the Slav people and popularized. It appeared first in its Latin form in tenth-cen-

teren en Wijsbegeerte, vol. 119 (Bruges, 1955). For the trade with Moslem Spain, see also "Traite et esclavage dans la vallée de la Meuse," *Mélanges Félix Rousseau* (Brussels, 1958), pp. 673–686. For slavery in the Italian medieval colonies, see my articles, "Aspects de l'esclavage dans les colonies médiévales italiennes," *Hommage à Lucien Febvre,* (Paris, 1954), II, 91–103; "Esclavage et ethnographie sur les bords de la Mer Noire (XIIIᵉ et XIVᵉ siècles)," *Mélanges Van der Essen* (Brussels, 1947), I, 287–298; "La colonie vénitienne de Tana, centre de la traite des esclaves au XIVᵉ et au début du XVᵉ siècle," *Studi in onore di Gino Luzzatto* (Milan, 1950), II, 1–25; and the relevant articles listed in note 5 to the Introduction.

[3] C. Verlinden, "Précédents et parallèles européens de l'esclavage colonial," *O Instituto de Coimbra,* CXIII (1949), 1–41.

[4] C. Verlinden, "L'origine de sclavus=esclave," *Archivum latinitatis medii aevi,* XVII (1942), 97–128.

tury Germany. It seems curious at first that an Arab equivalent, *siklābi* (plural *sakāliba*), in Moslem Spain, appeared at the same time. The reason for this is that at that time an important commercial current brought large numbers of Slav slaves, captured or bought on the eastern frontiers of Germany, over western Europe to the Spain of the Caliphs of Córdoba and from there to the rest of the Moslem world.[5] This trade ended in the eleventh century, or at least took a different direction. *Sclavus* and *siklābi* were arrested in their semantic evolution in the countries where they had first appeared. *Sclavus* suffered an eclipse and *siklābi* assumed in Arabic the more restricted meaning of eunuch.

But in the thirteenth century *sclavus,* meaning slave, reappeared, this time in Italy, whence it spread across the whole of Europe. At that period the Italians were, in fact, the initiators of a new trade current which fed the Mediterranean world in particular. They began to import into Italy Slav slaves who came from southeastern Europe and from the shores of the Black Sea. The Slavs became once more the object of a very active trade, so much so that soon their name began to be applied to all the nonfree. From Italy Slav slaves spread to the South of France and eastern Spain, where *sclau* in Catalan became the general term for a slave in the fourteenth century. In the Castilian political complex and in Portugal, on the other hand, there were never any Slav slaves because those regions played a much smaller part in the economic life of the Mediterranean. The result was that the term *esclavo* or *escravo* appeared in these countries much later.

This fact puts these countries—which are of direct interest to us in this chapter and which were familiar with slavery without interruption throughout the Middle Ages and during the colonial era—in a very special position. In the tenth century, in the Christian countries of the Iberian Peninsula, the vocabulary for slavery was still completely that of Antiq-

[5] See my article "Traite et esclavage dans la vallée de la Meuse."

uity. The terms *servus, mancipium, puer,* and *puella* were used, as in Rome. These words indicated equally the Christian slaves, successors of those of the era of the Visigoths, and the prisoners of the Moslem wars, reduced into slavery, who had become more and more numerous since the beginning of the ninth century. The slaves stemming from their Visigothic predecessors gradually developed into the state of semifreedom and were replaced by the Moslem nonfree, men as well as women. Even conversion to Christianity did not bring the latter freedom; only a land concession which took them out of domestic service could allow them a relative rise in social status. These Moslem slaves were called *sarracenus* and *maurus* in the Latin texts of the time.

At the beginning of the *Reconquista,* in the Christian regions of the Iberian Peninsula, the only Moslems were prisoners who had become slaves. Therefore *maurus* and *sarracenus* could only mean slave at that time. This was to change progressively, but especially from the beginning of the reign of Alfonso VI of Castile. The Christians at that time made a real leap toward the south. Their crushing advance brought them into regions where the Moslem population was very dense for that epoch, and they even captured, in 1085, the ancient Visigothic capital, Toledo. It was absolutely impossible to think any longer of enslaving such vast numbers. Certainly Moslem slaves remained numerous during the Middle Ages but they came from the razzias into Moslem territory in the course of the almost constant hostility along the frontiers where, even when the Christian and Moslem states were at peace, their subjects were not. What is important is that the captive Moslems did not come from the regions where the Christians went to settle.

Besides the Moorish slaves there were more and more free Moors from then on, like the *mauri pacis* of the *fuero* of Cuenca at the beginning of the thirteenth century or even at Teruel at the end of the preceding century. In Salamanca and Ledesma the *fueros* mention free Moors described as *engos.* In the beginning there were even autonomous Moorish communities like that of Tudela in Aragon in 1115. And also, attempts were made to establish a *modus vivendi,* at least in economic matters, between Christians and Moors, as at Calatayud in 1131. But everywhere there was a tendency toward conversion and, as a result, in the cities, toward assimilation at the various levels of Christian urban society, while in the rural areas evolution brought about the integration of the Moslems into the various layers of peasant society. A varying degree of tolerance continued to maintain communities of Mohammedan subjects of Christian sovereigns throughout the Middle Ages, but with this important nuance: beginning in the thirteenth century, the *repartimientos* superimposed everywhere on the Moslem population which was not assimilated into Christian society the hierarchy of a seigneury or domain controlled by the conquerors. Moslem slavery in Castile, therefore, continued to exist chiefly in the frontier zones; in the interior of the country it became more and more rare, but it did not disappear.

From the end of the thirteenth century, Aragon and Portugal were both cut off from direct contact with what was left of Iberian Islam. Both of them maintained slavery but fed it henceforth from different sources. In Aragon, especially in Catalonia and Majorca, both of which played an active part in Mediterranean trade, slaves would be mainly imported from the Levant and the Black Sea. In Portugal slavery underwent a period of vegetation but then took on new strength with the beginning of expansion in Africa. This evolution again was reflected in the vocabulary of the institution. In Mediterranean Spain, the slaves imported from the east of the Mediterranean basin and the area of the Black Sea became increasingly numerous during the fourteenth century; at this time the Latin term *sclavus* and its Catalan equivalent *sclau* became prevalent. In Portugal neither *sclavus* nor *escravo* became common before the fifteenth century; but this same century saw the appearance of *negro* or *guineu,* to-

gether with *mouro,* which delayed the complete triumph of
escravo for some time but indicated the even more important fact that, as of that time, in Portugal, the most common
kind of slave was the African. The Portuguese settlements in
Africa then were merely trading stations, like Arguin and,
later, Mina in Ghana. Up to a certain point, then, one could
say that in Portugal colonial slavery began before colonization. Spain had participated in this African trade from the
beginning of the fifteenth century, not at first by importing
Negroes, but by reducing to captivity the Guanches, the
natives of the Canary Islands, who today have disappeared.

Such in broad outline was the state of slavery in the Iberian countries at the time that they threw themselves into the
prodigious adventure of discovering and colonizing America.
Before we become involved in the adaptations of that institution on the western shores of the Atlantic, let us look briefly
at the societies with slaves which were to begin colonization.
The Italian colonies in the Levant had been slave colonies
during the Middle Ages. Slaves had been employed on the
Venetian sugar plantations of the Cornaro family in Cyprus
as in the Genoese alum mines of Phocaea on the Anatolian
coast, and there are many other examples. These slaves came
from the Levant or the shores of the Black Sea. When the
Portuguese and Spaniards began the colonization of the
Atlantic archipelagoes, their slave manpower was supplied by
reducing the natives of neighboring black Africa to slavery.
Black slaves were also found in the metropolis, but more so
in Portugal than in Castile. There were 9,950 slaves in Lisbon out of 100,000 inhabitants in 1551, 10,470 in 1620, and
the enormous majority of them were black. In Seville there
were 6,327 slaves in 1565. These were mainly Negroes who
had been bought and Moors captured in raids on North
Africa, as well as some Turks. In Cádiz in 1616, there were
500 Negro slaves as opposed to 300 captive Moors. But in
Madrid, only the nobles possessed Negroes, Moors, or Turks
up to the middle of the seventeenth century. It is nonetheless

true that slavery continued a parallel existence in the metropolises and in the colonies during the whole colonial era, since it was not abolished in Portugal until 1869, and the freed slaves even existed as a legal class up to 1878. In Spain the import of slaves into the metropolis from the colonies was prohibited in 1836.[6] In France emancipation *ipso facto* of similar slaves was decreed in 1818, and in Sicily there were still Moslem slaves in 1812. Thus in Europe there had been not only medieval precedents but also modern parallels of colonial slavery.

If one considers the uninterrupted succession from medieval slavery in Europe to the colonial slavery of the Italian possessions in the Levant and the Atlantic islands of the two Iberian states, then slavery in America was only an adaptation to the new milieu. It is this adaptation which I now wish to examine by comparing it with its medieval precedents.

A problem concerning slavery arose almost immediately in Spanish America as far as the native populations were concerned. From the first contacts of Columbus with the Indians in the Caribbean zone, a distinction was made between those who "had a disposition" to submission, as he wrote in his letter to Santangel in February 1493, and those who resisted. The conquerors and colonists considered at first that they had the right to treat as slaves all the natives they captured, either individually or in groups, as a result of war expeditions. Slaves originating in the Antilles were soon sent to Spain to be sold there, and those who sent them surely had no scruples concerning their place of origin. It is certain that at the beginning *encomenderos* sent to Spain for sale natives who had been given them in *encomienda*. This must have been rare, though, for they were faced with the problem of how to treat the native population just as Spain had had to face this problem with the Moslem population when the *Re-*

[6] For modern slavery in the Iberian countries, see my book *L'esclavage dans l'Europe médiévale*, I, pp. 835 ff.

conquista reached the zones where Moslems were more numerous than the conquerors. There could be no question of enslaving the whole subjected population. Besides, in America, the Crown was immediately opposed to it for religious as well as political and fiscal reasons. The Crown, supported by the Church, wished to integrate the natives into Christian society, which implied submission to royal authority on a relatively equal footing with the other subjects of the Crown. After 1503 the government strove to achieve this result by the use of the *requerimiento:* the as yet unconquered natives were asked "to become Christians and convert and be incorporated into the communion of the faithful and under our obedience".[7] They were promised they would live in peace, and efforts were made to maintain what I have called elsewhere "colonial peace"[8] with the other native populations. If the *requerimiento* were not successful, however, it was considered legitimate to reduce to slavery the natives who were taken prisoner in the subsequent hostilities; this is not to say that if an entire population were subdued after such hostilities it could be reduced to slavery. At this point certain provisions began to operate in favor of that population. On September 16, 1501, for example, in a message addressed to Governor Ovando,[9] personal freedom and a certain freedom of movement were guaranteed to the natives by the Crown; their goods were also protected since their lands were not distributed among the Spanish colonists, who were moreover threatened with penalties if they did not observe these provisions. The conquered Indians were regarded as subjects of the Crown; as such they owed a tax and certain services, which would be guaranteed by designating certain locations

[7] R. Konetzke, *Colección de documentos para la historia de la formación social de Hispano-America* (Madrid, 1953), I, 14 ff.

[8] C. Verlinden, "Pax Hispanica en la America colonial," *Historia,* XIV (1958), 5–17; and "Le requerimiento et la paix coloniale dans l'Empire espagnol d'Amérique," *Recueil de la Société Jean Bodin,* XV; *La Paix* (Brussels, 1961), 397–414.

[9] Konetzke, *op. cit.,* no. 6, pp. 5–6.

for that purpose. This system was legalized by the Ordinances of Burgos of 1512 and by subsequent provisions concerning the good treatment of the Indians, such as the Ordinances of Granada of 1526.

In Spanish America, as in Spain during the last centuries of the *Reconquista,* therefore, native slavery was a characteristic of frontier regions, that is, regions bordering on areas of as yet unconquered people. However it is obvious that, as in Spain, slaves coming from these regions were, through trade, scattered in limited numbers to the interiors of the Spanish possessions. The conquered Indians of the interior must not have been particularly surprised by this, for native societies had known slavery as the result of war before the Spanish conquest. As the unconquered zones gradually disappeared, however, and as all the native peoples were integrated into the empire, native slavery as a result of frontier war diminished and eventually disappeared completely. Then the king's peace reigned everywhere and the conquest was henceforward called "pacification," as in the ordinance concerning the good treatment of the Indians enacted by Philip II in 1573. Finally, war against the natives was banned from the Spanish empire in 1680 with the issuing of the Recopilación de Indias, which expressly stated "that war may not be and cannot be waged on the Indians of any province to make them receive the Holy Catholic faith and give us obedience (III, 4, 9)." War had in effect become useless, and native slavery was, by the same decree, banned in the whole vast world ruled in America by the *Pax Hispanica.*

All this does not mean that the native populations were not still treated very badly sometimes. But were the peasant populations of Europe everywhere and always treated much better? Here we are dealing with yet another trait inherited by societies of the *ancien régime* from the Middle Ages. It was no longer a question of slavery, however, but of various shades of serfdom, or at least of what survived of that regime

of semifreedom which had for so long been the dominant
condition of the rural population of Europe. In America an
analogous condition began to characterize almost the entire
native population, with one difference: the racial opposition
between master and Indian, complicated by the archaism and
petrification generally inherent in colonial societies, maintained a sort of colonial serfdom at a level of harshness that
had long ago disappeared in Europe. It is certainly true that
such harshness sometimes implied a condition not far re-
moved from slavery, but the legal regime was distinct and the
authorities were aware of their responsibility. As of December 20, 1503, they had declared that the natives of America
were "free and not subject to *servidumbre.*" [10] This latter
term denoted slavery; it did not exclude personal dependency
of natives working on a domain.

Rebellion on the part of peoples of a different race was
always punished with slavery in the Middle Ages. The same
had been true for the conquered Moslems in Spain and even,
during the Aragonese monarchy, for the Sardinians. In America the Indians who converted to Christianity but revolted
against the Crown did not escape this fate. Moreover there
was a tendency to interpret rather broadly the notion of rebellion, and natives who in fact were not rebels were marked
with the red iron of slaves. To avoid the abusive use of the
branding iron it was decided in Mexico on August 24, 1529,
that the iron "would be put in a chest with two locks and two
keys, different one from another, of which one would be kept
by the Reverend Father in Christ Fray Juan de Zumárraga,
bishop of Mexico City," [11] whereas the other would be in the
hands of justice.

---

[10] *Colección de documentos inéditos, relativos al descubrimiento,
conquista y colonización de las antiguas posesiones españolas de
América y Oceania* (42 vols.; Madrid, 1864–1884), XXXI, 209.

[11] *Colección de documentos inéditos relativos al descubrimiento,
conquista y organización de las antiguas posesiones españolas de
ultramar* (25 vols.: Madrid, 1885–1932), IX, 103.

The fact that the native societies were slave societies had the effect for a time of prolonging slavery in America. The Spaniards actually bought slaves from the natives. But royal authority intervened in this too. In Peru on October 26, 1541, Charles V decreed that no Spaniard "may dare to redeem or buy from the said Indian chiefs and leaders and other persons native to the said province which were at peace and subject to us, the Indians which they hold subject and for their slaves, and if anyone redeems or buys them, they have lost them and the slaves are given for free, so that they may do that which they desire and hold for good." [12] But it was not only in the new colonial society and not only for the Spanish colonists that the Crown wanted to eliminate this source of slavery; it was also in the native communities, inasmuch as they were still ruled by their own customs. In fact penal slavery was very widespread in these communities, as it had been before the conquest. However, a decree of 1541 forbade the Peruvian chiefs to continue to reduce natives to slavery, for, being subjects of the king of Castile, they were obliged to live according to Spanish laws.[13] Here there is absolutely no parallel with the situations which existed in medieval Spain. The Moslem communities that lived under Christian rule in Spain scarcely knew slavery, since the enslavement of Christians was impossible, and the possession of non-Christian slaves by Moslems was not legal and therefore only existed in exceptional cases with an actual or legal privilege.

Since the middle of the sixteenth century one of the tasks of the "procurador general de los indios," in New Spain was to bring before a judge the claims of slaves to freedom. This was stipulated by a decree (*cedula*) of July 7, 1550,[14] which gives fairly good proof of the degree to which Indian slavery

[12] Diego de Encinas, *Provisiones, cédulas, capitulos de ordenanzas, instrucciones y cartas* (4 vols.; Madrid, 1596; reissued Madrid, 1946), IV, 367.

[13] *Ibid.*   [14] *Ibid.*, p. 376.

had receded in Mexico. However, in the frontier zones, the ancient legislation still prevailed or was even expressly reintroduced. Thus, in 1608, in Chile, the legality of enslaving the Araucanian prisoners was recognized.[15] It is true that the free Araucanians did the same to the Spaniards. Curiously, there existed in these regions a temporary slavery of young natives up to their twentieth year—"as happened with the Moors of the Kingdom of Granada," said the decree which allowed their enslavement. But conversion entailed emancipation, which marks a progress over medieval slavery. The enforced sale of Indian children by their parents was equally practiced in these regions, and their purchase by Spaniards was expressly forbidden in 1697.[16] Similar situations had not existed in the metropolis in the Middle Ages, but they were frequently mentioned in the deeds of sale drawn up in the Italian colonies of the Levant, especially in the Genoese and Venetian settlements on the northern shores of the Black Sea where Tartar parents used to sell their children quite frequently to Christian merchants.

Thus, in the South of Chile, the war against the Indians, despite the interdiction of the Recopilación of 1680, continued to feed slavery. Slavery also kept the war going. To put an end to this vicious circle it was finally decided to forbid the enslavement of prisoners—a curious reversal of the habitual results and causes which marked how exceptional the situation that continued to prevail in Chile at the end of the seventeenth century had become.

It is worth noticing that enslavement of prisoners was regional and scarcely affected the whole empire. It was a long time since Indian slaves had been exported to Europe. In the case of Chile, it is also obvious that the central authority intervened to prevent the sale in other parts of the

[15] R. Konetzke, "La esclavitud de los indios como elemento en la estructuración de Hispano-America," *Estudios de historia social de España*, I (1949), 472.

[16] *Ibid.*, p. 474.

Hispanic-American world. The Crown thus remained faithful to its general policy of hostility to enslavement of Indians. If there was some departure from it in Chile, it was under the influence of local colonists, then as always and everywhere uncompromising in their rigorous attitude toward the indigenous peoples struggling for their freedom. This extremism was not shared by the metropolitan government. The latter saw in the *Pax Hispanica* the supreme goal to be attained. Just as there was no place in the Spanish empire for civil war, there was also no room for slavery, its bitter fruit. This proves that, if the legislation against the enslavement of the natives was important, if the action of the defenders of the Indians was generous, nevertheless it was exclusively the establishment and maintenance of colonial peace which provided the necessary and imperative conditions for this legislation and action. Contrary to what might be thought, no colonial society has been able to exist by enslaving the entire native population. Indigenous slavery and colonization are, when the accounts are reckoned, contradictory. This is one of the great laws of colonial society in all times.

But of course colonization did not exclude slavery, provided it was reserved for the nonindigenous, for the imported slaves. And this presents the immense problem of black slavery which I can only treat briefly.

As far as its precedents are concerned, let us note that such slavery had already existed in the Middle Ages, throughout the Mediterranean world. Especially in the fourteenth and fifteenth centuries numerous Sudanese and Guinean slaves were brought to the shores of the Mediterranean by trans-Saharan caravans and then sold to Christian merchants who spread them into eastern Spain, southern France, and Italy. In reality the Portuguese of Henry the Navigator merely rerouted this trade. From a trans-Saharan trade with Moslem and Italian intermediaries they developed a direct maritime trade without intermediaries, exactly as they would do later for the spices from the Indies. From both sides the Moslem

and Italian merchants were eliminated. But the Portuguese
changed the black slave trade from a Mediterranean into an
Atlantic commerce. Thenceforth, to obtain supplies of Negroes, like supplies of pepper and spices, one had to pass
through Lisbon.

The Negro slave in the Middle Ages was primarily a domestic slave. Now he became primarily a plantation slave.
Slave plantations had already existed in the Middle Ages, especially the sugar plantations in the Levant, but they had
rarely employed Negroes. When the Portuguese and Spaniards began to exploit intensively the archipelagoes and islands of the Atlantic, they had recourse to Negro slave manpower, which was used chiefly in the cultivation of sugar in
Madeira, in the Canaries, and on São Tomé. From there, by
a connection which can often be followed in detail, the agriculture of the plantation was to pass to the Antilles and to
Brazil, and with it black slavery.

This presented no sociopolitical problem in America. Enslavement of Negroes could not compromise the "colonial
peace." They were not indigenous. The problem was not in
America but in Africa, and there, during the whole of the
ancien régime, colonization never actually penetrated into
the interior. There were trading stations along the coasts
where both blacks and whites lived off the traffic in people
from the interior. This situation continued throughout the
ancien régime, as did colonial slavery in America. It is curious
to note that during this period the legitimacy of enslaving the
Negroes was very rarely questioned. Laws controlling black
slavery were commercial, agricultural, laws of the domain—
in other words, economic laws, not limiting measures, and
even less abolitionary.

Abolition of the trade, if not of black slavery in America,
only began to be talked about when the colonial powers had
set foot in the interior of Africa. Then relations between
colonists and colonized became in Africa what they had long
been in America: it became impossible to continue to enslave

the indigenous African population if a nation wanted to maintain and develop colonization in Africa. Certainly the great abolitionists were magnificent figures, as were the great theologians who had defended the Indians. They did not, however, bring about the end of black slavery. Their efforts contributed to it; but what made the triumph of their ideas possible was that it became necessary for the "colonial peace" to reign in Africa in order to facilitate exploitation. Instead of sustaining a marginal economy in the literal sense of the term—that is, an economy almost exclusively limited to trade along the coast—the black continent would, in the nineteenth century, yield its interior riches to the appetites of the colonial powers. The latter had to abolish the Negro traffic in order to be able to profit from Africa. Moreover they had, in the meantime, lost interest in America, which had largely escaped the control of the Spaniards, Portuguese, French, and English. The Iberians had monopolized or controlled the traffic as long as they had dominated the Atlantic. Each new maritime power had then tried to control both the ocean and the trade in Negroes. The Dutch had not been able to break the ebony chain which linked Angola and the Congo with sugar-producing Brazil, but the English obtained the *asiento* in the treaty of Utrecht. In the nineteenth century, interests were no longer centered in America; it was then that it became possible first for the Negro traffic and then for slavery to disappear.

Only in 1871 did the Spanish Cortes (parliament) decide to forbid slavery after 1880 in what was left of the empire. True, Spain had forbidden the slave trade in 1820, and Portugal had decided to do so in 1836, although Brazil, its ancient colony, had gone before it along this road since 1831. We know that the last Brazilian emperor, Pedro II, imposed in 1871 the law of "free belly," which assured the emancipation at birth of children of slaves, and that he proclaimed total emancipation in 1888; this action cost him his throne. In the Antilles where Haiti, since the beginning of the century, had forged in blood the political liberty of a nation of emancipated slaves, the progressive suppression of slavery was also the cause of social and economic trouble. Attempts were made to relieve difficulties by importing other nonaborigines, generally Asiatic. Legally these were not slaves, although their economic condition was often scarcely better. Africans were even imported once again, but now they were called "free workers" although their misery was such that one could see in them new victims of the slave trade. When international opinion became aware that, in fact, a kind of slavery was being practiced again in the Antilles, the importing of Africans and other nonaborigines was brought to an end. But it had lasted long enough to substitute for plantation slavery, the sad monopoly of the blacks, a multiracial plantation proletariat whose living conditions were extremely poor. The emancipated blacks held a place in it, and more and more it became the situation of the indigenous population in continental America where a plantation economy already existed or was developed by the diversification of cultures. Sugar in fact was no longer sole king; the improvement in the standard of living in Europe as a result of industrialization created outlets for new agricultural products suited to production on plantations. At the same time this production was no longer an American monopoly. Plantation economy spread to other tropical and subtropical regions of the world, to Asia as well as Africa. The rise of a plantation economy in Africa was a result of the suppression of black slavery in America, in itself a result of the intensification of the colonial undertaking in Africa. In Asia the introduction of a plantation economy was due entirely to the industrialization of Europe, a factor which of course exerted its influence equally in Africa and America.

So far as slavery is concerned, the cycle of continuities and adaptations now ceased, as did its racial and cultural results. Thenceforth the worker on the plantation, whatever the color of his skin, was a proletarian, at first agricultural then gradually industrial, as production became intensified by the development of technique. Improvement in his living conditions depended thenceforth on technology, whose advance determined the decrease in his physical discomfort and finally the increase in his salary. This situation constituted an enormous difference from slavery. No technical progress in the course of the Middle Ages and the *ancien régime* had determined the disappearance of slavery: neither the shoulder collar of the draft animals, as Lefebvre des Noëttes mistakenly thought, nor the water mill nor the windmill. The rudder was no more decisive in banishing slavery from the galleys than the process of amalgamation in abolishing enforced labor in the mines of the New World. It was only when the sources of the slave trade dried up as a result of the need to establish "colonial peace" first in America and then in Africa that slavery died out. "Colonial peace" itself was born of the desire to make possible intensive economic exploitation with the collaboration of the indigenous population. This collaboration, to be effective, had to maintain the native in his place, and it forbade slavery. These developments operated in America and Africa successively, with results that were manifested on both sides of the Atlantic. Every time the drying up of the sources of the slave trade was the determining factor. When one current of the trade petered out in the Middle Ages it was replaced by another. Once it became evident that indigenous freedom was imperative in America, black slavery was utilized in those places where, as in the plantation economy, slave manpower was considered essential. But when the African source of the slave trade ran out, the cycle was closed. The era of world industrial economy had been entered, and the last traces of the economy of the *ancien régime,* inherited from the Middle Ages, had to disappear, as its political and social organization had already been abolished. Henceforth improvement in the human condition was bound to the development of industry and technology; it no longer had anything to do with the trade of man by man that had made slavery possible, first in Europe and then in America.

I believe that this chain of events, which played so large a part in the transformation of American society, and of other societies that have passed, in different forms, through analogous stages of evolution, must be shown, since it helps to connect that evolution with the great world forces of continuity, and also of renovation. These forces control the relations of men through time and across space, and the historian, in the end, always comes back to them when he wishes to do what, after all, is his primary task: understand in order to explain.

3. Western Civilization and Atlantic Civilization*

During the period between the Renaissance and the Enlightenment Europe's colonial expansion began to transform Western civilization into an Atlantic civilization. Its foundations, laid in Antiquity and fortified in the Middle Ages, endured in the form given them by the Middle Ages and constituted the basis of Atlantic civilization in the modern era.

To speak of the history of classical Antiquity and of the Middle Ages is to speak of the history of Europe, a history which is by no means centered in the Atlantic. But which Europe or which different Europes as situated in space and time should concern the historian? Ancient and medieval Europe was constantly growing and being displaced; Western civilization was already expanding and continued to do so until it became an Atlantic civilization in the modern and contemporary eras.

It is interesting first to consider the difference between geographic and historic Europe. Europe in the atlases is very clearly defined and consists of a nonvariable entity. Here we find maps, separated from the others, which represent the zone enclosed by the Atlantic Ocean and the Ural Mountains, with a division into numerous states; the fact that all the states appear on one map makes one think that there is something which unites them and which in turn distinguishes

* Translated from "Civilización occidental y civilización atlantica," *Atlantida,* IV (1966), 278–297.

thcm from the rest of the world. But from a purely geographic point of view these maps are deceptive. The Ural Mountains are not really very high, and the great plain, called "Baltic" in Europe although it really begins much to the west of the Baltic Sea, continues into the great expanse of northern Asia as far as the shores of the Pacific, across the infinity of Siberia. This circumstance is translated in the Soviet system into the political form given to the Union of Soviet Socialist Republics, all of which are theoretically equal, be they found to the east or to the west of the Urals. This theoretical equality is not sufficient to conceal differences of administrative "consideration," but it does reveal and underscore the unity of the metropolis and of the colonies, a unity which is the more solid for being continental and not divided into different sections by oceans and seas, as was the case in the traditional colonial empires that are now disappearing. As far as power relations are concerned, the frontier of the Urals has been insignificant for centuries. Its example is enough to demonstrate that intellectual customs whose origin is not geographic but pedagogical and technological have nothing in common with the idea of historical unity as it can and should be conceived by the historian. If terrestrial globes were used as frequently as maps framed in books, the idea of a frontier at the Urals would no doubt never have been applied.

The historical concept of Europe is by nature very different and much more complicated than that of Europe in the atlases. It has varied and still varies in its geographic application. In other words, the historic continent which we can term European has been applied in the course of time to different zones, coincident more or less with the divisions of the Europe of the atlases, exceeding its limits in certain zones and not reaching them in others. Moreover, the historical notion of Europe has been diluted into a broader historical conjunction which could only be born of the expansion of the population of certain sections of Europe, of the fusion and cultural progress of its civilizations within new physical and anthropological mediums.

Greece

We know that the Greeks were the first to speak of Europe, but in essence this name had a mythological meaning. It is curious to think that, according to the Greeks, the maiden Europa was snatched away by Zeus, father of thought; we can see in this a symbol of the part of Greece in the formation of the earliest outline of the concept of Europe. Greek thought was the first to conceive of Europe, still very small, as opposed to the Asiatic Orient. But that same thought was impregnated with the Orient, and because of this, Zeus assumed in the myth of Europa the barbaric form of the divine bull, so close to the zoomorphic gods of ancient civilizations on the other side of the Mediterranean. Moreover, the Greek god carried off Europa and took her far away, just as the Europe of the Greeks stretched from Asia Minor to Greece proper, jumping from island to island over the emerald belt of the Aegean Sea, passing from Greece to Sicily and southern Italy or, on the other side of the Mediterranean, to Cyrenaica in Africa. This original Europe in the atlases comprises only the extreme southeast of the continent, and it is difficult to separate it from its North African extension. It is important to make the distinction that Europe from its very beginning was continually expanding to the west until it reached Mediterranean France and Spain. It was not only occidental but mobile, dynamic, with all that these qualities imply in the way of advances and withdrawals. It is obvious that all civilizations have passed through phases of expansion, but compared with Europe they appear static; none has known such a constant and full expansion in its world ascendancy; none has overcome so many obstacles with such great skill. This has been taking place ever since Greek Antiquity and is still occurring.

The Greek polis was the first model of a specifically European political form, that is to say of a democracy, in the sense that power came from the whole citizenry, was exercised by men elected by them, and was controlled and, when necessary, limited by them. This is one of the most important elements of the historical context first of Europe and then of the Atlantic world. We can consider this attitude toward democracy a necessary criterion in determining European historical unity. Wherever this attitude is not present, the idea of European and Atlantic historical unity does not apply or has ceased to apply, although it might be reintroduced. The process of understanding democracy by the essential factors involved in the idea of the polis can determine whether a zone belongs to European and Atlantic civilization.

Among the characteristics of Greek civilization which foreshadow and prepare the way for European civilization we should study three, at least, which possess a distinctive, essential, and permanent value. Two of them are of a positive nature and the third is of a negative and dangerous type.

A primary positive characteristic is maritime and colonial expansion. Greek ships carried into the West their message of civilization, of which the Greek colonies were the radiating centers. One of Greece's most imperative legacies to Europe was that, during the Roman era and in the Middle Ages, it would continue to colonize in the same way, so that later its message was carried by the great oceanic expansion to the other side of the Atlantic, and, in its most external but perhaps most operative aspects, across every ocean and toward every continent.

A second positive achievement of the Greeks was the birth of the spirit of analysis, which established the basis for the development of European knowledge. The real "wonder of the Greeks" was rooted in the rapidity, the dynamism, the restless vitality with which they assimilated the disorderly acquisitions of the preceding Oriental civilization in order later to develop them, adapting and integrating them into order. For them the world was order, cosmos, whether it concerned nature or society. Intelligence must dominate in order to understand and then shape. This faith in intelligence is characteristic of Europe despite its temporary eclipses, usually caused by interruptions from the barbaric exterior.

The negative factor in Greece, with its terrible consequences, was the division, the opposition of the lesser states to the historical unity, to the unity of civilization. The struggle among the city-states enabled first the Macedonians and then Rome to destroy Greece itself. So influential were these internal divisions on Europe that their legacy eventually brought to an end Europe's chances of material expansion and then endangered its very existence. Fortunately for Greece and for Europe, the worst danger came only after they were absorbed into more extensive historical unities, born of the fusion and cultural progress of their civilizations: the Roman world in Antiquity, and the Atlantic world in our day. Thanks to these broader worlds, which have an analogous historical significance, it has been possible to continue to hear first the message of Greece and then of Europe.

Rome

The Romans created a Mediterranean Europe around their *mare nostrum*, relying heavily on North Africa and the Near East, but at the same time—and this is most important from the point of view of historical continuity—expanding to the North as far as the Rhine and the Danube, and even including England and a part of Scotland. But this Europe which was slightly African and Asian, especially from a geographic perspective, was more "European" than the Europe of the Greeks, since it included within its civilization a considerable portion of the Europe of the atlases. In the broad area engulfed by the Roman Empire at its point of greatest expansion in the century of the Antonines, it spread its Greco-Roman civilization with an intensity and a profundity of penetration which decreased the further it receded from the Mediterranean. We have already mentioned the main Greek outlines of that civilization; they became permanently established, although part of what constituted their peculiar distinction was lost. The Romans were less artistic, less learned, less philosophical, and even less skilled sailors than the Greeks, but with the creation of the Empire they were able to put an end to the struggles between the city-states and to establish the Roman peace for a considerable time, a peace which was based on conquest and on military and administrative colonization, but also on law. These three features will occupy our attention in the paragraphs that follow.

The Roman conquest, as we have seen, achieved the expansion of Europe in space. Into the history and civilization it had inherited from Greece and the Orient through assimilation, it introduced a considerable portion of the Europe of the atlases, until that time sunk in prehistory, so to speak, and foreign to the superior civilization which Rome was spreading around the Mediterranean, and extended that Europe to the frontiers of the Rhine and Danube, as far as Antoninus' wall and the farthest lands of the Picts and the Scots. The transalpine zones of Europe were, until then, an extension of the seminomadic civilizations of the great steppes of the north and center of the Euro-Asiatic continent. They seemed to belong more to Asia than to Greco-Roman Europe. When the Roman conquest reached the Rhine, the Danube, and England, there arose between these zones and Rome a relationship based on opposition in everything which encouraged urbanization, organization, and continuity with the Greco-Roman heritage. In reuniting the Near East and the Europe of that time in one political and cultural whole, the Roman conquest laid the foundations for the spread in the West and in Europe of Christianity, which otherwise might have continued as a Jewish heresy. The importance of the Roman Empire in understanding the Christianization of Europe cannot be overestimated. The Roman conquest made possible, historically speaking, the Christian conquest, and made Christianity a permanent and essential element of the European and Atlantic historical context.

The Roman military and administrative colonization was a colonization over land, somewhat analogous to the Russian colonization of Siberia. Like the latter, it welded the colonized zone to the metropolitan area without breaking continuity. By establishing camps and hubs of military support in the conquered areas, Rome created distribution centers for its language and civilization. The existence of countries in Europe with a Latin language is due to Roman colonization, and ultimately the twenty republics of South America are similarly a continuation of the inheritance of Roman Europe. It was Roman administration which gave to a great part of Europe its administrative structure: the Roman *pagi* and *civitates* provide the foundation for the counties and bishoprics, points of departure for the subsequent administrative units. The construction of Roman villas throughout the Empire was due both to Roman colonization and to assimilation, or rather to cultural progress of the indigenous social elite toward the ways of living of the Roman administrators and military leaders. Where churches were built throughout the zone affected by the Roman conquest, their model was the Paleo-Christian architecture of Mediterranean tradition. The circulation of goods and ideas through these vast areas was made possible by the Roman roads, which had been necessitated by military and administrative colonization. The communication system of Europe belonged to Roman Europe. The part which remained outside the scope of Roman civilization bore no more trace of it than the Asia of the steppes and forests.

Rome's conquest and colonization spread the concepts of

Roman law throughout Europe to the degree of granting citizenship to all the inhabitants of the Empire at the beginning of the third century of the Christian era. There was a systematized law in the Empire which was absolutist in its public aspect. In its private form it constituted a more elaborate legal system than had yet existed in any part of the world. This inheritance was also a permanent acquisition of the European world first and of the Atlantic world later, since nowhere was there a private system of law which protected man more efficiently. That this inheritance was modified through the incorporation of important elements of Germanic origin is only the natural outcome of cultural progress and by no means affects its inmost nature. The same absolutist public law which has, on various occasions and during long periods of European evolution, constituted a threat to and sometimes even an interruption of democracy, presented positive aspects which helped to assure the permanence of the European heritage. There were periods, in fact, in which the notion of the Empire constituted the main political and cultural characteristic of the truly European world; later, when the absolutism inherited from the Roman law of imperial times appeared in the framework of the national state, it became an obstacle to the flourishing of a democratic society.

The Roman world had a wide influence on the barbarians, the peoples of the undeveloped world of those times. When the absence of normal succession threw the Empire into anarchy, the barbarian world took over again and Europe was on the point of becoming Asiatic, since the German invaders came from the part of Europe without communications, without cities, without law, and without Christianity—in effect, an extension of the Asia of the steppes. Then began the Middle Ages; but, to the great good fortune of European historical continuity, the dark Middle Ages of the historians of the Renaissance and the Enlightenment only lasted a short time.

The Church

Initially continuity was assured almost solely by the Church. Not only did it diffuse the Christian message, which was its natural function, but it assured the transmission of ancient culture over the centuries. Beside its normal, daily religious duty, this was undeniably the Church's greatest work, and it was of vital importance for Europe and for Atlantic civilization. That Europe was not absorbed by the barbarians, that it did not regress into the Asia of the steppes and forests, may be attributed to the Church. All that persisted of knowledge, of literature, and of science was transmitted through the Church, whose language continued to be Latin, the only one at that time, outside the Byzantine world, that enabled ideas and thoughts of any degree of refinement to be transmitted. The Germanic or Romance languages were not yet literary, nor were they even written for a large period. The only literate people were the clerics; they carried on whatever remained of the rationality of ancient culture. Although many monks and priests were indeed ignorant and superstitious, it was only among them that the few enlightened minds of the time were to be found. With the collapse of the Western Empire at the end of the fifth century, the Church assumed its unifying function and some of its administrative functions. The bishop became the *defensor civitatis* of his episcopal city and also, in the ancient sense, of the area around it, that is to say of his bishopric. While the German kings struggled continuously among themselves and while the terrible confusion in which the whole world was plunged increased, the bishops and superiors of the monasteries continued to maintain their close relationship and began to have an increasingly intimate connection with Rome, whose bishop became the head of the Western Church, mainly because henceforth there was no emperor on his side. The basileus of Constantinople did not receive the title of emperor from his own subjects, although effectively he was the highest ruler, though weak, inefficient, and incapable of protecting Europe and the ancient heritage. Finally the Pope of Rome set opposite him a Western colleague and a rival in the person of the King of the Franks, who was crowned Emperor in Rome on Christmas in 800.

That Pope Leo III, in making Charlemagne the first Emperor of the West, carried out a truly European measure has not been sufficiently stressed. The decadent Roman Empire had shown itself incapable of protecting Europe from the invasions of the Germans, driven on by the Huns coming out of the heart of Asia. The basileus managed to save the remains of the Empire of the East and assure the survival there of a kind of Christianized hellenism, but he could not prevent his state from being constantly encroached on and sometimes crossed by bands of barbarians. He was even less capable of protecting the West from elements which had threatened it for some time. In fact, waves of barbarians continued to cross from Asia into Europe. The Turko-Mongolian nomads harried the Slavs who, in turn, pushed the Germans. Some had passed far beyond the borders of the semibarbarous, semi-Christian European West which the Church had with great difficulty organized and disciplined through the action and sometimes the martyrdom of its bishops and missionaries. The Lombards were installed in Italy, not only on the plain which bears their name, but much beyond, in the duchies of Spoleto and Benevento which encircled and threatened the very seat of pontifical authority. The Franks had been in opposition to the Avars since Merovingian times and their Germanic neighbors, the Saxons, constantly threatened their land and sea frontiers, while the Germans from Scandinavia began to move to the south in long ships which carried them, a little later, as far as North America. The combination of these threats constituted a new barbaric wave as fearful as that which some centuries before had brought about the fall of the Roman Empire of the West.

The papacy then rendered Europe the enormous service of strengthening the prestige and authority of the King of the Franks, the strongest of the German-Christian sovereigns, by making him Emperor. Thus was formed a western European block under the combined authority of the Pope and the Emperor. This is not the place to study the actual partition and sphere of action of both powers; but it is certain that, as early as the time of Charlemagne, western European thought was kept alive primarily in the minds of the men of the Church. That the West was for them more Christian, or more Catholic—in its opposition to Byzantine Orthodoxy—than European, or in other words more religious than political, does not interest us here. But we must not forget that the only unifying force until then had been religion, and the union between that religion and the only political power capable of defending it was strong enough to preserve the European West. This was how, one might say, the Orthodox East became separated from the Catholic West. That separation is a fact; but it merely represents acknowledgment of the situation that had developed in the course of the centuries between the fall of the Roman Empire of the West and the imperial crowning of Charlemagne. It was a question of providing Europe with the best possible self-protection, since not to do so would certainly have meant the loss of all Europe to the barbarians in the very near future.

Indeed we must not lose sight of the fact that Europe was not only threatened by the successive waves of barbarians that Asia hurled ceaselessly at its back, from the east and from the north, but it had also retreated constantly before Islam in the south. The Christianity of North Africa, which had with some effort remained united to Europe until the seventh century, was being absorbed by the Moslem empire, and in 711 the Visigoth ruler of Spain, recently converted from Arianism to the faith of Rome, was in turn overthrown. In 732 a Frank, Charles Martel, saved Europe *in extremis,* in Poitiers, pushing back the frontier of Islam to the Pyrenees.

With Charlemagne it regressed to the Ebro, thanks to the warriors whose adventures would much later be chronicled in the *Chanson de Roland*. But the Mediterranean was lost, and the Moslem fleets pillaged the coasts of the Christian world, subjecting the inhabitants to slavery. Islam occupied the large islands and established itself on the shores of the continent. Even the basileus of Constantinople governed on an island surrounded by a sea of hostility, Slav to the north and soon to the west, Islamic to the south and east. The creation of the Empire of the West was a final effort to preserve Christianity when the Church and the West had almost no other choice, and no chance to retreat.

Feudalism

The task imposed on the Empire was superhuman, and Charlemagne's successors perished before it, mainly because they did not understand the European scope of the task; they acted as leaders of groups of the faithful in the German tradition rather than as leaders of the state. The kings of Germany managed, again with the help of the Church, to keep their followers faithful to a certain degree, whereas the king of France and the king of the central zone which lay between the two large Carolingian states—an area to which the Imperial Crown had been bound for some time—were abandoned by their retinue. The faithful at that time became vassals, through a system which attempted to establish power relations by law and to which was given the name of feudalism.

Certainly the feudal regime contributed to the preservation of the notion of the state, and, interpreted by a strengthened monarchy, would result finally in a centralized state. But for a time, it meant the political collapse of a vast section of western Europe in which it had taken hold. Soon France and Lorraine were devastated by waves of Norman—that is, Scandinavian—invasions, which again plunged them into the darkness of chaos where only the monasteries, frequently plundered, and the episcopal towns, isolated and surrounded by walls built from the remains of ancient monuments, constituted islands of civilization among the roaring waves of brutality and barbarism.

Germany, although battered along its frontiers, was better able to resist this onslaught, and again the Church came to an agreement with it, transferring the imperial crown to the head of its king. This alliance was not a perfect solution, but by erecting a barrier against the barbaric waves coming from the East, it enabled the West to recuperate and gain strength to expel the invaders. The survival of the French royalty and the beginning of the *Reconquista* in Christian Spain were mainly due to the fact that the rear guard of France and Spain was protected by the Germanic kings, who had inherited the conception of the empire supported by the Church. On the other hand, the fact that England, dominated by the Germanic races and the Scandinavians, was able to remain Christian and European was the result of the direct action of Rome from the time of Gregory the Great and of the support of Celtic Christianity, less affected by the barbaric invasions and reunited around its monasteries, from which a missionary movement would soon extend over most of the European continent.

What was the extent of Europe at the time of the Ottonian Emperors? In Germany the European frontier at that time ran along the Elbe and was thus further east than its position under the Roman Empire. France began to recover little by little. In Spain a small Christian group resisted in the North in the hope of forcing Islam southward in the centuries to come. In Italy the Pope ruled protected by the Emperors. Otto II and Otto III experienced more and more forcibly, the call of the Mediterranean and of classical culture. After the "Carolingian renaissance" there was an "Ottonian renaissance," which was particularly important in the history of art. Central Europe was submerged in barbarism, and this force was strong enough to separate the European West completely from Byzantium, an ever more insulated island in a sea of Slav and Moslem hostility.

But the more Western and diminished Europe of that time began again to radiate a certain strength by means of its missionaries. The Germanic people of Scandinavia began to receive them, and gradually the same occurred in central Europe where the Hungarians, of Asian origin and recently settled, were among the first to be converted. Earlier, Rome and Byzantium had confronted each other in this area. Now the Hungarians became Catholic and the Slavs of eastern Europe and the Balkans passed to Byzantine Orthodoxy, with the exception of those evangelized from Germany. In this way the European West of the tenth century showed, by its religious expansion, that the Church, together with the empire, had effectively protected it and enabled it to store up energy, the first exterior signs of which were visible in the missionary work. From this point of view Byzantium's chances for the conversion of pagans seemed just as good, but all the energy of the basileus was soon absorbed in fending off a new Islamic wave, that of the Seljuk Turks whom Byzantium could not have resisted without the support of a renewed West.

The eleventh century in western Europe was, in fact, a period of demographic development and extraordinary vitality after the terrible centuries of the invasions. For this reason the Investiture Conflict—which put the pope who supported the Cluniac reform and the independence of the clergy in opposition to the Emperor, the head of the imperial Church whose high dignitaries were appointed by him—does not merit, from the point of view of European historical continuity, the importance too often given it by traditional historiography, which has concentrated too much on the idea of State or of Church and on the opposition of those two forces. If the destiny of Europe had truly been endangered by the struggle between Pope and Emperor, then Europe would not have been able, in the eleventh century, to create cities where none existed, to bring back life to those that had survived since Antiquity, to drive the Islamic fleet back to the coast of Africa and the Levant, and to resume trade over a great area, first in the Mediterranean and later in eastern and central Europe. Europe in the eleventh century was a Europe that was developing on the exterior and consolidated within.

The Bourgeoisie

In addition to the Church, the kings, and the great princes, free towns began to play their part about this time, first of all in the countries that had formed the heart of the Roman Empire, especially in Italy. The citizens, primarily merchants, soon had artisans working for them. Together they created within the ancient cities, close to or adjoining the monasteries and fortresses of the lords and princes, new suburbs with markets surrounded by alleys, where artisans were grouped together by their specialties and, soon, by corporations. Their interests were already very different from those of the ecclesiastical or laic dignitaries on whom they were dependent. They accumulated reserves of money which enabled them to raise their voices; they claimed rights, set up urban governments which they elected and which the bishops and lords, laymen and ecclesiastics, had to recognize. It seemed, to a certain degree, that the polis or *civitas* was in the process of being reborn. The merchants of the Italian cities sailed far into the Mediterranean and their ships soon formed fleets in Amalfi, Pisa, Genoa, and Venice. The ancient Byzantine duke or doge came to an agreement with them; he became their chief, since he was the representative of the basileus, who was unable to assert his authority. In some cities the alliance of the head of the local church with the bourgeoisie kept for him his power and wealth for some time, until he had to abandon the direction of affairs after some political mistake. The fleets of the merchant towns expelled the Moslem ships from the central and western Mediterranean, or at least prevented them from leaving African waters. They would soon transport the crusading armies to the Orient.

With the appearance of the municipality, representative government was reborn. Thus a tradition from ancient Europe, repressed for centuries first by absolutism and then by barbarism, took on a new life. This tradition, despite some eclipses brought about by a return to absolutism, would not again be broken. It would continue as a permanent characteristic of European and later Atlantic historical unity and would differentiate these from other civilizations. Initially, representative government would only exist in the various municipalities of the countries, and the urban governments would not collaborate among themselves. But the economic interests of the urban bourgeoisie in certain zones created bonds and associations which began in the northern countries of Europe and were called hansas. The Flemish Hansa of London grouped together a series of commercial companies from cities which are now Belgian or French but were then trading with England, where their members bought wool in the fairs in order to manufacture cloth in their cities. In western and northern Germany, the hansa of the commercial cities, united around Lübeck, would ultimately dominate the Baltic and establish subsidiaries in the zone between Novgorod in Russia, Bergen in Norway, London, and Bruges; for a long time this hansa controlled the salt trade between the ports of the Atlantic coast of France and the Baltic.

Economic associations made their political power felt in the cities and reclaimed from the feudal monarchies of the early Middle Ages a part of the control which the newly established parliaments exercised over the governments. Political society was now divided into estates: clerical, noble, and bourgeois. The princes had allied themselves with the citizens of the cities in order to combat the feudalism of the nobles and ecclesiastics, but precisely because of this, they did not succeed immediately in bringing about the return of absolutism. They had to devote their attention to their administration, which became more complex as their power spread, and for this reason they needed taxes. They could only turn to parliament to obtain them, that is, to the Estates General, where representatives of the three estates entered into discussion with the princes and used the vote on taxes as a means of exerting pressure on the Crown. Thus the ordinary citizen found the means of making his voice heard through his representatives.

But soon the richest citizens began to administer the property of the princes, since by agreement among the capitalist groups, funds would be advanced to the princes so that they would not have to depend for money exclusively on the vote of the Estates. The great nobility, subdued by the ever stronger royalty, lost its property to the Crown, which could live, at least in part, upon the income from its royal domain, augmented by the credit granted by the financiers. The kings and great princes—who had become small monarchs in Germany and Italy as the Empire weakened in passing from one family to another after the Great Interregnum —would soon renounce completely or partially the principle of voting direct taxes and would themselves establish indirect taxes: excise taxes, transportation taxes, bridge and road tolls, and so forth. But they did not dare suppress the parliaments, although they no longer consulted them. The representative government would lose its actual power through the work of the rulers who succeeded in inculcating absolutism, but it would not be abolished and would sooner or later reassume its functions, in some cases with enough strength to destroy the monarchy. Thus, although momentarily obstructed in the exercise of its power, the representative government would continue to be a part of the European inheritance and its essential and determinative feature from a political point of view. Neither Byzantium nor the Orthodox principalities of Russia, absorbed one after the other by the Muscovite tzars, had known such an institution as a parliament or Estates General. Combined with orthodox Christianity, this despotism without representative control characterized them sufficiently to place them outside the European historical unity. This unity, in the later Middle Ages, extended over an area from Scandinavia to Spain and Portugal, from France to Poland, from the shores of the North Sea in England and the Low Countries to the shores of the Baltic in Germany, and as far as the Ionian Sea in Italy.

The whole zone gradually became urbanized. The bourgeoisie played an increasingly large part from an economic point of view, and its richer members began to form part of the nobility. One of the most important sociological characteristics of the European historical unity of those times was a social mobility which fared better in some countries and in some periods than in others, but which eventually destroyed the forces which tried to oppose it, as happened in France at the end of the eighteenth century. Compared with this truly European Europe, the eastern part of the Europe of the atlases was as rigid in its social framework as it was despotic in its system of government. Moreover it was technologically backward compared with historical Europe. The rise of the bourgeoisie had provoked in the latter countries a laicism in the culture which permitted a growing development of the natural and applied sciences. These terms might seem anachronic to the noninitiated when used in reference to the period prior to the Renaissance, but historians now know that the Renaissance would have been impossible without the renewal in sciences and technological achievements of the later Middle Ages. This progress, we repeat, was possible exclusively because of the secularism of the culture, as a result of the rise of the bourgeoisie. Out of this social stratum, so essential to the historical notion of Europe, was to come the Renaissance, the scientific revolution of the seventeenth century, and the Enlightenment of the eighteenth century. Henceforth the function of defending culture had passed from the Church to the urban bourgeoisie.

Maritime Transportation

The most economically and technically advanced country of the early Renaissance was, without doubt, Italy; but it lacked political unity, partly as a result of the extraordinary rise of the urban bourgeoisie. The latter managed to set up city-states, of which the most powerful were Genoa and Venice, where great capital was accumulated as a result of the then most important technological superiority: Italy's highly developed system of maritime transportation. The demographic increase had enabled historical Europe to gather crusading armies, but it was the Genoese and Venetian fleets which carried them to the Levant and to what was left of the Byzantine Empire. They carried the food supplies of the armies and later the supplies for the Christian principalities and colonies founded after the First Crusade in Palestine, starting with the Fourth in what remained of the Byzantine Empire, both in the center and south of continental Greece as well as in the Aegean islands and on the coasts of Asia Minor. The Genoese and Venetians were also granted lands in Palestine and Greece and on the islands. The Venetians received in Palestine a great part of the seigneury of Tyre, which they immediately devoted to the production of sugar cane. After the fall of the Latin Empire of Constantinople, the Genoese acquired the ancient city of Phocaea on the coast of Asia Minor where they began to mine alum, a substance which at that time was absolutely necessary for the European textile industry. Some of the Italian possessions were of considerable extent. Thus Venice owned Crete, and at the end of the thirteenth century, Genoa penetrated as far as the Black Sea where it managed to acquire a series of possessions on the southern coast of Russia and as far as the Caucasus, the most important of which was Caffa in the Crimea. This region had formerly been inhabited and settled by the Gazars (Khazars), and for this reason the Genoese administrative service gave it the name of Imperium Gazariae. The office that administered it was called Officium Gazariae, which can be translated Colonial Office. If this colonization, Italian around the Black Sea and the Aegean, Franco-Italian in Cyprus, and Franco-Catalan in central and southern Greece, had been able to continue, the technological, political, and social backwardness of these areas would have been overcome, and they would have passed from the Europe of the atlases to historical Europe in whose prosperity they would have shared. But a new invasion prevented this, an invasion which again separated Russia and the Balkans from Europe at a time when the colonization of the later Middle Ages was on the point of bridging the gap that separated them.

This invasion by the Ottoman Turks achieved what neither the Mongols of Genghis Khan nor those of Tamerlane had been able to achieve. The latter had been unable to put an end to the Byzantine Empire by taking Constantinople, where the Westerners had become the indispensable commercial intermediaries, while their colonies disseminated the progress which was a part of the truly European civilization. If the Italian colonies had survived along the shores of the Black Sea, Russia would not have had to wait until the time of Peter the Great to learn to use Western techniques. If the Turks had not conquered Cyprus, it would have continued to be one of the foremost producers of sugar cane, as it was under the Lusignan dynasty and on the plantations of the Cornaro family from Venice. There would have been in Russia and in the Balkans a mercantile bourgeoisie with all the political and cultural consequences implied thereby.

The Turkish advance closed the straits leading to the Black Sea by capturing Constantinople in 1453. The sea, first to the north and then to the south of those straits, passed to Turkish control, and the Italian fleets, and obviously the western colonies as well, were shut out. To the south Venice managed to remain in Crete, in some points of the Morea, and in the Ionian islands until well into the seventeenth century. Genoa withdrew definitively from the Levant and turned toward colonization in the Atlantic zone but under the flags of Portugal and Spain. In another direction the Turks penetrated into the heart of central Europe, and Suleiman the Magnificent managed to lay siege to Vienna in 1529. Islam had carried out a new offensive action, even more impressive than its first attack in the eighth century, when it had reached Poitiers. Just as it had managed to remain in Spain for centuries, now it would retain its dominance throughout the Balkan Peninsula and a great part of central Europe; thus the Europe of the atlases lost much more this time than during the Arab invasion. Since the Turks had rapidly built powerful fleets, they were on the point of obtaining control of the Mediterranean and after the failures of Charles V against Tunis and Algiers, only the victory of Philip II in Lepanto was able to hold them back.

The Discovery of the Atlantic

In the meantime Europe had found a brilliant compensation for the loss of the Levant by turning westward, toward the Atlantic. The process of becoming Atlantic had its most important results in the modern and contemporary era, but its germ came from the later Middle Ages, a period which appears more and more to have had the strongest influence on deciding the future possibilities of Europe and on maintaining its historical heritage and adapting it to new necessities.

In the thirteenth century Italian navigation had begun to link the Mediterranean with the North Sea along the Atlantic coasts. After greatly helping the Spanish and Portuguese in their efforts to become seafaring nations, the Italians, especially the Genoese, whose interests were being directed more and more to the West, were strengthening western European trade along the French coast and from there as far as the ports of Flanders and England. They seemed for some time to move around continental western Europe as around a great heap of lifeless wood, onto which they hurled sparks of fire that scattered in every direction until everything was set ablaze with a fresh commercial impetus. This impetus, moreover, was brought to life from within by the development of land trade centered first around the fairs of Champagne and then around those further and further to the interior of the continent, in expectation that the great commercial centers such as Bruges, Lübeck, and later London would become permanent international markets. In Portugal, which would be the first Western state to plunge into colonization, it was the Genoese who organized the navy. In 1317 King Denis appointed to the admiralty Manuel Pessagno, a great Genoese merchant who was very active in trade through the straits of Gibraltar and as far as the North Sea. For six generations the Pessagnos (the name was changed to Pessanha in Portugal) were admirals in that country. One of their Genoese collaborators founded, in the name of Portugal, the first European colony in the Atlantic, on two islands of the archipelago of the Canaries. At the same time other Genoese were admirals of Castile; and the most famous of all of them, Christopher Columbus, discovered America for Ferdinand and Isabella. Meanwhile the Portuguese had explored the whole of the African coast. In 1487 Bartolomeu Dias rounded the Cape of Good Hope, and in 1498 Vasco da Gama reached the Indies. The Atlantic became the key to all the oceans of the globe. Whoever controlled it could sail to the Indian Ocean, by way of the Cape of Good Hope, or discover the Pacific, crossing from east to west as did Magellan, and on his death his lieutenant Elcano.

In the beginning this control was shared, since the East and the Indies fell to the Portuguese and the West and America to Spain. The Spanish colonial efforts are of greater interest to us, from the point of view of historical continuity, than the

Portuguese, especially since the latter, during the greater part of the sixteenth century, were mainly active beyond the Cape of Good Hope. In little more than fifty years, the Spanish, setting out from the Antilles, created an enormous colonial empire which extended from Mexico as far as Argentina and Chile, while the Portuguese only occupied a few points along the coast of Brazil. The indigenous societies soon began to assimilate European civilization, and, whatever the brutalities that accompanied this process, there is no doubt that living conditions in the American continent were progressively improved to a level incomparably superior to what they had been, even in the great Indian states, before the discovery. Moreover, the mixture of races and cultures created in Latin America a kind of extension of Europe which acquired a culture and features whose common European basis was readily apparent. This culture constituted the most important factor of progress of this new, specifically Atlantic, human composition.

In 1580, the accession of Philip II of Spain to the Portuguese throne made Spain a world empire whose sovereign reigned from Madrid to Acapulco. Spain was linked by its own vessels to the Philippines, while the ships of its Portuguese subjects plied the seas from Lisbon to Goa and the Indies, via Bahia in Brazil and the innumerable establishments of the African coast. But in 1588 the destruction of the Invincible Armada by Elizabeth's seadogs put an end to Spain's exclusive control of the Atlantic, the key to the oceans.

The result of the Spanish defeat by the English was to be a second wave of European Atlantic colonization. England began to found colonies along the eastern coast of North America, colonies which would form the starting point of the future United States. France became established, although less firmly, in Canada, and even Holland and Sweden held possessions for some time in the territory of the present United States—the former in New York (at that time New Amsterdam) and in the valley of the Hudson, and the latter in the valley of the Delaware—while the English and Dutch both set foot in the Lesser Antilles and later on the northern coast of South America. The English colonies along the Atlantic coast, which, in the course of the seventeenth and particularly the eighteenth centuries, began to constitute the melting pot which is currently the United States (that is to say that the European population became diversified as colonization expanded), were by far the most important of the new European colonies to be born in America during the second wave of colonization. The United States and Canada, which became English in 1763, were even more mixed than South America, from a racial point of view, and they appeared as a kind of projection of Europe on the other side of the Atlantic.

Thus, from the beginning of American colonization, the European historical unity was increasingly the principal component of a broader historical unity born of Europe's expansion into the Atlantic zone of civilization. Africa is fatally linked to this zone by the early and even present maritime transportation systems, since its economic connections with the rest of the world have been vital to its existence from the moment when European expansion forced it into contact with the exterior world. The situation today is even more serious, since the independence of the African colonies has increased their need for communication with the rest of the world through the traditional European communication systems.

But in the case of Africa, what happened was that economic ties with the outer world and cultural progress of civilization had scarcely begun when most of it reached independence. On the other hand the massive contribution made by the European population to America has made of this double continent a new Europe, which initially was almost completely receptive, as far as civilization is concerned, to the older European historical unity. Later, as the colonial empires disappeared from American soil at the end of the eighteenth and the beginning of the nineteenth centuries, the ties with Europe became closer and on a more equal level. The prodigious economic surge of the United States in the nineteenth century, and even more in the twentieth, has made it the most powerful land in the Atlantic zone of civilization, a zone in which, as happened once before to Greece in respect to Roman Europe, the mother of the arts and thought has continued to be the European historical unity, as it came to be defined in the course of time. For their part, the American nations, formerly colonies, became increasingly important, and their power in the common attainment of an Atlantic civilization is constantly increasing to the point where the United States has now surpassed the technological level achieved by Europe.

The historian does not pretend to see into the future, but even if, by a still unforeseeable evolution, the portion of the Europe of the atlases detached today from the historical unity were no longer a threat, it would benefit not only that Europe of the maps which has never been a historical unity, but also the immense zone which extends from the American Pacific to the Russian or Siberian Pacific. And therefore, even in such a zone, the European historical unity, as we have seen it expanding and contracting in the long stretch of history, would always appear as the fount of the historical traditions which would constitute the basis of the different cultures there existing, as can be seen at present in the Atlantic area. Only in the perspective of the common work achieved around the Atlantic does the past of Europe's historical unity acquire true meaning. All that has prepared this work and perfected it is European, and yet it is also increasingly Atlantic. All that was not a part of it is not European, but could one day be Western, belonging to a West which from a geographic point of view could merely be a name, since it would apply from Canada to Tierra del Fuego, and from the Pacific to the Pacific, all across America, Europe, and northern Asia. But this is the concern of statesmen, not of historians.

PART II
Early Italian Colonization

4. Some Aspects of Slavery in Medieval Italian Colonies*

Throughout the Middle Ages slavery was, as we have seen earlier, the normal condition of a considerable part of the population along the Christian shores of the Mediterranean. The various Moslem states along the African, Asian, and even European shores of that great sea also possessed a fairly numerous slave class. Just as the Christians would enslave great numbers of Moslems captured by them in the course of raids or privateering, so too the Moslems never missed an opportunity to do the same to the enemies of their faith. Thus Moslem slaves were numerous in Italy, in Christian Spain, in the South of France, and in the Byzantine Empire, just as there was no shortage of Christian slaves in Moslem Spain or in North Africa. Moreover, in both the Christian world and Islam there were also slaves from two different sources: Negroes from central Africa and whites or Mongols from the Balkans, eastern Europe, and the Caucasus. Such at least was the situation during the thirteenth and the two succeeding centuries, the period that concerns us in this chapter.

Under these circumstances it is hardly surprising that when the Italians began to establish colonies in the eastern Mediterranean their policy toward slavery conformed both to the tradition of their own country and to that of the Byzantine Empire or Islamic states it had inherited.

The first medieval colonies created by Westerners in the

* Translated from "Aspects de l'esclavage dans les colonies médiévales italiennes," *Hommage à Lucien Febvre* (Paris, 1954), II, 91–103.

eastern Mediterranean are the seigneuries which rose up in Palestine after the First Crusade.[1] From the beginning the Italians were interested in exploiting these colonies either commercially or agriculturally.

Genoa's colonial empire may be considered to date from Bohemond of Antioch's concession made July 14, 1098. The Genoese received at that time, eleven days after the capture of the city, the church of St. John and the square in front of it, thirty houses, a fonduk, a well, and permanent exemption from all taxes.[2]

Bohemond's rival, Raymond of Toulouse, conquered Tortosa, again with the help of the Genoese, and the latter, the Pisans, or the Venetians had a share in the capture of Acre in 1103, of Gibelet in 1104, of Tripoli in 1109, and of Beirut in 1110. As a general rule the Italians, in compensation for the naval and other forces they put at the disposal of the conquerors, would receive a third of the city and sometimes a considerable portion of the rural area surrounding it, as we have seen in the case of the Venetians and the seigneury of Tyre.[3] In some areas they cultivated cotton or sugar cane with the help of the indigenous serf or slave manpower.[4] The importance of this manpower and the role it played has not been sufficiently explored; we need many more studies like Josuah Prawer's (although he is not dealing with slavery in the particular work cited above). Moreover, the dividing line between the legal status of the various rural populations in Palestine has often been drawn too sketchily. Pierre Christin

---

[1] J. Prawer, "Colonization Activities in the Latin Kingdom of Jerusalem," *Revue belge de philologie et d'histoire,* XXIX (1951), 1063–1118. Prawer has shown previously, in a work published in Hebrew, the Venetians' association with agricultural colonization in the seigneury of Tyre from 1123 on. In this seigneury which numbered some 114 villages, the Venetians possessed 21 villages in their entirety and held a third of the ground in 51 others.

[2] R. S. Lopez, *Storia delle colonie genovesi nel Mediterraneo* (Bologna, 1938), pp. 82 ff.

[3] See note 1 above.   [4] Lopez, *op. cit.,* p. 96.

in his *Etude des classes inférieures d'après les Assises de Jérusalem* is too hasty in his conclusions when he says: "The Christian Lords found in this part of Asia (Palestine) lands exploited for the benefit of the Turks and Syrians by the indigenous slaves who were Moslems, Greeks, or Christians." [5] First of all there was certainly no uniformity in the legal status of the rural population under Islamic rule and, secondly, the Christian regime was not a plain copy of the latter.

Members of the rural classes were designated "villeins" in the Assizes of Jerusalem, and, in actual fact, the Assizes of the *High Court* attached little importance to them since trading could involve "villeins, animals or some other chattel." [6] The Bans and Ordinances of the King of Cyprus, however, made a distinction when speaking of "all the villeins, men and women, and the slaves (*esclas*), men and women, and all kinds of beasts." [7] Villeins, then, were not slaves, since they were contrasted with the *esclas,* and moreover they had to pay a capitation fee.[8]

The *esclas* were domestic slaves, who acquired their miserable condition either by birth or as the result of having been captured in a raid. Similarly whoever hid a runaway slave could be reduced to slavery, as could whoever let himself be

[5] (Poitiers, 1912), p. 83. On p. 81 the author talks of the *parici* of Cyprus as slaves, although they are clearly semifree and subject to capitation and a system of farming with payment in kind (⅓ of the harvest) as well as heavy forced labor (two days a week). Cf. Académie des Inscriptions et Belles-Lettres, *Recueil des historiens des Croisades* (17 vols.; Paris, 1841–1906), I: *Lois: Assises de Jérusalem—Assises de la Haute Cour,* ed. Arthur A. Beugnot (1841), 207, n. 1.

[6] *Recueil des historiens,* I, part IV ("Livre de Philippe de Novare"), chap. 43, p. 519.

[7] *Ibid.,* II: *Lois: Assises de Jérusalem—Assises de la Cour des Bourgeois* (1843), part III ("Bans et ordonnances des rois de Chypre"), sec. 31, no. 4, p. 377.

[8] Christin, *Etude des classes inférieures,* p. 87. For the capitation fee see the Cyprian Charter of 1210 reproduced *in Recueil des historiens,* I, 403, n. b.

sold as a "saracen." Finally the Assizes also recognize slavery as a penalty for debt.[9] As for their condition, slaves were obviously not allowed to be proprietors or witnesses. They were not able to form marriage contracts. They were actually looked upon as chattels, and if they received the benefit of any legal protection it was in the interests of their master. Thus, if a doctor, while caring for a slave, killed him, he owed the master a replacement. If he crippled him, he was obliged to take him into his own service and pay the master his price.[10]

Many citizens of the Holy Land owned slaves. A sale could be rescinded if a slave were discovered to have certain physical defects, such as epilepsy or leprosy. Certain provisions of the Assizes of the Burgesses concerned the presence of slaves on ships, others, thefts committed by them.[11] They could also become "frangoumates" or freed slaves,[12] either by a verbal act of freeing in the presence of witnesses, or by inheritance, or by baptism, but the regulation was not absolute in the latter case.[13] Moreover, the freed slave continued to be bound closely to his patron and could not, for example, take him to court.[14] He could even be enslaved again for in-

---

[9] Christin, *op. cit.*, pp. 121 ff.   [10] *Ibid.*, pp. 127 ff.

[11] For example: "If the slave of any citizen should steal something from his master and the master's neighbor or anyone else either receives the stolen property in his house or hides the escaped slave or persuades the slave of another to escape, and the master is able to prove by two legitimate witnesses that he has corrupted his slave and that this man was the cause of his flight and theft, then he may sue him for the theft of the slave and the man owes either another slave or the cost of the slave and compensation for what the runaway slave took from his master in simple payment, as the penalty of double payment does not apply in the kingdom of Syria" (*Recueil des historiens,* II, 159).

[12] *Ibid.*, part III ("Bans et ordonnances des rois de Chypre"), sec. 31, no. 3, p. 375.

[13] Christin, *op. cit.*, pp. 140 ff.

[14] *Recueil des historiens,* II, "Assises des Bourgeois," XVI ("Now listen to the penalty to be paid by any male or female slave who should sue his master"); this is obviously a question of freemen and not slaves.

gratitude, but a child born to him during his freedom continued, in this case, to enjoy freedom.

I have cited these provisions of the Assizes, even though they are considerably more recent than the Christian establishment in Palestine and even the much later Crusade kingdom of Cyprus, only to give an idea of the condition of the slaves in these regions and thus make up for our present ignorance of all that concerns slavery in the Italian colonies of the Holy Land. Moreover, the general characteristics I have mentioned are sufficiently constant to apply both to Palestine and Cyprus.

In the thirteenth century the Genoese replaced the semi-commercial, semi-agricultural economy, which was common in the Italian colonies in the Holy Land during the preceding century, with an economy of colonial trading posts. The Venetians, on the other hand, after the break-up of the Byzantine Empire following the Fourth Crusade, acquired whole territories, the most important of which was Crete. From then on, the aspect of slavery which most interested the Genoese was the slave trade. The Venetians, although they played an equally important role in the slave trade, also regarded the slaves as manpower for their agricultural colonies. The situation changed again after the fall of the Latin Empire of Constantinople in 1261. The Genoese began at that time to establish a chain of more important possessions in and around the Aegean and Black seas, and instead of just trading posts, they now held entire islands and fairly extensive stretches of land. They now utilized slaves for the same purposes as the Venetians had used them earlier. The Crusade kingdom of Cyprus, on the other hand, continued to experience in matters of slavery conditions similar to those found in Palestine in the twelfth century. Since the Venetians, and to a lesser extent the Genoese, succeeded to

Cf. *Recueil des historiens,* II, 29: If it happens that the freeman, that is he who was a Saracen slave and became a Christian, wants to sue. . . ."

the Lusignan of Cyprus, we obviously cannot neglect a brief study of slavery in that great island of the eastern Mediterranean.

Unfortunately modern historians know relatively little about the internal history of the Venetian colonies in the thirteenth century. There is little to be gleaned in this connection from the synthesis devoted to Venetian colonial history by Bruno Dudan,[15] and there are very few monographs or even published extant documents dealing with the thirteenth century. Only from the beginning of the fourteenth century do we have some knowledge, and even in this period a great deal remains to be done.[16]

We know a little more about slavery in the Genoese colonies, thanks mainly to G. I. Bratianu,[17] who has gathered in his studies on Genoese commerce in the Black Sea at the end of the thirteenth century precious data concerning slavery in the Crimean colony of Caffa and in Pera, the Genoese quarter of Constantinople.

In Caffa, on April 28, 1289, Ansaldo Gattilusio, a member of an important family of Genoese merchants, sold to another Italian a slave called Balaban, "de proienie Maniar," which presumably means that he came from Madjar on the Kuma.[18] He had been imported to Caffa, the Byzantine Feodosiya, from Sorchati or Sorcat in the center of the Crimea, controlled

[15] *Il dominio veneziano di Levante* (Bologna, 1938).

[16] In 1959, Prof. F. Thiriet helped to fill this lacuna with *La Romanie vénitienne au moyen âge: Le développement et l'exploitation du domaine colonial vénitien (XIIe–XVe siècles)*, Bibliothèque des Ecoles Françaises d'Athènes et de Rome, no. 193 (Rome, 1959). He has also published several volumes of documents in the series Documents et Recherches sur l'économie des Pays byzantins, islamiques et slaves et leurs relations commerciales au moyen âge, published by the Ecole Pratique des Hautes Etudes, Paris.

[17] *Actes des notaires génois de Péra et de Caffa de la fin du XIIIe siècle (1281–1290)*, Académie roumaine, Etudes et recherches, II (Bucarest, 1927), and *Recherches sur le commerce génois dans la Mer Noire au XIIIe siècle* (Paris, 1929).

[18] Bratianu, *Actes*, p. 178 and *Recherches*, p. 229.

by the Tartars since the time of Genghis Khan. The price
is given in aspres, a coinage then much in use in the whole
Black Sea area. The notarized deed that is our evidence was
drawn up in the *loggia* or fonduk (warehouse) of the Genoese
at Caffa, in the presence of witnesses among whom figured
the syndic of the Genoese community at Caffa. Two days
later, before the same notary, a slave was sold who was described as white and only fourteen years of age. The name
given to him indicated that he was a Moslem.[19] On May 2,
1289, again before the same notary, a Genoese sold to a
Greek lady residing in the extremely cosmopolitan Caffa, a
little slave girl of ten, "de proienie Jarcaxa," which meant
that she was Circassian, one of that lovely Caucasian race
which, up to the nineteenth century, had the sad privilege of
providing slaves for merchants from every region.[20] The next
day, an Abkhas of thirty years was sold by one Genoese to
another. On May 5 a male slave from Tapizasco, Syria, was
sold by a merchant, a member of the important Genoese family of the Lercari, to one of his fellow countrymen. On May
11, 1289, a man named Spinola acquired a young Circassian
aged eleven years. Five days later another little girl of the
same age was described as brown, which may have meant
that she was a Mongol, for in that region dominated by the
Tartars, parents frequently did not hesitate to sell their
own children to Italian traders. The majority of Caucasian
slaves, however, were victims of raids organized by enemy
mountain tribes or by Tartars from the plain.

On May 20 another Caucasian, this time a Lezghian ("de
proienie lachi"), was sold, still in the presence of this same
notary. He was only ten and was described as "brunetum,"
which shows that the qualifying adjectives should be interpreted with care, since in this case it was out of the question

[19] Bratianu, *Actes,* p. 179.

[20] See F. de Foulon, *La Russie en Asie Mineure* (Paris, 1840), p. 78
and L. de Mas Latrie, *L'Officium Robarie,* Bibliothèque de l'Ecole des
Chartes, LIII (Paris, 1892), pp. 266 ff.

to think of him as a Mongol. Perhaps the color of his hair was being referred to, as in a deed of the following day in which one Usodimare from Genoa acquired a little boy eight years old, white with blond hair, called Mikhail, which obviously meant that he was Christian and perhaps a Russian. On May 26 a little Circassian girl, described as "olivegna" (olive-colored), ten years old, was sold in the presence of a drago-man who acted as witness. On May 27 it was the turn of a Bulgarian girl of eighteen or twenty years who bore a Greek first name, Kali. Perhaps she acquired it from a previous master of that nationality, for the Greeks were fairly numer-ous at Caffa. One of them, called Theodore of Kalamit, sold, on May 30, 1289, a Hungarian slave of thirty years whose name indicated he was a Christian. The majority of these buyers and sellers are known to us only by their name. On June 6, however, one of them is described as a grocer. He was selling a little Circassian of twelve. And in the presence of the same notary, the long line continued, composed primarily of young girls and boys. The Circassians pre-dominated, but from time to time there appeared a different race. Thus on July 12, 1289, a furrier sold to another repre-sentative of the same trade a white Zyguian, called Martin, and therefore a Christian, ten years old. Sometimes even the origin indicated by the notary remained mysterious. This is true in the case of a young boy, ten or twelve years old, who was sold on May 19, 1290, by a Venetian to an inhabitant of Pontremoli and who was said to be "de proienie de Cevia." [21]

In each of these sales the deed included the names of seller and buyer, the price, a receipt, and a waiver of any exception "non numeratae pecuniae." Then came the donation of any eventual appreciation and the waiver of the clause which, in Roman law after Diocletian, permitted the seller to rescind

[21] Perhaps Cevia means Serbia? Information concerning all of these transactions is taken from Bratianu, *Actes,* pp. 183–185, 189, 194, 197, 198, 200, 208, 242, 294.

the sale for damages of more than half the real value of the object.

To obtain an idea of the importance of the slave trade at Caffa, it is necessary to remember that in 1289, in addition to the notary from whom we have taken the preceding deeds— and who drew up in that year a total of thirty concerning slaves—there were twenty-seven other notaries in that city, without counting the ships' scribes. Moreover we do not have the deeds of the notary for the whole year. [22]

Similarly, in Pera, the slave trade at the end of the thirteenth century was extremely active. Bratianu published, for the year 1281, thirteen deeds taken from only two notaries. But we have evidence of nineteen other notaries for that same year, and no doubt they too drew up a fair number of deeds concerning slaves.

In the documents for Pera the age of the slave was indicated, but the origin was mentioned less often. This can evidently be explained by the fact that Pera was even further than Caffa from what might be called the hunting grounds, and the sellers were no longer as well informed about the origin of their captives. The sale of young boys and girls in any case was still very common.

Among the deeds concerning Pera there appears a document, dated August 30, 1281, that deserves special attention. In it we read that someone called Bulgarino from Piombino, described as a count of the Byzantine Empire, freed his slave Sair Rezem of Alexandria for 17 gold hyperperes. The slave paid with his earnings ("peculium") for his freedom and he received all the rights of a Roman citizen ("floride civitatis romane"). The former master renounced all rights of patronage and pledged, under a penalty of 100 gold hyperperes, to see that his slave's freedom was respected by everyone. This Sair Rezem was perhaps a merchant of Alexandria who had been captured at sea and who had continued to do business at

[22] *Ibid.*, p. 34. The sale in 1290 cited above comes from another notary.

Constantinople for his master, thereby earning a store of grace money with which he was able to buy his freedom.[23]

Further south, on the coast of Asia Minor, in Lesser Armenia, the Genoese were engaged in a slave trade that was governed by a privilege granted by Leon III of Armenia on December 23, 1288, by the terms of which prior dues on slaves were abolished, and Christian slaves could not be sold by the Genoese to the Moslems.[24] The Genoese had engaged in the slave trade in this area even before the conclusion of this treaty. By a deed notarized on March 12, 1274, the prior of the Genoese church of St. Lawrence at Ayas, at the end of the Gulf of Iskenderun, sold to the son of the Genoese consul there a slave girl called Fatima, and this was done in the presence of the Chancellor of the King of Armenia. The price was given in Armenian dirhems. The new master acquired absolute rights over the slave: "to do with her all you wish, according to the customs and habits of other masters." [25] By another act of April 14 of the same year a buyer guaranteed not to yield his slave to a Saracen in accordance with the aforementioned treaty concluded between the Genoese and the King of Armenia. On June 10, 1274, a Genoese, no doubt on his death bed, freed "for the good of his soul," in separate deeds, two female slaves.[26]

I will end this series of deeds concerning Lesser Armenia with an extraordinary document dated March 31, 1279. It describes a situation that was not pure and simple slavery,

---

[23] *Ibid.*, p. 147.

[24] *Historiae patriae monumenta: Liber iurium reipublicae Genuensis,* II (Turin, 1857) col. 184. See *Recueil des historiens des Croisades: Documents arméniens,* I, 752; and M. J. de Saint-Martin, "Décret ou privilège de Léon III, roi d'Arménie, en faveur des Génois en l'année 1288, tiré des archives de Gênes," *Notices et extraits des manuscrits de la bibliothèque du roi et autres bibliothèques,* XI (1827), 114.

[25] C. Desimoni, "Actes passés en 1271, 1274 et 1279 à Aias (Petite Arménie) et à Beyrouth devant des notaires génois," *Archives de l'Orient latin,* I, (1881), 456.

[26] These two examples are from *ibid.*, pp. 477, 490.

but in a strange way resembled it and doubtless could only be explained by the particular social conditions prevalent in colonial trading posts. We read in it of a woman called Cerasia Ciciliana, who promised to cohabit with a certain Jacobo Porcho "like a good woman, without having anything to do with another person that is bad, either lying with another man or letting myself be known carnally by another." She was to be satisfied with the clothes, shoes, and food given her, and agreed to do all that was asked of her and not to leave his service. If she did not observe the obligations she contracted, she recognized Porcho's right to cut off her nose, hand, or foot and to put her in chains. If she wished to become a nun, however, the deed was nullified. Porcho, for his part, agreed to pay her 400 Armenian dirhems when she wished. This unusual contract must have seemed too extraordinary even to the two parties concerned since we learn from a marginal note that it was annulled some days later. No doubt its equivocal nature, halfway between the sale of a slave and a work contract, led the notary to advise the parties to renounce it.[27]

Now let us turn to Cyprus, where a series of deeds concerning slaves were passed before a Genoese notary in the port of Famagusta between 1299 and 1301.[28]

The merchant Salveto Pessagno, a member of a Genoese family which played a large part in Atlantic trade—particularly with England—and which provided Portugal with a series of admirals from 1317 on, died in Famagusta toward the end of the century. The inventory of his possessions, drawn up on February 2, 1300, indicated that he owned two Greek slaves who were griffins or half bloods and who were about to be redeemed, as well as two other slaves, one of

---

[27] *Ibid.*, p. 520.

[28] Desimoni, "Actes passés à Famagouste de 1299 à 1301 par devant le notaire génois Lamberto di Sambuceto," which appeared in *Archives de l'Orient latin,* I (1882), and was continued in *Revue de l'Orient latin,* I, (1893).

whom came from Genoa.[29] This merchant thus had in his service four domestic slaves.

On March 13, 1300, Ugolinus de Messana, a banker, sold a young Negro, imported from Spain, aged twelve years. He had bought him in the Famagusta market ("in publico cridagio Famaguste") for 129 white bezants and passed him on to a fellow countryman for the same price. On March 31 a young Saracen of nine years was sold to an inhabitant of Savona, Liguria, for six gold florins and one white bezant. On April 9 a Genoese living in Famagusta freed a woman slave and her children, two boys and a girl, on condition that she remain another five years in his service. On April 22 a Slavonian girl of sixteen or eighteen years was freed. On July 1 there took place the sale of a slave "de provincia Cervia," a Serb no doubt, with her little boy. She was twenty-four years old. She had to serve her new owner for five years, after which time she would be freed. During this period, however, she could be sold. Her son could not be sold to a person called Nicolaus Cavazuti, who may have been his father, for less than 300 white bezants, a very high price. Another curious point of origin is mentioned in a bill of sale passed July 7, 1300, in which the widow of an inhabitant of Nicosia gave up an olive-hued woman slave "de proienie Mazarabi." She may have been a Mozarab from Spain, since we have already found mentioned a young Negro imported from that country. In fact it is worth remembering that there were a lot of Catalan merchants in Cyprus at that time. Then again on August 1, 1300, a slave from Smyrna was freed.[30]

To complete the picture of the extraordinary ethnic mixture which colored slavery in Famagusta at this time, let us

[29] "Two griffin slaves from Marvasia who are for redemption. Also another slave who was given to that same Salveto, as has been mentioned. Also another slave who is called Tartarinus and who came from Genoa" (Desimoni, "Actes passés à Famagouste," *Archives,* I, 28).

[30] Information concerning these transactions is taken from *ibid.,* pp. 49, 51, 54, 61, 86, 92, 107.

mention a deed of September 8, 1300, in which two members of the Genoese Spinola family sold to a Jew of Palermo six Jewish male slaves for a sum total of 700 white bezants. That this proved to be a case of redemption can be seen from a deed of the same day in which the six Jews agreed under oath not to flee Famagusta before having reimbursed their fellow Jew from Palermo for all the money he had spent. The latter retained the right to sell them if they did not fulfill this obligation. On September 25, five of the six Jews appeared once more before the notary and agreed jointly to pay 241 hyperperes to the Jew from Palermo or to his son at Candia within eight days, failing which they could be sold as slaves.[31]

Finally, a will dated December 21, 1300, and two deeds of the same day give us a fuller picture of domestic slavery as it was practiced by the Genoese settled in that port. In the will a man called Januinus de Murta, who no doubt belonged to the family which, several decades later, was to provide Genoa with its second democratic doge, bequeathed to his freed slave, Mariona, a little house and fifty white bezants. Another slave received the same amount; a third, a Negress, had to serve de Murta's wife for four years and then she, too, would be freed and would receive a small house, ten barrels of wheat, and a bed with bedding. She was freed by a special deed, as were her brother and her daughter. Thus Januinus de Murta possessed at Famagusta alone a total of six slaves, of whom five were women and one a man.[32]

Cyprus, as we can see from the variety of ethnic origins of the slaves already mentioned, was a center of the slave trade, a meeting point of widely diverse commercial currents. The princes of the French house of Lusignan who reigned in Cyprus were very much aware of this. In 1311 a memoir concerning the means of reconquering the Holy Land and destroying the power of the sultans of Egypt was handed by

[31] Desimoni, "Actes passés à Famagouste," *Revue,* I, pp. 83, 115.

[32] *Ibid.,* pp. 343, 347, 348.

an envoy from the king of Cyprus to Pope Clement V, during the Council of Vienne.[33] This document drew attention to the necessity of intercepting and searching Christian ships which were exporting slaves into Egypt, where they went to feed the battalions of the famous Mamelukes.[34] These Mamelukes, the text added, were imported into Egypt from Turkey, that is to say from Asia Minor, and from the regions around the Black Sea. They constituted the mainstay of the Egyptian military power.[35]

The Cypriot merchants themselves, especially the Famagustans, were playing an active part in this traffic. They would seize the inhabitants of the islands of the Aegean Sea as slaves and maintain constant traffic with Egypt, even at a time when communication with Moslem countries was expressly forbidden by the papacy. The popes returned constantly to this question, for example in 1317, 1323, 1329, 1338, and 1425. French and Catalans also participated in this traffic, but the greatest slave traders seem to have been the Genoese. The Sultan of Egypt had already obtained, under Michael Palaeologus, the right of free passage through the Bosporus, and he used to send his own Moslem or Christian agents into the Black Sea region. He maintained agents at Adrianople and Gallipoli, both important stages in the journeys of slaves destined for Egypt, who were carried by both Christian and Moslem vessels. Sometimes the cargoes numbered as many as two or three hundred heads. Each year some two thousand male slaves between the ages of

[33] L. De Mas Latrie, *Histoire de l'île de Chypre sous le règne des princes de la maison de Lusignan* (Paris, 1852), II, 118 ff.

[34] "A number of galleys should be sent which would seize evil and false Christians who are carrying to the Saracens soldiers, i.e. Mamelukes, wood, iron, pitch, food and other goods which they need" (*ibid.*, p. 119).

[35] "Since the land of Egypt would not produce strong soldiers if it did not have these same Mameluke boys who are brought to it from Turkey and the Black Sea, I urge that the Sultan's power be weakened by intercepting this trade which is harming Christians" (*ibid.*, p. 120).

teu and twenty—Tartars, Circassians, Greeks, Albanians,
Slavonians and Serbs—were brought to the Sultan of Egypt.
Five to six thousand of these slaves were permanently settled
in Cairo and were taught soldiering.[36]

The fact that the Genoese played one of the most important roles in this traffic and that Cyprus was often the port of
call is evident in a commercial treaty concluded on April 18,
1365, between the Ligurian republic and the island kingdom
where this traffic was expressly forbidden.[37] But such prohibitions were useless, as is evident from a letter dated
February 13, 1434, and addressed to the Pope by the government of Genoa.[38] The latter was trying to clear its subjects of
censure for exporting to Egypt baptized slaves from the
Black Sea colonies. The Genoese emphasized the treaties they
had made with the princes of the neighboring regions; [39]
furthermore, a law stipulated that, on their embarkation, the
slaves had to be counted and presented to the bishop, who,
accompanied by priests and laymen, came on board, called
each of the slaves in turn, and asked them to what country
they belonged, whether they were Christians, and whether
they would not like to embrace Christianity. Whoever agreed
was disembarked and sold to another Christian who approved
the slave's conversion. If such practices were not maintained,
the document goes on, there would be worse abuses in the

[36] *Ibid.*, pp., 127 ff.

[37] "Except that the said Genoese may not take out of the said kingdom of Cyprus things forbidden by the Holy Mother Church for
the sake of carrying them to the areas subjugated to the Sultan of
Babylon [Egypt]; such things are weapons, iron, wood, and slaves for
trade in that place" (*Historiae patriae monumenta,* II, col. 741).

[38] N. Jorga, *Notes et extraits pour servir à l'histoire des croisades au
XVᵉ siècle* (Paris, 1899), I, 566.

[39] See, for example, the treaties of 1380 and 1387 concerning the
possessions in the Crimea and at Pera, the obligatory transit point to
Egypt, in Sylvestre de Sacy," Pièces diplomatiques tirées des archives
de la République de Gênes, *Notices et extraits des manuscrits de la
bibliothèque du roi et autres bibliothèques,* XI (1827), 52, 58, 63.

colonies of Trebizond, Tana, Vosporo (now Kertch), Phasis (Poti, in the Caucasus), and in other trading posts on the Black Sea. If, in 1434, Genoa still felt the need to justify itself, the fact indicates the tremendous importance of the slave traffic between the Genoese colonies around the Black Sea and Egypt.

The Venetians had already been participating in the slave trade in this area for a long time. I have studied elsewhere in detail, using notarized Venetian deeds as my source, the role of the Venetian colony of Tana, at the mouth of the Don, as a center for the slave trade in the fourteenth and fifteenth centuries.[40] From Tana the Venetians transported great quantities of slaves to the whole of the Mediterranean world and especially to Venice. Cargoes of two hundred slaves at a time were not exceptional.[41] As late as 1427 the Venetian senate was discussing a matter of four hundred slaves "both male and female" which galleys coming from the region of Tana were supposed to be bringing to Venice.[42]

But none of the Venetian colonies played as important a role in the slave trade as Crete. Unfortunately the documents concerning the trade remain almost entirely unpublished and are available only in that very rich source, the Collection of the Notaries of Candia in the State Archives of Venice. I have gathered a great number of texts on this subject which it is impossible to summarize here.[43] I will limit myself to several comments concerning one special aspect: the role played by Catalan sailors and merchants in the slave trade in Crete.

[40] C. Verlinden, "La colonie vénitienne de Tana, centre de la traite des esclaves au XIVe et au début du XVe siècle," *Studi in onore di Gino Luzzatto* (Milan, 1950), II, 1–25.

[41] *Ibid.*, p. 3.   [42] Jorga, *op. cit.*, p. 462.

[43] Many of these are cited in my study on slavery in Venetian Crete: "La Crète, débouché et plaque tournante de la traite des esclaves aux XIVe et XVe siècles," *Studi in onore di A. Fanfani* (Milan, 1962), III, 593–669.

The proximity of the Catalan duchies in Greece and the role of the Almogavares explained, to a great extent, the importance of the activity of the King of Aragon's subjects as slave traders in Crete. From the beginning of the fourteenth century the Cretan notaries are full of information on this subject.

Thus, on July 9, 1301, before Benvenuto de Brixano, notary at Candia, an inhabitant of Negropont sold to a doctor of Majorca "one of my slaves of Greek origin called Leone whom we captured at Samos." [44] On October 12, 1304, a Catalan from Barcelona sold to a fellow citizen a female slave "de partibus Romanie" bought in Turkey. This formula concerning a purchase from the Turks recurred so frequently that we are tempted to believe that it served as a cover for acts of piracy committed by Christians at the expense of other Christians.

Two documents from 1317 testify to the sale, by someone called Domenicus Berengo, of two Greeks bought from the Catalan Company of the Almogavares, which was operating at that time in Greece.[45]

The notary Giovanni Similiante registered on October 1, 1332, the sale made by Guillelmus Simon, a Catalan from Perpignan, living in Thebes, to the notary Johannes Gerardus of Candia, of a Greek woman whom the seller declared he brought from Thebes. The slave was originally "de partibus Despotatus," that is, from Epirus. This Guillelmus Simon seems to have been a specialist in the slave business, for, on the same day and before the same notary, he completed thirteen other bills of sale.

On December 19 of that year, the same Cretan notary registered fifteen sales made by two Catalans, one from

[44] Collection of the Notaries of Candia, B. IX, 141, State Archives of Venice. This deed has been published by R. Morozzo della Rocca in *Fonti per la storia di Venezia*, section 3, Archivi notarili (Venice, 1950), p. 81, no. 220.

[45] Collection of the Notaries of Candia, Notary Stefano Bon, State Archives of Venice.

Barcelona, the other from Perpignan. On March 24, 1333, Guillelmus Simon of Thebes, whom we already know, completed no less than twenty-two bills of sale. On May 22 someone else sold no fewer than twenty Greeks, men and women. Somewhat later, before one notary alone, six Catalans sold eighty-nine slaves in six days. Obviously, then, Candia was a very important slave market for them and for many other merchants from different parts of the medieval world. It was, moreover, a crossroads on the route to Egypt, since we already know that the Catalans were active in the slave trade with Egypt.

The documents I have mentioned give an idea of the very real importance of the slave trade in medieval Italian colonies in the Levant. But there is one further aspect of medieval colonial slavery which should be mentioned here: the uses to which slaves were put.

Among the slaves whose sale is attested by the notarized deeds, there were certainly many who were destined for domestic service, but a good number found other work in the colonies. In Crete alone, we know that slaves were employed in the cultivation of the *casalia* in the interior of the island, together with villeins or half-free men. They would often escape and take refuge elsewhere. This we learn from a debate in the Venetian senate in 1393.[46] That same year, because some *casalia* were still not cultivated, the senate decided to grant financial aid to those who would contract to undertake for two years the importation of male slaves under fifty years of age.[47] The decision was confirmed in 1397.

[46] "It is decided that if any slave or villein, male or female, of anyone should leave his master's casale and should in any way go to another casale, then he to whose casale the said villein or slave, male or female, has gone, must pay one hundred hyperperes" (H. Noiret, *Documents inédits pour servir à l'histoire de la domination vénitienne en Crète de 1380 à 1485*, Bibliothèque des écoles françaises d'Athènes et de Rome, no. 61 [Paris, 1892], p. 53).

[47] "Since . . . several casalia remain uncultivated . . . and it is good, and indeed useful to provide that the aforesaid casalia and other

These documents are sufficient evidence that the slaves also played a part in the agrarian economy of the Italian colonies, for what we have seen in Crete was true in Cyprus,[48] in Chios—in short, everywhere where the territory controlled by the Italians was large enough to provide an important agricultural economy. In this aspect, as in many others, the medieval Mediterranean colonial economy bears characteristics that prefigure the colonial economy of modern times in the Atlantic region.[49]

----

places can be worked . . . our government of Crete . . . will decide that whoever undertakes under public contract to import into our aforesaid island of Crete a great number of male slaves who are below the age of fifty years should have a loan of three thousand hyperperes" *(ibid.,* p. 54).

[48] On Cyprus, in the Cornaro sugar plantations, they employed mainly slaves of Arab or Syrian origin; see G. Padovan [G. Luzzatto], in *Capitalismo coloniale nel trecento,* I (1941), 62 ff.

[49] C. Verlinden, "Les influences médiévales dans la colonisation de l'Amérique," *Revista de historia de America,* December 1950; pp. 440–450; "Le problème de la continuité en histoire coloniale," *Revista de Indias,* X (1951), 219–236; "Le influenze italiane nella colonizzazione iberica (uomini e metodi)," *Nuova rivista storica,* XXXVI, (1952), 254–270; "Les origines coloniales de la civilisation atlantique: Antécédents et types de structure," *Journal of World History,* I (1953), 378–398.

5. The Italian Colony of Lisbon and the Development of Portuguese Metropolitan and Colonial Economy*

In two articles that appeared in 1931 and 1932, Dr. M. A. Hedwig Fitzler attributed a certain importance to the influence exerted by the Italians on the Portuguese economy in the Middle Ages and at the beginning of modern times.[1] In 1953 two historians, Professor Virginia Rau of the University of Lisbon and Professor B. W. Diffie of City College, New York, took issue, at times quite violently but for the most part justifiably, with what Dr. Fitzler wrote concerning a number of "commercial companies." [2] They too mention in passing certain Italian influences. Naturally, like the German author, they cite the privilege granted by King Denis of Portugal in 1317 to the Genoese Manuel Pessagno whom the king appointed admiral,[3] and they even mention the privi-

* Translated from "La colonie italienne de Lisbonne et le développement de l'économie métropolitaine et coloniale portugaise," *Studi in onore di Armando Sapori* (Milan, 1957), pp. 617–628.

[1] "Uberblick über die portugiesischen Uberseehandelsgesellschaften des 15.–18. Jahrhunderts," and "Portugiesische Handelsgesellschaften des 15. und beginnenden 16. Jahrhunderts," *Vierteljahrschrift für Sozial- und Wirtschaftsgeschichte*, XXIV (1931), 282–298, and XXV (1932), 209–250. Cf. in this connection C. Verlinden, "Italian Influence in Iberian Colonization," *Hispanic American Historical Review*, XXXIII (1953), 199–211.

[2] "Alleged Fifteenth-Century Portuguese Joint-Stock Companies and the Articles of Dr. Fitzler," *Bulletin of the Institute of Historical Research*, XXVI (1953), 181–199.

[3] J. Martins da Silva Marques, *Descobrimentos portugueses* (4 vols.;

lege granted by Alfonso IV "to the Florentines" in 1338.[4]
These matters were of only secondary importance for them,
however; otherwise, they would most certainly have studied,
if only briefly, a series of documents all dated about the same
time which appear, together with those already mentioned,
in Silva Marques' valuable collection. I do not intend to
examine these documents in detail in this chapter, but I
consider it essential to point them out to anyone interested
in Italian commercial expansion in the later Middle Ages
as a whole, and particularly in the influence of the Italians
on Portuguese expansion.

On December 4, 1341, Alfonso IV granted a privilege to
Alberto Moncassela, a merchant of "Prazenssa de Lombardia"
(Piacenza), the terms of which were rather similar to that
granted in 1338 to the Florentine Company of the Bardi.[5] In
both cases individual or collective safe-conducts were granted,
but toward the end of Alfonso IV's reign (1325–1357), general privileges must have been granted to the Genoese, Milanese, and Piacentines, since Peter I confirmed them—unfortunately without quoting the text—on June 22, 1357, in favor

---

Lisbon, 1944), publishes a series of documents which constitute a virtual
cartulary of the Pessagnos as Portuguese admirals in the fourteenth
and fifteenth centuries. These documents deal with Manuel, Bartolomeu,
Lançarote, Manuel II, Carlos, and Lançarote II. Of special interest here
are documents 37–45, 47, 48, 78, 89, 185, 196, 361, and 380 in Vol I. See
too L. T. Belgrano, "Documenti e genealogia dei Pessagno Genovesi,
ammiragli del Portogallo," *Atti della Società Ligure di Storia Patria*,
XV (1881).

4 Rau and Diffie, *op. cit.*, p. 183. The text is found in Silva Marques,
op. cit., I, 53, no. 57. Actually the "privilege" was a safe-conduct granted
to Beringel Omberte and Nicolau Bertaldi, as well as to the merchants
of the Bardi Company present in Portugal and trading there. H. V.
Livermore draws attention to the clause concerning the nomination of
a consul but emphasizes the hybrid character of the document ("The
Privileges of an Englishman in the Kingdoms and Dominions of Portugal," *Atlante*, II [1954], 9).

5 Silva Marques, *op. cit.*, I, 75, no. 68.

of those same merchants who probably had been demanding such measures since his accession to the throne.[6]

On March 7, 1363, the Piacentine, Genoese, and Milanese merchants in Lisbon, together with the Cahorsins, obtained an additional privilege.[7] Until that date these merchants had appointed one of themselves to supervise the loading of their ships. The King of Portugal, however, had recently appointed a special official to control the loading of all vessels in the port of Lisbon. The privilege of 1363 granted the Italians and Cahorsins exemption from this control.

Two years later, on December 4, 1365, Alfonso IV's decree concerning the Genoese, Milanese, and Piacentines was confirmed and extended to the Lombards.[8] This same document also contains a prohibition from participating in the local retail trade, as was often the case for foreigners in the Middle Ages.

In 1370, on October 25, King Ferdinand, the last representative of the old Burgundian dynasty that had reigned over the country since the kingdom's origin, concluded a treaty with Genoa concerning the damages to be paid by Portuguese corsairs to Genoese merchants whose vessels had been captured, together with their cargo consisting largely of cloth from the Netherlands and the north of France. The agreement was ratified by the Genoese government on the following January 15.[9]

Continuing our chronological summary, let us point out a decree dated July 3, 1380, to the cloth merchants of

[6] *Ibid.*, p. 105, no. 84, for the Genoese in Lisbon. For the Milanese and the Piacentines nos. 85 and 86 (p. 106). No doubt these privileges were still safe-conducts, but this time they were extended to all the merchants of a particular Italian state. What allows us to think so is a document of this kind granted the Catalan merchants on August 1, 1362. See *Ibid.*, p. 115, no. 101.

[7] *Ibid.*, pp. 116–117, no. 102.

[8] *Ibid.*, pp. 118–119, no. 104. In addition to the Italians, this decree also concerned the Catalans and the French.

[9] Silva Marques, *op. cit.*, I, 128–134, no. 116, and 136–138, no. 119.

Piacenza and Genoa. It deals with certain benefits granted them concerning the measuring of cloth [10] and can be compared with those guaranteed them in 1363 concerning the loading of ships.

Apart from the act in 1365 that excluded Italians from the retail trade, there were scarcely any decrees which did not broaden their rights and improve their status. However, in 1390, foreigners were forbidden to sell in the country and buy outside of Lisbon any merchandise except wine, figs, and salt.[11] On August 25, 1391, the Genoese, Piacentines, English, and "others" found themselves forbidden to sell cloth on the retail market and to buy, from within the country, honey, wax, and nearly all goods sold by weight.[12]

After the appearance of Florentines in the Portuguese records in 1338, so far only Milanese, Piacentines, and Lombards are mentioned, and more often Genoese. But one must not think that the Venetians did not play an active role in Portugal. A privilege dated June 26, 1392, concerning their convoys of galleys, suffices to prove the contrary.[13] Nevertheless, the position of the Genoese and Piacentine merchants seems to have been more important, especially in Lisbon itself. A law of June 18, 1395, had repeated the regulation forbidding foreigners to participate in anything other than wholesale trade. They could not sell merchandise outside of Lisbon, but they were permitted to transport it from there to Algarve. Except in Lisbon and Algarve, they were only allowed to purchase wine, fruit, and salt.[14] There seems to have been a fairly strong feeling of xenophobia at this time, for on July 26 of that same year John I of Avis took the merchants of Genoa and Piacenza under his own special protection. They had encountered some hostility from the inhabitants of Lisbon, and the King ordered his judges to protect them. They also retained the right to

[10] *Ibid.*, pp. 168–170, no. 145.   [11] Livermore, *op. cit.*, p. 11.

[12] Silva Marques, *op. cit.*, II, 308, no. 191.

[13] *Ibid.*, pp. 197–198.   [14] Livermore, *op. cit.*, p. 11, n. 3.

decorate the doors of their shops with green drapes, the sign
that they had cloth for sale, as they had always done until
recently when the drapes had been torn down.[15] This hostility
on the part of the national merchants and the special protection accorded by the King implied that they were a powerful
group.

We have mentioned the connections of the foreigners with
Algarve at the end of the fourteenth century. These connections strengthened, and some Italians established their
homes there. Thus it was that on January 16, 1404, the Genoese Giovanni della Palma was granted the right to establish
a sugar-cane plantation in that region.[16]

As the final document in this series concerning the Italians
up to the period of the great discoveries, and to return to the
Florentines, we will cite a letter of January 9, 1429, by which
the government of Florence thanked the King of Portugal
for the warm welcome he had given the Florentine galleys
on their journey to Flanders.[17] From then on, the Florentine
convoys that were heading for the north of Europe, like the
Venetian ships, began regularly to stop in Portugal.[18]

The documents we have mentioned suffice to prove that
the commercial activity of the Italians in Portugal was
extensive even before Henry the Navigator took over the
leadership of the movement toward expansion.[19] Some of

[15] Silva Marques, *op. cit.*, I, 606, no. 190, and Livermore, *loc. cit.*
[16] Silva Marques, *op. cit.*, I, p 217, no. 208. Cf. C. Verlinden,
Précédents médiévaux de la colonie en Amérique (Mexico City, 1954),
p. 51.
[17] Silva Marques, *op. cit.*, II, p. 326, no. 208.
[18] A. Grunzweig, "Le fonds du Consulat de la Mer aux Archives de
l'Etat à Florence," *Bulletin de l'Institut Historique Belge de Rome*, X
(1930), 24 gives a list of ports of call drawn up in 1447. Apart from
the Spanish ports of San Felíu de Guixols, Palma, Valencia, Jávea,
Villajoyosa, Denia, Alicante, Almería, Málaga, Cádiz, and Coruña, only
Lisbon is mentioned in Portugal.
[19] Until 1434 the Portuguese were only interested in the archipelagoes of the Canaries, the Madeiras and the Azores, which had been

these privileges, moreover, retained a practical value for many centuries, and they still formed a part, in the eighteenth century, of the series of decrees which the Genoese regarded as the basis of their status in Portugal.[20] Similar collections of privileges have been gathered for other national groups trading in Portugal, such as the English, the Flemings, and the Germans.[21]

Now let us return to the studies of Dr. Fitzler, Professor Rau, and Professor Diffie; insofar as they concern Italians appearing in documents, Rau's and Diffie's article did not prove that Dr. Fitzler's usage was unjustified. However, we should hasten to say that this is not always true, and therefore the German author's work should not be completely accepted without verification. On the other hand, some of the documents used by Dr. Fitzler contain information concerning the activity of the Italians which seems to have been misread

---

discovered during the fourteenth century thanks to Italo-Portuguese collaboration. In 1434, Gil Eannes rounded Cape Bojador, and from that moment began the exploitation and soon the colonization of the African coast. See, for example, B. Penrose, *Travel and Discovery in the Renaissance, 1420–1620* (Cambridge, Mass., 1952), pp. 37 ff.

[20] This is particularly true of the documents of March 7, 1363, and July 3, 1380, mentioned above. They appear in a collection called "Privilegi concessi dai Re del Portogallo alla nazione genovese," compiled in 1769 and kept in the State Archives of Genoa.

[21] For the English, see Livermore, *op. cit.*, pp. 7, n. 1 and pp. 18 ff.; this collection dates from the seventeenth century. For the Flemings and Germans, see J. Denucé, "Privilèges commerciaux accordés par les rois de Portugal aux Flamands et aux Allemands (XVe et XVIe siècles)," *Arquivo historico portugues*, VII (1909), 310 ff. and 377 ff. This collection follows a copy dated 1644. There must have been a Flemish fraternity in Lisbon even before 1414. Alfonso V granted the Flemings their first privilege in 1458. See Livermore, *op. cit.*, p. 19, n. 4, and Denucé, *Inventaire des Affaitadi, banquiers italiens à Anvers de l'année 1568* (Antwerp, 1934), p. 91, n. 4. The first individual privilege was granted the Germans in 1452 and published by J. H. Cassel, *Privilegia und Handelsfreiheiten, welche die Könige von Portugal ehedem den deutschen Kaufleuten zu Lissabon ertheilt haben* (Bremen, 1771).

by her critics. This is particularly the case where coral fishing is concerned.

Dr. Fitzler talked of the Milanese devoting themselves to this activity in the thirteenth century, but the references she supplied are not accurate.[22] She is correct in noting that, in 1443, a five-year monopoly was granted Bartolomeu Florentim and Jean Forbin. Rau and Diffie give us the exact source of this fact [23] but they seem unaware, as Dr. Fitzler is not, that the people concerned were Bartolomeo Marchionni of Florence and Jean Forbin of Marseille,[24] two very important merchants who had successfully formed a company between them.[25] Moreover, Forbin's activity in coral fishing was known outside of Portugal.[26]

In 1456, a monopoly for the export of cork was granted to Pedro Diniz and Martim Leme (a Fleming from Bruges [27]), and a few days later to an Italian company composed of Marco Lomellino, Domenico Scotto, and Giovanni Guidotti.[28] The two privileges would in fact seem to relate to one single company, for in 1466 an account mentions Leme side by side with the Italians.[29]

Marco Lomellino was described as "Genoese residing in our city of Lisbon" in the second document dated June 21, 1456. In return for a fee of 2,000 dobras, he received a ten-year monopoly for the purchase of cork in the kingdom and

[22] Cf. Fitzler, "Portugiesische Handelsgesellschaften," p. 219, n. 1, and Rau and Diffie, *op. cit.,* p. 188, n. 2.

[23] F. M. de Sousa Viterbo, "A pescaria do coral no seculo XV," *Arquivo historico portugues,* I (1903), 318–319.

[24] Fitzler, "Portugiesische Handelsgesellschaften," p. 210.

[25] P. Peragallo, *Cenni intorno alla colonia italiana in Portogallo nei secoli XIV, XV, e XVI,* 2d ed. (Genoa, 1907), p. 101.

[26] F. Reynaud, *Histoire du commerce de Marseille* (Paris 1951), II, 546, 703.

[27] Fitzler, "Portugiesische Handelsgesellschaften," p. 222.

[28] Sousa Viterbo, "O monopolio da cortiça no seculo XV," *Arquivo historico portugues,* II (1904), 41–52.

[29] *Ibid.,* and A. Braamcamp Freire in *Arquivo historico portugues,* VI (1908), 359–360.

the right to export it by land and sea. He was also permitted
to seize any amount of cork bought or exported by any other
merchant. He was allowed to enter into partnership with
anyone he wished. If he died before the expiration date of
the monopoly it would pass to his brother Daniel. As for the
profits, the king retained for himself one-third, to be assessed
from the firm's books. The capital was divided into twenty
parts, eleven of which were owned by Lomellino and his
brother; Domenico Scotto, also from Genoa, held five parts,
and Giovanni Guidotti of Florence owned the remaining
four.[30]

After studying this monopoly, Rau and Diffie concluded:
"In any case this was in no sense a 'company' with joint-stock
characteristics as Dr. Fitzler claims." To tell the truth, I
found no such opinion in Fitzler's account of the contracts
of 1456. Certainly we are dealing here with a commercial
company of the type that was formed in Italy at that time.
The one of 1456 is little different from the Societas Alumi-
num which was operating the Pope's alum mine at Tolfa
about this time and sold the whole of what it produced.[31]
Raymond de Roover had no hesitations in calling this operation a "company." [32]

It is extremely clear after reading Rau's and Diffie's
article that what Fitzler says of the various "colonial companies" in which Henry the Navigator must have played a
part strains the texts terribly, or even, in some cases, invents
them! [33] Does this mean that what she wrote concerning the

[30] See Peragallo, *op. cit.*, pp. 96–97.

[31] G. Zippel, "L'allume di Tolfa e il suo commercio," *Archivio della
Reale Società Romana de Storia Patria*, XXX (1907), 5–51, 389–461;
and J. Strieder, *Studien zur Geschichte kapitalistischer Organisationsfor-
men* (Munich, 1925) pp. 168–183. In 1466 the Medici acquired shares
in the company as mentioned in the contract analysed by Zippel on
p. 405 and by Strieder on p. 170.

[32] *The Medici Bank: Its Organization, Management, Operations, and
Decline* (New York, 1948), p. 46.

[33] Rau and Diffie, *op. cit.*, pp. 191–195.

company for wood from Brazil deserves the same reproaches? This company began with a monopoly granted to the Portuguese merchant Fernão de Noronha in which several foreigners were to have a share.[34] Rau and Diffie have shown that Fitzler has confused with these facts dating from the sixteenth century others concerning the eighteenth century which have nothing to do with them.[35] But they themselves seem somewhat vague on the topic. In actual fact the text of the contract is unknown. Only a privilege granted to some German merchants in 1503 speaks of the "ships of the contract of Fernam de Loronha" and of "the time of his contract ending in 1505." [36] It was only for the arming of the ship "Bretoa" which went to Brazil in 1511 that Noronha (or Loronha) became associated with Bartolomeo Marchionni and his nephew, Benedetto Morelli, both from Florence, and with an unknown Portuguese.[37]

Thus it is obvious that the "commercial companies" which Dr. Fitzler considered so numerous in Portugal in the fifteenth and sixteenth centuries were actually limited, as far as can be traced in documents, to the one for coral in 1443 and the one for cork in 1456. But what is surprising is that, in both of these cases, Italians played a part in these companies. This fact has not been sufficiently emphasized, and moreover, even if we accept the first part of Rau's and Diffie's conclusion about the importance of foreign—in this case Italian—participation in Portuguese commerce of the fourteenth and fifteenth centuries, it is impossible to agree with them that they were only family business and temporary partnerships, not share companies.[38] Nothing of

[34] According to Fitzler this contract dates from 1502 ("Portugiesische Handelsgesellschaften," p. 241), and according to Rau and Diffie, from "early in the sixteenth century" (p. 196).

[35] Rau and Diffie, *loc. cit.*

[36] A. Baiao, *Historia da colonização portuguesa do Brasil* (3 vols.; Oporto, 1923), II, 325.

[37] *Ibid.*, p. 343.   [38] Rau and Diffie, *op. cit.*, p. 199.

this sort can be seen from an examination of the companies of 1443 and 1456, and besides Italian technique had long ago passed that stage.

It would be worth while at this point to assemble some data concerning the Italians who played a part in the Portuguese metropolitan and colonial economy of the later Middle Ages and especially toward the beginning of modern times. The book by Prospero Peragallo, *Cenni intorno alla colonia italiana in Portogallo,* the second edition of which was published in Genoa in 1907, is certainly valuable but difficult to obtain. It is, moreover, an alphabetical catalogue intended for consultation, not reading, and it does not deal only with the merchants. Actually, despite Peragallo's work, the role of the Italian merchants in Portugal has not been given the importance it deserves in either the history of Italian commerce or that of Portuguese economy. I do not intend to fill that gap in this short chapter. I wish merely to point out some of these merchants.

The most frequently mentioned of the Italian merchants in Portugal is Bartolomeo Marchionni. The one who appeared in 1511 among the outfitters of the ship "Bretoa" is another Bartolomeo Marchionni, presumably a relative of the man encountered around 1443 in connection with the coral agreement. No doubt it was the second of these namesakes who was given the task of supplying Pero da Covilham and Afonso de Paiva with money during the course of their voyage in search of India and Prester John.[39] On August 21, 1498, Manuel the Fortunate, when he endeavored to ensure that Portuguese nationals had priority in the exportation of sugar from Madeira, made an exception in favor of Bartolomeo Marchionni and Girolamo Sernigi, both of them from Florence; in 1501 the former was still taking an active part in that trade.[40] On the other hand, he was

[39] P. Peragallo, *op. cit.,* p. 101.

[40] *Raccolta Colombiana,* 15 Vols., Vol. II (Rome, 1893), part 3, p. 183.

also involved in the slave trade in Rio dos Escravos in West Africa. According to the accounts of the Casa dos Escravos for the period from June 15, 1486, to December 31, 1493, Bartolomeo Marchionni paid 6,300,000 reis for a license to trade for the first two years.[41] In 1489 and 1490 he paid up 500,000 of the 1,100,000 reis he owed for the second of these two years. In 1492, he paid 2,200,000 reis in partial payment of the dues he owed from trading in Rio dos Escravos during the years 1493 to 1495, in return for which he obtained an extension of his license. If we add up the sums of money paid out by the Florentine and those realized in sales by the Casa, it becomes apparent that Marchionni's license enabled him to corner a considerable part of the trade. During the period under examination, Marchionni must have imported 1,648 of a total 3,589 slaves.[42]

Apart from Africa and Brazil he was involved in trade in India. Marchionni joined with others, it would seem, in the equipping and loading of a ship (*nau*) for the expedition commanded by Pedro Alvares Cabral, who is known to have reached Brazil on his way to India. Domenico Pisani, the Venetian envoy, informed the government of Venice of this on July 27, 1501, from Lisbon. "This ship which has entered" he writes, "belongs to Bartholomeo the Florentine, together with the cargo which consists of: about 300 jars of pepper, 120 jars of cinnamon, 50 or 60 jars of lacquer, 15 jars of benzoin." [43] But of course this account is not altogether true, for on June 26 Gian Francesco Affaitati had written that the outfitters were "the gentleman Alvaro, together with Bortolo the Florentine and Hironimo and a Genoese." The

[41] A. Braamcamp Freire, "Cartas de quitação del Rei D. Manuel," *Arquivo historico portugues*, II (1905), p. 477, no. 404.

[42] For details of the calculations see C. Verlinden, *L'esclavage dans l'Europe médiévale*, I; *Péninsule Ibérique—France*, University of Ghent, Werken uitgegeven door de Faculteit van de Letteren en Wijsbegeerte, vol. 119 (Bruges, 1955), pp. 625–627.

[43] *Diari di Marino Sanuto* (58 vols.; Venice, 1879–1902), IV, cols. 99 ff.

first man was the brother of the Duke of Braganza, the second Marchionni, the third Girolamo Sernigi, and the fourth may have been Antonio Salvago.[44] In 1502 Marchionni had another ship in the convoy commanded by João da Nova; he unloaded from it at least 400 tons of spices, and in 1503, 2,100 to 2,200 quintals of spices were brought from India to him.[45] This is the way it went from year to year up to 1518.[46] Thus we are dealing in this case with an Italian merchant of great scope who for more than thirty years played a very prominent part in Portuguese colonial trade. It is worth noting that the Marchionnis, before becoming involved in colonial trade, had, at least since the partnership formed in 1443 for coral fishing, been engaged in undertakings relative to Portuguese metropolitan economy.

We have already seen that in the agreement concerning cork passed on June 21, 1456, the chief partner was the Genoese Marco Lomellino. Other Genoese of the same name, Urbano and Battista Lomellino, had been established on Madeira since the end of the fifteenth century. The former owned a sugar plantation (*engenho de assucar*) near Porto de Seixo and, together with a compatriot named Luigi Doria, controlled a vast agricultural domain. These Lomellinos of Madeira were the first of a noble family which played an important part in the eighteenth-century wine trade. Others who had settled in Lisbon began to import coral in the second half of the sixteenth century, which was in turn re-exported to India.[47]

In our study of Bartolomeo Marchionni we found that he,

---

[44] *Ibid.*, col. 66. Cf. Peragallo, *op. cit.*, p. 104.

[45] *Diari di Marino Sanuto,* IV, cols. 544 ff. and V, col. 131.

[46] Peragallo, *op. cit.*, p. 106.

[47] *Ibid.*, p. 98. A certain Giovanni, a Leonardo, and a Sisto Lomellino exported sugar from Madeira to Genoa from 1496 on. See D. Giofré, "Le relazioni fra Genova e Madera nel primo decennio del secolo XVI," *Studi Colombiani,* III (1952), 483. For the Dorias of Madeira see Peragallo, *op. cit.*, p. 69. Several of them owned sugar-cane plantations.

too, had been involved in exporting sugar from Madeira, and that in 1498 the King of Portugal had granted him and another Florentine, Girolamo Sernigi, an important privilege. That same year Sernigi went to Guinea on his own ship.[48] It is he, again, who on July 10, 1499, sent news from Lisbon to Florence of the return of Vasco da Gama, by means of a long letter included in Gian Battista Ramusio's collection *Delle Navigazioni e Viaggi*.[49] It is therefore not at all surprising to find him associated with Marchionni on the occasion of Cabral's expedition. In 1503 Giovanni da Empoli set out for India in a ship belonging to Albuquerque's fleet, which had been equipped by Sernigi, together with Luca Giraldi, the Gualterottis, and the Frescobaldis. In 1510 Sernigi seemed to have supreme control of equipping the four ships which Diogo Mendes de Vasconcellos took to Malacca.[50] Various Florentine men of business were on board, notably Lunardo Nardi and, once more, Giovanni da Empoli. The following year Girolamo Sernigi became a citizen of Lisbon, and, in 1515, he was so far assimilated as to have become "a Portuguese nobleman." [51]

Gian Francesco Affaitati is another Italian who seems at first to have been involved in the sugar trade from Madeira,[52]

[48] *Raccolta Colombiana,* II, part 2, p. 82.

[49] The letter is reprinted in *Ibid.,* p. 113.

[50] Francesco Guicciardini wrote from Spain to his brother Luigi on June 17, 1513: "One of Girolamo Sernigi's ships is coming [from Malacca] very richly laden and another three of Girolamo Sernigi's ships remained at Malacca to load there and if they return to harbor, they will be very richly laden. This one which has arrived carries the capital for all four; more than sixty or seventy per cent profit; thus, if they all come, you see that miracles follow" (*Raccolta Colombiana,* I, part 3, p. 215).

[51] Before 1511 he was "a resident of our city of Lisbon." In that year he becomes "citizen," while in 1515 King Manuel commands that "he and all his descendents, should have all the honors, privileges, freedoms, graces, rewards, exemptions and immunities which noblemen have or should have" (Peragallo, *op. cit.,* p. 158).

[52] Peragallo, *op. cit.,* p. 27.

but, from 1502 on, he was active in trade from India. His agent, Matteo da Bergamo, was aboard one of the ships of Vasco da Gama's second expedition. This expedition brought Affaitati 5,000 ducats in return for a capital outlay of 2,000, as he wrote to his brother Luca in Cremona in 1503.[53] In a later convoy he had a twelfth share in two ships.[54] Meanwhile he continued trading in Madeira, but this did not prevent him from faithfully conveying information on Portuguese commerce to the government of Venice in numerous letters, a great number of which have been preserved by Marino Sanuto in his diary.[55] The merchant dynasty of the Affaitati is known to have continued playing a decisive role both in Portugal and in the Low Countries.[56]

In talking of Marchionni's trade with India we mentioned Antonio Salvago of Genoa. He apparently belonged to the same family as the Giovanni Salvago who is known to have guaranteed a debt incurred by the Bishop of Algarve to Alvaro de Braganza during the reign of John II (1481–1495).[57] Antonio Salvago himself bought 200 quintals of spices in 1502 and fitted out a 200- to 250-ton boat to send to India with the convoy the following year.[58] Is it the same man who, in 1498, obtained from the King of England the right to load wool for export "to foreign countries overseas through and beyond the strait of Morocco (Gibraltar)"?[59] A certain Luca Salvago later owned a sugar-cane plantation on Madeira.[60]

All the merchants we have mentioned so far were independent traders and generally possessed large fortunes. Here now are two agents.

Let us begin with the most famous, Giovanni da Empoli.

[53] *Diari di Marino Sanuto,* V, col. 133.

[54] Letter of September 26, 1502, in *ibid.,* IV, col. 663.

[55] *Ibid.,* IV, V, VI.

[56] See Denucé, *Inventaire des Affaitadi, passim.*

[57] "Acting as guarantor [was] a certain Genoese who is called João Salvajo" (Peragallo, *op. cit.,* p. 148).

[58] *Diari di Marino Sanuto,* IV, col. 545 ff.

[59] Peragallo, *op. cit.,* p. 148, n. 2.   [60] *Ibid.,* p. 149.

We have already seen that he embarked for India in 1503. He was at that time in the service of Marchionni.[61] He set out again in 1510 on a ship equipped by Girolamo Sernigi, with whom we are familiar, but this time he also did business on his own account to the extent of 7,000 cruzados.[62] During his third voyage he died at Canton while acting as the king's own representative.[63] This is typical of the rise of a commercial agent who was exceptionally gifted, as can be seen from his documents.

Lunardo (or Leonardo) Nardi was also employed by Bartolomeo Marchionni. He had taken part as an agent in the expedition sent to India in 1501, and he worked on the preparation of the 1502 convoy, but he never engaged in business on his own account, "because" he said, "I don't want to seize more than is put before me." [64] This did not prevent his being greatly appreciated by Albuquerque for his work in India after 1510. The latter wrote to the king, "I have more faith in the counting house of Bartolomeo [Marchionni] with his Leonardo, than in all the agencies and agents in India." [65] No greater praise could have been made of Italian collaboration in Portuguese colonial economy, nor could its importance have been indicated more strongly.

[61] *Ibid.*, p. 72.   [62] *Raccolta Colombiana,* II, part 3, pp. 180 ff.
[63] Peragallo, *op. cit.,* p. 74.
[64] *Diari di Marino Sanuto,* IV, col. 545 ff.
[65] *Cartas de Affonso de Albuquerque* (Lisbon, 1884), p. 104.

6. Italian Influence on Spanish Economy and Colonization during the Reign of Ferdinand the Catholic*

Ramón Carande, whose fine books on the Spanish economy of the sixteenth century have so greatly enriched our knowledge, has made a brilliant study of economic life under the Catholic Kings.[1] He presents a picture of a Spain very low in capital precisely at the outset of its period of great discoveries and of the first colonial undertakings of great breadth. This is not the place to determine whether Spain's position in international trade at that time, and for some time previous, enabled its kings to obtain from within the country a large part of the maritime and financial means such an elaborate expansion would imply. Such a task would in fact involve a survey of the whole history of external trade on the peninsula in the Middle Ages. But even setting aside this extremely important question, I am astonished that Carande, who forty years ago devoted a remarkable study to Seville as an international market and had concentrated in particular on the part played by Italians, especially Genoese, did not consider at all what might have been their participation in the econo-

* Translated from "Les influences italiennes dans l'économie et dans la colonisation espagnoles à l'époque de Ferdinand le Catholique," *Fernando el Catolico e Italia,* V° Congreso de Historia de la Corona de Aragón, *Estudios,* III (Saragossa, 1954), 269–283.

[1] *Carlos V y sus banqueros* (3 vols.; Madrid, 1943–1967). See also by the same author "Sevilla, fortaleza y mercado," *Anuario de historia del derecho español,* II (1925), 233–401.

mic and colonial boom which, whatever he said, did mark the reign of the Catholic Kings.

The economic activity of Italians in Spain exerted a great influence, which was first felt in the twelfth century, and its effects continued at least into the middle of the seventeenth century. I have dealt separately with the principal aspects of it in a series of articles and I will not go into them here.[2] I wish to concentrate exclusively on the period of Ferdinand the Catholic, a period of capital importance as much from a Spanish as from an Italian point of view.

I wish to show, by a series of examples, that Ferdinand took a personal interest in commercial relations with Italy. These examples are taken from the period after 1483, a year that marks the break in relations with Venice following the formation of a league against that city.

On January 2, 1484, Ferdinand, an Italian prince himself, commanded the viceroys, the *magistri racionales,* and the *magister portulanus* of Sicily and Sardinia to allow the subjects of the king of Naples and the states of the League to export "from whatever ports and docks they wish of our said kingdoms of Sicily and Sardinia, even those reserved for us and our court, all deliveries of grain, barley, vegetables, and other foodstuffs which they wish to export . . . so that they might supply, with these and other foods, the war which . . . is being waged against Venice." This passage, like those which follow, from the magnificent series of *Documentos sobre relaciones internacionales de los Reyes Católicos,* com-

---

[2] C. Verlinden, "De Italiaanse invloeden in de Iberische economie en kolonisatie (XIIe–XVIIe eeuw)," Mededelingen van de Koninklijke Vlaamse Academie voor Wetenschappen, Letteren en Schone Kunsten van België (Brussels, 1951); "Le influenze italiane nella colonizzazione iberica (uomini e metodi)," *Nuova rivista storica,* XXXVI, (1952), 254–270; "Italian Influence in Iberian Colonization," *Hispanic American Historical Review,* XXXIII (1953), 199–211; "Modalités et méthodes du commerce colonial dans l'empire espagnol au XVIe siècle, I: La question des influences italiennes," *Revista de Indias,* XII (1952), 249–276.

piled by Count Antonio de la Torre,[3] is more political than economic. It shows, however, that the King was careful to maintain, despite adverse circumstances, a traditional trade, essential to the prosperity of his possessions in southern Italy: the trade in grain.

One peninsular zone important for commercial relations with Italy was Valencia. On February 10, 1484, Ferdinand commanded the general bailiff of Valencia, in compliance with the papal bull against the Venetians, "to expel all Venetians who are in our kingdoms and prevent our subjects from trading in goods to all of Venetian birth." A Venetian ship which was no doubt part of the regular convoy (*muda*) to Flanders had to anchor in Valencia. It could not obtain a safe-conduct and was not allowed either to load or unload or take on supplies.[4] Nevertheless the act of December 29, 1483, had to be observed, which allowed Venetian merchants, in accordance with international trade law of the times, a period—admittedly very short—of fifty days in which to leave the royal territories. On the other hand the King was thinking about the future and the resumption of normal commercial relations with Venice. This can be seen from a decree of January 8, 1485, in which Ferdinand enjoined the authorities of Valencia to take certain measures in favor of Venetian merchants who were living in that port. "We have learned that in this city of Valencia there are several Venetians, who were left by the Venetian galleys when they left the shores of the city," the document said. Did this refer to the last Venetian convoy admitted regularly before the rupture of commercial relations, or had these relations already been re-established, since the peace treaty was signed on July 7, 1484? We cannot decide on the basis of this one text, but in any case the King declared that the Venetians in question "with their goods and their possessions wish to leave and go to Venice. And since it is our will that they may leave with

[3] II (Barcelona, 1950), 9.   [4] *Ibid.*, p. 18.

their goods and possessions, without any penalty at all, for this reason we charge and order strictly that they should and are permitted without any hindrance or delay to leave and load on whatever ships and vessels the aforesaid goods and possessions." [5] And so a Biscayan ship had to take them to Venice.

On the other hand, the King had some months ago indicated that the measures taken against the Venetians were extremely unfavorable to the trade of the kingdom of Valencia, and of Catalonia and Sicily. On March 31, 1484, in a letter to the King of Naples, he truly showed an economic and fiscal realism of his own and even defended his point of view testily, taking into account what he presented as the balance sheet of his subjects with the whole of Italy. Again I will let the document, speak for itself:

With respect to the response of Your Serenity concerning the prohibiting the Venetians to trade, saying that it will not harm our receipts and balances, nor our vassals, it seems to us that Your Serenity does not answer what we wrote to you concerning this matter. For we, understanding from that moment [it had only taken the King three months to understand the results of the rupture] the great interest which we had in them and the great disadvantages and losses which would derive from this prohibition of commerce to our real earnings, especially in the Kingdoms of Sicily, Valencia and the principality of Catalonia, we desired to write to you and pray you that Your Serenity in consideration of this matter would give an order and would act in such a way with those of the aforesaid League that the aforesaid damages and interests would be satisfied.

The King endeavors to clarify his thoughts further: he wants an indemnity in cash for the losses suffered:

Likewise, inasmuch as you know that it is not possible for those of the aforesaid League to pursue trade in those said Kingdoms like the Venetians nor can they by trade make reparations for the said damages nor any part of them, which damages, by being so

[5] *Ibid.*, p. 179.

much and so great that because of our necessities and burdens are almost impossible to tolerate, we have requested to write to Your Serenity about it, praying that after due consideration of all of the above and other things in relation to them, inasmuch as the said damages and interests, as has been said, cannot be compensated through similar trade or negotiation, you should give an order and require those of the League so that the damages can be satisfied and made up to us in money.

Moreover, Ferdinand even threatens to lift the measures against the Venetians and to refuse the ships requested by Naples under the pretext of the war with Granada.

This letter shows that the King, and his contemporaries generally, considered that the three zones of his states which were particularly concerned in the trade with Venice were Catalonia, the kingdoms of Valencia and of Sicily. It also proves that, for these areas, the King seemed to be of the opinion that the Venetian trade was more important than anything. Finally it emphasizes the fact that the Catholic King's diplomacy was as much economic as purely political.

At that time political relations with Genoa were bad, as they had so often been in the later Middle Ages between the Crown of Aragon and the ligurian republic. On May 30, 1484, Ferdinand sent from Córdoba a decree to the governor of Valencia which would leave one to suppose at first glance that the already tense commercial relations would for a while become impossible.

We have had news from Genoa that, because Don Francisco Torrelles has taken with his galleys a son of the Doge of Genoa, the said Doge has occupied and seized all the possessions of our vassals who did business in the said city of Genoa, despite the fact that they held guarantees and safe-conducts from the said Doge and Commune of Genoa. And since, therefore, the guarantees given to our vassals are not valid, it is not right that our guarantees should be valid for Genoese merchants who are living, trading, and owning houses in this city and kingdom, so that it has been decided that, since they have seized the goods of our vassals and imprisoned their persons, we shall do the same in our kingdoms.[6]

A similar decree was sent to the viceroy of Majorca.

This proves that the regions of Aragon where the Genoese were most numerous at that time must have been Valencia and Majorca, since there was no similar decree for Catalonia.

Aragonese policy of the time indicates that Genoese trade was vital for Mediterranean Spain, for, despite poor political relations, commercial connections had been maintained until then by means of individual safe-conducts. Moreover, even in Valencia, the decree does not seem to have been carried out, since on October 27, 1484, five months after the first order, the King had to repeat it. Obviously commercial connections had been maintained, for on both sides merchants had given securities. Here is what the King said:

We have sure news that in Genoa our subjects are so closely confined that they may not go to the gate of the town, nor within a hundred steps of it, despite the fact that they have given securities. . . . For this reason I charge and command you, with all my heart, that you seize in person all the Genoese merchants residing in your city and have them deposit in your power the six thousand ducats, for which they have given securities.[7]

It is clear that even then agreement was not yet impossible. Besides, the practice of granting safe-conducts continued. We know this from a decree of January 25, 1487, in which Ferdinand cancelled all the safe-conducts granted the Genoese and Corsicans throughout the kingdom of Aragon, except for those resident in his domains.[8] In other words, the door remained wide open for relations with Liguria, even under the appearance of strictest severity. Moreover the 1487 document showed that the people of Nice specialized in contraband with Genoa wherever it proved necessary or profitable. During all this time the Catalans maintained normal consular

[6] *Ibid.*, p. 61.   [7] *Ibid.*, p. 128.   [8] *Ibid.*, p. 385.

relations with Genoa,[9] which would be enough to explain why orders concerning the arrest of Genoese and confiscation of their property were not carried out in that principality. The war seemed to have little effect on normal business relations. Doubtless this was because such relations were tacitly protected by the authorities, which emphasizes their importance and makes us think that, despite what Ferdinand had written on this topic to the king of Naples, business relations with Genoa must have been at least as extensive as those with Venice. Besides, for whomever knows the orientation of Venetian, as well as Genoese, trade, to raise this question is to begin an answer which can only be favorable to Genoa, since, in any case and apart from the loss of almost all its Levantine possessions, Genoa, as opposed to Venice, was henceforth oriented almost exclusively toward the West.

My aim in this chapter is not to carry out a systematic study of the economic politics of Ferdinand the Catholic with regard to the Italian republics. I simply want to emphasize that the documents published by Antonio de la Torre enable one to grasp the intensity of commercial relations even in time of war and that, apart from the large number of decrees concerning Genoa and Venice, there are also documents which are of particular interest for Florence and Naples, as well as for Sicily, an actual Aragonese territory. The third volume contains a whole series of safe-conducts granted to Genoese merchants resident in Spain, whose precise location is not mentioned. There is even a case of naturalization involving Oberto Spinola, the formula of which deserves to be remembered, since it is used again and again in Spain as well as in the colonies:

We accept you, the said Ubertus Spinola, with all and every one of your possessions in vassallage and as a natural subject and we

[9] Ferdinand to the Doge of Genoa, August 22, 1485 (*ibid.*, p. 225); Ferdinand to the Council of Barcelona, September 24, 1485 (*ibid.*, p. 231).

welcome you in the number and company of our other subjects, so that you will reside and be counted among our natural subjects as if you were born in any city of our Kingdom of the Crown of Aragon.

The object of such naturalization is obvious, for the text goes on to say:

And if something in favor of the Genoese or against them, in general or particular, should be legislated or ordered or admonished by us or by our officials and subjects in said Kingdom, that statute, ordinance, or warning scarcely includes you or embraces you.[10]

Again, the aim was to maintain commercial relations in spite of all opposition.

I have commented on the texts I have just quoted, and to which I could easily have added, with the objects of localizing some important centers of Italian commercial activity in Spain and of showing that the Catholic King was constantly concerned about trade with Italy.

While we are discussing the Aragonese political complex, I would like to mention one aspect of the work of another Spanish historian, Manuel Ballesteros, who studied the part played by John Cabot in Spain.[11] He has shown that Cabot, who possessed Venetian nationality at that time, lived in Mediterranean Spain from 1491 to 1493, that he very likely traded with Valencia, as so many other Italians did, and that he had drawn up and submitted to the King a plan for the improvement of the harbor equipment of Valencia. That this plan was not implemented at the time does not concern us here, but rather that Cabot showed himself a technician. This is a characteristic we find repeated in the activities of many other less well known Italians in Spain or in the colonies.

[10] *Ibid.*, III (1951), 401.
[11] "Juan Caboto en España: Nueva luz sobre un problema viejo," *Revista de Indias*, 1943.

Now let us shift our attention from eastern Spain to the south of the peninsula and examine a genre of documents very different from the decrees and orders of the royal chancery from which we have been drawing our information.

The notary archives of Seville are very precious but unfortunately nearly exclusively known through the *Catalogo de los fondos americanos del archivo de protocolos de Sevilla,* published in 1930 by the Instituto Hispano Cubano in Seville. In 1935, however, Roberto Almagià, extracted useful information from the catalogue concerning Genoese merchants, bankers, and outfitters in Seville during the first two decades of the sixteenth century,[12] and his compatriot Pietro Gribaudi the following year contributed an article to the *Bolletino della Società Geografica Italiana* entitled "Navigatori, banchieri e mercanti italiani nei documenti degli archivi notarili di Siviglia." Both scholars concentrated their attention on the economic activities of many Genoese and of some Florentines in Seville and on their participation in the first commercial relations with America. The aim pursued by these two Italian historians had more relevance to the history of geography than to that of economy. Essentially they were trying to increase our knowledge of the milieu surrounding Columbus; the actual techniques of business and its financing obviously interested them less.

Some years earlier a French historian, A. E. Sayous, who had completely ignored the role of the Genoese in previous works devoted to trade between America and Spain, gave his attention to these problems.[13] I believe the method he

[12] "Commercianti, banchieri ed armatori genovesi a Siviglia nei primi decenni del secolo XVI," *Rendiconti Accademia dei Lincei,* Classe di scienze morale, storiche e filologiche, series VI, vol. XI (1935), 443–458.

[13] His earlier articles include "Origen de las instituciones económicas en la América española," *Boletín del Instituto de Investigaciones Históricas,* VII (Buenos Aires, 1928) and "Partnerships in the Trade between Spain and America and also in the Spanish Colonies in the sixteenth century," *Journal of Economic and Business History* I (1928), 282 ff. He utilized notarial deeds from Seville in "Le rôle des Génois

followed was mistaken, and I think I proved this in lectures I gave at the Instituto Gonzalo Fernández de Oviedo at Madrid, which were published in the *Revista de Indias*.[14] But, even if Sayous was wrong in considering the methods of Spanish colonial trade out of date, and even if he did not take into sufficient account the evolution of commercial technique in the later Middle Ages both in Spain and in Italy—which made him overestimate the influence of the *commenda* and the Italian companies—nevertheless it remains clear that the Italian influence, especially the Genoese influence, was enormous in the financing of business, and the boom in colonial trade, and as a result in colonization itself, would have been much slower had not Italian money been associated with the bravery of the conquistadors, through the Italian merchant colonies in Seville and in the southern half of the peninsula. Our attention is bound to be held by these problems of financing even after the study of many documents concerning the Genoese in the notary archives of Seville has been made from the texts themselves.[15]

Since the Seville documents are sufficiently recognized as sources for the economic activity of Italians in Spain and in the colonies at the time of the Catholic Kings, I need not insist on this point further. This is not true of certain analogous sources concerning other metropolitan or colonial regions.

---

lors des premiers mouvements réguliers d'affaires entre l'Espagne et le Nouveau Monde (1505–1520)," *Comptes rendus de l'Académie des Inscriptions et Belles-Lettres,* 1932, pp. 287–298, and "Les débuts du commerce de l'Espagne avec l'Amérique (1503–1518), *Revue historique,* CLXXIV (1934), 185–215.

[14] See note 2 above. The second part of this work is entitled: "Paiements et monnaie en Amérique espagnole," *Revista de Indias,* XII (1952), pp. 249–276, and similarly refutes certain views formulated by Sayous in other works.

[15] This has been done recently by my former student Ruth Pike in her book *Enterprise and Adventure: The Genoese in Seville and the Opening of the New World* (Ithaca, N.Y., 1966).

Apart from Seville, Cádiz and Jerez held an extremely important place in Genoese activity, and their role has been studied in two works by H. Sancho de Sopranis.[16] He has drawn up a list of the Genoese to be found in Cádiz, Jerez, and Puerto Santa María between 1460 and 1500. He classified them as citizens, residents, and transients and counted 53 of them. At Jerez: 14 citizens, 4 residents, 2 transients—20 in all; at Cádiz: 18 citizens, 1 resident—19 in all; at Puerto: 6 citizens, 2 residents, 6 transients—14 in all. This might seem relatively few, but actually all the documentation comes from only one notary, Hernando de Carmona, who held office in Jerez and, moreover, the author only had access to a small portion of the deeds of this notary, which cover only a fraction of the period 1483–1484. Among these Genoese are some quite important men, particularly the Adornos, the Spinolas, the Cataneos, the Centurionis, the Dorias, the Grimaldis, the Marruffos, the Negros, the Salvagos, Usodimare, Vivaldi, Cabron—who colonized the Canaries—and others.

What Sancho has done is to point out and catalogue men. The next step should be to look at their work and get to know their trade and above all their methods, but to do this the deeds which mention them must be published. We can see from Sancho's research that some of these Genoese went to the Canary Islands and to Barbary, that they imported grain from Sicily, or exported fruit and other goods to England and Flanders. They also hired out their ships to the king for use in war. Some of them were money-changers like Niculoso Merlessyn and Niculoso Espindola, who appear in a document of 1484. Unfortunately numerous other documents are simply mentioned or analyzed so briefly that an economic historian can obtain no precise information from them. But

[16] *Los Genoveses en Cádiz antes de 1600,* Sociedad de Estudios Históricos de Jerez de la Frontera, no. 4 (Larache, 1939), and "Los Genoveses en la región Gaditano-Xericiense de 1460 à 1500," *Hispania,* VIII (1948), 355–402.

even so, in addition to the transport of grain from Sicily, an operation of considerable scope, and the trade with Barbary, we get glimpses of shipbuilding, wine-trade, fishing in Morocco, and, on a simpler level, the work of Italian artisans in Andalusia. It would be very useful if these documents were available in their entirety, especially since we could learn from them, not only about the economic activity of Italians on the peninsula itself, but also in that trial laboratory of colonial matters—the Canary Islands.

It is to this Atlantic archipelago, where the Spaniards, both Castilians and Aragonese, had been active since before the middle of the fourteenth century, that I now want to turn my attention. Efforts are being made at present under the competent direction of Elias Serra Rafols of the University of La Laguna, by a valiant group from the *Revista de historia* at Tenerife. Many documents and studies of this area have recently become available in the volumes of this journal and in the series Fontes rerum Canariarum, and the archipelago has the unusual good fortune to possess notary archives which go back to the very beginning of its colonization.

Dr. Manuela Marrero has made a study of the economic activity of the Italians, and again particularly the Genoese.[17] She is concerned with the period between 1496 and 1509, when the colonization and development of the archipelago were proceeding very actively. In 1496 Alonso de Lugo founded a company with royal authorization and the participation of Italian capitalists, especially Genoese, for the conquest of the island of La Palma. The capitalists, several of whom were already established on other islands of the archipelago, were often reimbursed by concessions of land, which they would irrigate and use for sugar-cane plantations, as in some Italian colonies of the Levant and in Sicily. These enterprises too were sometimes operated by companies.

Manpower was provided partly by the slave trade in which

[17] "Los Genoveses en la colonalización de Tenerife," *Revista de historia,* no. 89 (1950), 52–65.

the Italians as well as the Spaniards participated, thus continuing a tradition which goes back to the Middle Ages in the Mediterranean countries.[18] Black slaves were imported from the African continent, and some of the ships which went in search of them were Genoese.

Trading conditions were quite primitive at first, and they remained so for some time in America as well because of the lack of currency. In 1498 a municipal ordinance of Tenerife made possible payment in wheat and barley.[19] The Genoese immediately took part in the cereal trade, and they granted loans to all classes of the population. We see them at the head of vast land possessions, received from the very man who undertook the conquest, Governor Alonso de Lugo. One of them, Matteo Vigna, is particularly well known to us. He, together with some fellow countrymen, invested considerable sums of money in the conquest and supplied provisions to the troops. The Crown gave him the duty of partitioning the land, for he knew the Canary Islands well, having previously settled on Grand Canary Island, in the occupation and colonization of which his compatriot Pedro Fernández Cabrón had collaborated since 1480.[20] He was a reasonable manager and a good technician. He brought in, no doubt from Italy, equipment for drying up the marshes.

Another Genoese, Battista Ascanio, came from Cádiz, where Hippolito Sancho de Sopranis also came across him [21] and where he occupied the important office of city alderman

[18] See my book *L'esclavage dans l'Europe médiévale*, I: *Péninsule Ibérique—France*, University of Ghent, Werken uitgegeven door de Faculteit van de Letteren en Wijsbegeerte, vol. 119 (Bruges, 1955).

[19] *Acuerdos del cabildo de Tenerife (1497–1507)* (La Laguna, 1949), no. 62.

[20] M. Fernández Navarrete, *Colección de los viajes y descubrimientos* (Madrid, 1825) II, 397–399, and F. Pacheco, F. Cardenas, and L. Torres Mendoza, *Colección de documentos inéditos, relativos al descubrimiento, conquista, y colonización de las antiquas posesiones españolas de América y Oceanía* (42 vols.; Madrid, 1864–1884), XXXVIII, 83–88.

[21] "Los Genoveses en la región Gaditano-Xericiense," p. 396.

before becoming constable-major of Tenerife. A third man, Cristóbal de Ponte (Cristoforo da Ponte in Italian), actually became a lord, possessed a fortress, and held it by the authority of the king, with all the duties it involved. He subenfeoffed lands, as a Genoese colonist of the Levant would have done.

Apart from these Genoese there were some Romans, Lombards, and Venetians in Tenerife, though admittedly they were far less numerous. All, or almost all, had brought capital which aided the rapid boom in agriculture, industry, and trade in the Canaries. Without Italian support development would certainly have been much slower.

In addition to the texts used by Dr. Marrero in her 1950 article, she kindly made available to me the transcription of others. On October 26, 1506, Giovanni Giacomo de Carminatis, a Lombard merchant, and Bartolomeo da Milano, both of them residents of Tenerife, gave a commission to Giovanni Rondinel or Rondinelli, a Florentine merchant living in Seville,[22] another proof of the close relations existing between the Italians of the archipelago and those of Andalusia. On January 26, 1508, Cristóbal de Ponte, whom we already know as landlord and feudal lord, acknowledged that he owed 36,000 maravedis to the Council of Tenerife for the rent of the inn at Garachico for a period of six years.[23] It is obvious that this powerful personage did not disdain any form of profit-making. Moreover it would seem that his business affairs were not faring well and that he was obliged to use every means to attain his ends. In fact, by a deed of March 30, 1508, we learn that, being in the debt of another Genoese, Francesco de Riberol who lived at Seville, de Ponte sold him, through the agency of Cosimo de Riberol, the former's brother, half of the sugar-cane plantation, lands, and vineyards which he owned in the realm of Dabte in

[22] Notary archives of Tenerife. Notary Sebastian Paez, no. 2 (1506–1509), fol. 24r.

[23] *Ibid.*, fol. 536r.

the island. In future the whole operation would be developed as a company.[24] The deed of partnership has so far eluded the investigations of Dr. Marrero, so we have no exact idea of the administration of the plantation. Another document shows that, before reaching this agreement, da Ponte had had to grant his creditor an interest in kind, payable in sugar to the extent of 200 arrobas a year.[25]

It is of primary importance that we become better acquainted with the economic development of the Canary Islands at the time of the Catholic Kings, for these islands, as I have already mentioned, served as a sort of trial laboratory for more than one aspect of the colonial methods used later in America. Professor Robert Ricard of the Sorbonne, has pointed out, admittedly for a later period, a particularly interesting example of direct connection in the sugar industry. He cites a royal schedule of April 23, 1569, dealing with the organization of the sugar industry at Puerto Rico. This schedule granted the authorities of the Canary Islands permission to send to Puerto Rico two "master sugar makers" who were living in the archipelago, two carpenters, two blacksmiths, and two boilermakers, who were put in charge of the machinery and management of the sugar mills.[26] We know, judging from the parallelism observed in the Portuguese empire and particularly between Madeira and Brazil, that similar influences were exercised even earlier from the Atlantic archipelagoes in the direction of the American possessions. In these exchanges, the archipelagoes formed the central pillar of the bridge across the ocean. The origin of the techniques as well as of the capital is often to be found first in Italy and in the Italian colonies of the Levant. We have seen examples of this in the Canary Islands concerning both sugar-cane plantations and vineyards, and the situation in the Portuguese colonies was the same. Duarte Pacheco

[24] *Ibid.*, fol. 325r.   [25] *Ibid.*, fol. 271r.
[26] R. Ricard, "Recherches sur les relations des Iles Canaries et de la Berbérie au XVIᵉ siècle," *Hesperis*, XXI (1935), 80.

Perreira was explicit on the subject of Madeira where the sugar-cane technique was imported from Sicily.[27] Moreover the sugar industry in Brazil was started with the help of Italian capital and technique.[28] Did nothing similar happen in Spanish America?

We must again look for the answer to the reign of the Catholic Kings. Las Casas tells us that the cane was introduced into the West Indies by Columbus when he left the Canary Islands during his second voyage. At that time the Italian influence was very strong in the Canaries, but unfortunately the history of the origins of sugar cultivation in Española is still rather vague. According to Herrera, the Hieronymite governors of this island granted a loan of 500 gold pesos for every sugar mill built, beginning in 1516–1518 and therefore after the death of Ferdinand the Catholic. But Gonzalo Fernández de Oviedo had earlier brought to Spain samples of American sugar.[29] We now know more about this initial period as far as the Italians are concerned and can see that the Genoese have influenced the early development.[30]

We have, moreover, pertinent information that quite a number of Italians went to the New World and even became citizens of colonial municipalities. Italian agents in the Caribbean sometimes profited from the distance to carry on private business with the funds entrusted to them by their compatriots of Seville. Whatever the situation, their intervention could only have been favorable to the development of Spanish colonial economy in the Antilles. Ferdinand the Catholic was perfectly aware of this. Herrera informs us, in

[27] *Esmeraldo de situ orbis* (Lisbon, 1892), pp. 57 ff. See also Chapter 1 above, p. 21.

[28] A. Marchant, *From Barter to Slavery: The Economic Relations of Portuguese and Indians in the Settlement of Brazil, 1500–1580* (Baltimore, 1942), p. 94.

[29] C. H. Haring, *The Spanish Empire in America* (New York, 1947), p. 252.

[30] See Pike, *op. cit.*, ch. VI, pp. 128–144.

fact, that when the Archbishop of Seville, faithful to the traditional doctrine of hostility to interest-bearing loans, thought to interfere in 1509 in the name of the Church against the Italians of Seville who were demanding excessive interest for transferring funds to America, the King immediately tempered the prelate's zeal. What other considerations but the benefit of colonial economy at its earlier stages could have guided royal politics in this case? It would be worth making a closer study of the dossier of this affair.

Men such as Giacomo and Tommaso Castellione lived for a long time in Española, the latter from 1509 to 1515. Similarly Girolamo Grimaldi was in Santo Domingo from 1508 to 1515. It is about such men that Prof. Ruth Pike has searched the archives of Seville.

I mentioned earlier in this chapter that the reign of the Catholic Kings was of primary importance in economic and colonial matters, as much from the Spanish as from the Italian point of view. This importance results from more than one factor.

During the epoch of the Catholic Kings, the Italians, especially the Genoese and to a lesser degree the Florentines, felt themselves more strongly drawn toward Spain than at any other time. Usually this attraction is explained in terms of Spanish colonial expansion. But that force would have had an equal influence on the Venetians, and the notary archives clearly show that they were influenced to a much lesser extent. In fact the Venetians both kept their former colonies in the Levant, or at least the most important of them, and continued to take a more important part than is generally realized in trade with that area. Fernand Braudel did not fail to draw attention to this point in his brilliant volume *La Méditerranée et le monde méditerranéen à l'époque de Philippe II* (Paris, 1949). In contrast, the Genoese had lost most of their colonies and wanted somehow to take part in colonization by means of an intervening power, at first in both the Spanish and Portuguese Atlantic archipelagoes, and then in America. Florentines and other Italians joined in the background of this movement.

Italian support was unquestionably well received, at least by the rulers. Ferdinand the Catholic, in particular, understood admirably the contribution Italian capital and techniques could make at that crucial time to his kingdom. Coming from the east of the peninsula, he was accustomed to look to the Mediterranean and Italy and considered economic relations with that country as obvious and natural. This attitude of mind dictated a similar policy in Andalusia, in the Canary Islands, and in America, when destiny put control of these areas into his hands. It was not a question then of a Castilian or even Spanish monopoly. No doubt the reason for this was that the capital and economic experience of the Italians, and especially of the Genoese, seemed indispensable. I would not dare, in the present state of our knowledge, draw the conclusion that this was owing to the poverty of Spain, as has so often been done, even in that country. I believe that there was considerable capital of commercial origin in Spain, but it came from traditional commercial currents which were difficult to deflect without opening the way to catastrophe. Italian capital and technique, on the other hand, especially Genoese, were deprived at that time of a good portion of their normal field of action as the result of the Turkish advance in the Levant and were in need of an alternative field of investment. This was provided by Spain and Portugal. By seizing this opportunity the Iberian monarchs were able to accelerate the rhythm of their colonial undertakings and to outstrip in this area the people of northwestern Europe.

Ferdinand the Catholic seems always to have understood this, as we have seen both in Mediterranean Spain in the years after 1480 and in Seville during the first decade of the sixteenth century. The King's economic politics was not traditionalist. He made a very great contribution in helping to graft onto the commercial economy inherited from peninsular Middle Ages the powerful support available from Italy.

But this Italian support had itself an inheritance from previous centuries, by means of which commercial and colonial economy created in the Mediterranean area was transferred to the vast Atlantic world.[31] Spain constituted an important stage on the route leading from medieval economy and colonization to those of modern times; that Spain was able to assume in this process the most important role was largely because a sovereign of Ferdinand the Catholic's ability was presiding over its destinies at the crucial moment when the possibilities were presented. To have moved then in the right direction constitutes one of the greatest claims to glory and one of the clearest proofs of the political genius of this exceptional prince.

[31] See chapter 1 above, pp. 3–10.

7. The Italians in the Economy of the Canary Islands at the Beginning of Spanish Colonization*

At the end of the Middle Ages and beginning of modern times, and with Seville, where the Genoese were particularly numerous, as their point of departure, the Italians began to exercise an economic influence on the growing Spanish colonial empire, first in the Canary Islands, the starting point of Spanish colonization, then in the Antilles, and finally in the Spanish possessions on the continent of America.

The work of several scholars who have studied the part played by Italians in Spanish economy and colonization has been documented in Chapter 6.[1] Much work remains to be done in this field, particularly the bringing to light of unpublished documents in the rich archives of Seville and Tenerife.[2] The collection of published works cited in Chap-

* Translated, with revisions, from "Gli italiani nell' economia delle Canarie all' inizio della colonizzazione spagnola," *Economia e storia,* VII (1960), 149–172.

[1] In addition to the works cited in Chapter 6, see my short volume *Précédents médiévaux de la colonie en Amérique* (Mexico City, 1954), pp. 19–24. For Italian influences at the beginning of Portuguese colonization see my article "Navigateurs, marchands et colons italiens au service de la découverte et de la colonisation portugaises sous Henri le Navigateur," *Le Moyen Age,* LXIV (1958), 467–497, and Chapter 5, above. On the development of the Spanish economy in the medieval period see my article "The Rise of Spanish Trade in the Middle Ages," *Economic History Review,* X (1940), 44–59.

[2] The Italian archives also offer precious elements on Italian commerce in Spain and the colonial Spanish empire, both at the end of the

ter 6 and in this chapter is sufficient to give quite a complex outline of the role of the Italians in the Canary Islands and to add a new page to the history of Italian economic expansion.

In addition to those in the article published in 1950 by Dr. Marrero[3] there is a list of Genoese and other Italians who occupied a position in the economy of Tenerife between 1496 and 1509, and it contains references to the notary deeds in which names of Italians appear. The first name on the list is that of a certain Antonio, called "Xinoves," who was considered to have settled permanently on the island of La Palma, for he was "estante," that is, resident without having acquired the qualification of citizen, in which case he would have been termed "vecino." Since the notary deed cited beside his name was not used in Dr. Marrero's article, she examined it at my request together with many other deeds which will be mentioned later in this chapter.[4]

From it we learn that a Portuguese by the name of Gonzalo Gil, also "estante," i.e., a resident of Tenerife, had given power of attorney to a "vecino" Alfonso de Nobledo on November 19, 1507, to receive, on behalf of Antonio and Luca his partner (*compañero*), a packing case containing two judicial sentences, two certificates, four bills of lading, and, lastly, four shirts and a long gown. The crate had been shipped by the Portuguese in a ship (*caravelon*) belonging to the Genoese. We are dealing, therefore, with a Genoese who

---

Middle Ages and at the beginning of modern times. See, for Florence and Prato, the notable analyses of F. Melis, "Malaga nel sistema economico del XIV e XV secolo," *Economia e storia*, III (1956), 3–68; "Il commercio transatlantico di una compagnia fiorentina stabilita a Siviglia a pochi anni dalle imprese di Cortes e Pizarro," *Fernando el Catolico e Italia*, V° Congreso de Historia de la Corona de Aragón, *Estudios*, III (Saragossa, 1954), pp. 131–206.

[3] "Los Genoveses en la colonización de Tenerife," *Revista de historia*, no. 89 (1950), 52–64.

[4] Archives of Tenerife, Notary Sebastian Paez, no. 2 (1506–1509), fol. 17r.

travelled through the Canary Islands, arranging transportation between them.[5]

On December 4, 1509, we again meet with Antonio, as captain "maestre" of a Genoese caravel. He now was giving full powers to his fellow countryman Battista.[6] The analysis made by the two scholars who edited this volume gives us no access to any further information, but no doubt it was a case of a general mandate without any special clauses. In any event, in a previous document, dated June 15, 1509, Antonio, captain of the caravel "Santo Espiritu," anchored in the port of Santa Cruz and hired the boat to the merchant Melchior Diaz for a load of pitch to be sent to Funchal, on Madeira.[7] The fee was 12,000 Madeira maravedis. On November 3 of the same year, again in Santa Cruz, Antonio put his ship at the disposal of a certain Pedro Párraga for the transport of wine.[8] Some twenty barrels (*botas*) were involved, each containing about 500 litres. No other load is mentioned. It would seem therefore that the Genoese's ship was a small one of about twenty tons, if we take the considerable dimensions of the barrels into account. The published summary says

[5] This fact was confirmed in a series of documents analyzed in *Protocolos del escribano Hernan Guerra,* ed. E. Gonzalez and M. Marrero, Fontes rerum Canariarium, VII (La Laguna, 1958). This notary kept records from 1508 to 1510.

[6] *Ibid.,* p. 50, no. 131.

[7] *Ibid.,* p. 297, no. 1347. The editors have arranged the entries in the order in which the deeds appear in the three volumes from which they were originally taken: *Archivo Historico provincial de Santa Cruz de Tenerife,* Protocolos, 13, 14, and 15. "In our extracts we have not held strictly to the chronological order in which the original documents were drawn up, and the order has been followed in which they are sewn in the volumes. Where this order does not correspond to the chronological order it is no doubt because it was arranged and grouped after the deeds were drawn up" (p. 19 of the introduction to *Protocolos del escribano Hernan Guerra*). The result is some uncertainty in consulting the collection. I will try to avoid any confusion when I have to deal with persons cited more than once in the deeds.

[8] *Ibid.,* p. 196, no. 949.

nothing of the landing places between which the cargo was transported.

On February 26, 1510, Antonio appears yet again. He undertook to transport to Madeira 300 quintals of pitch and 40 fanegas of grain, together with the two merchants who owned the cargo and their servants. The transport was fixed at 33 maravedis per quintal or per fanega.[9] And so it would seem that here we have a Genoese owner of a small ship known solely as a transporter between 1507 and 1510, whose activity was limited to the Canary Islands and the Portuguese archipelago of Madeira. He was a small-time operator who did not appear in Dr. Marrero's study.

In 1506, the name of one Blasino Romano appears in the notary archives.[10] He was not Genoese but Roman. We know that, together with his brother Giovanni Filippo, he had received some completely arid lands in the south of Tenerife (Valle de Güimar) in the hope that the two Romans would develop these lands "since they were men of means and would start to do this with efficient equipment." The document goes on to say that "they brought good money." [11]

The two Romans set up an "ingenio"—that is, a sugar-cane plantation; we know this from the same notary deed. In 1512 one of them bought a house in Santa Cruz.[12] They were agricultural managers who arrived in the Canaries with capital and equipment and showed they knew how to make use of barren land. On the other hand, it seems that they were also merchants, since the last deed to be quoted says that Giovanni the Roman assumed the title of merchant (*mercader*). Would this mean that he sold only the products of

[9] *Ibid.*, p. 314, no. 1311.

[10] Archives of Tenerife, Notary Sebastian Paez, no. 2 (1506–1509), fol. 617 r.

[11] See L. de la Rosa Olivera and E. Serra Rafols, eds., *El adelantado D. Alonso de Lugo y su residencia por Lope de Sosa*, Fontes rerum Canariarum, III (La Laguna, 1949), p. 121.

[12] Notary S. Paez, no. 10 (1510–1512), fol. 255r.

his plantation, or was his commercial activity of a broader range? In any case, these are examples of Italians whose economic activity was twofold, in the sense that they took part in both production and distribution, whereas in the case of the Genoese Antonio, his was a single activity in the form of a service.

Giovanni Giacomo de Carminatis was a Lombard merchant. We know that on November 11, 1506, a certain Juan de Llerena owed him 50 arrobas of sugar, "good, white, choice," in exchange for textile products (*ropa*) bought from him.[13] This sale of cloth was not exceptional in the Lombard's activity; six years later the Portuguese Tomé Diaz owed him 2,746 maravedis for certain textiles, and payment was completed after three months.[14]

It should, moreover, be noted that buying on credit must have been quite widespread, since, in the preceding example, even the payment in sugar was made six months after the consignment of the textiles. In both cases it was the Italian salesman who gave credit, which again proves that the Italians who settled in the Canary Islands were well known for their financial resources, whereas the Spanish were usually short of money or paid in kind.

Other notary deeds of Paez', which Dr. Marrero has been kind enough to copy out for us from unedited sources, show that Carminatis did not always do business alone but sometimes acted in partnership with his fellow nationals. For example, on November 26, 1506, he and another Lombard, Bartolomeo da Milano, both of them "estantes," gave, in complete agreement, full powers to the Florentine merchant Giovanni Rondinelli, resident in Seville.[15] We should point out that Carminatis, both in 1506 and six years later, was "estante" and not "vecino." It would therefore seem that he had absolutely no intention of settling permanently in the

---

[13] *Ibid.*, no. 3 (1505–1507), fol. 526r.
[14] *Ibid.*, no. 10 (1501–1512), fol. 277r.   [15] *Ibid.*, no. 2, fol. 24r.

Canaries and that he intended to return to his native Lombardy after acquiring a handsome profit. The same Carminatis appeared in partnership with two Genoese, Cosimo de Riberol and Tommaso Giustiniano, in a deed of 1507. The three Italians jointly bought 700 arrobas of sugar which would be consigned to them four months later, from a Spanish plantation in Tenerife. The price was 280 maravedis per arroba.[16] It is obvious that the Italians paid ahead of time the Spaniards of the plantation, who in turn pledged themselves to deliver the sugar for a sum equal to 700 times the 280 maravedis. Since the Italians paid in advance for the consignment they obtained the sugar at a lower price than usual, thus making a greater profit.

The Lombard Carminatis appeared a great many times in the deeds of Hernan Guerra studied by Gonzalez and Marrero in 1958. I would need no fewer than forty of these deeds to try to give a complete picture of the economic activity of this Lombard. In other deeds Carminatis simply figures as a witness. In 1509, he appeared as witness in a business deal of his Milanese partner's, Bartolomeo, who was to receive seven arrobas of sugar in return for textiles he had consigned to a certain Rubin Dumpierres, "vecino." The contract was drawn up on August 13 and the sugar was to be delivered at the end of September. It was, again, a sale on credit, but with a very short waiting period.[17]

A deed of that same year informs us that Carminatis possessed a store (*tienda*), which he may have owned or rented. The document mentions a plan for irrigation to be organized by a bricklayer (*cantero*). The price seems to have been 4,000 maravedis to be paid 1,000 maravedis in cash, a third in textiles to be bought from Carminatis' store or from that of the Genoese Tommaso Giustiniano, with the remainder to be

[16] *Ibid.,* no. 2, fol. 466r.
[17] Gonzalez and Marrero, eds., *Protocolos del escribano Hernan Guerra,* p. 146, no. 715.

paid by the Spanish client of the bricklayer on completion of the irrigation scheme.[18]

Carminatis was also involved in a series of real estate deals. On October 16, 1508, he sold a house for 24,000 maravedis to a merchant by the name of Alonso Donaire, who was to pay in money or in sugar by the end of September 1509, at a rate of 300 maravedis to an arroba of sugar. A mortgage was made on the house, but unfortunately the analysis of the document does not reveal much about it.[19] We know for sure that a blacksmith signed as guarantee. Was it he who raised the mortgage on the house? In any case, our Italian advanced 24,000 maravedis to his partner Donaire for one year. Earlier, on May 30, 1508, Carminatis had bought another house for 8,000 maravedis cash. He bought a third for 3,000 maravedis on August 13, 1509, and a final one, the date is uncertain, for 5,000 maravedis.[20] In effect he had, in two years, sold one house for 24,000 maravedis and bought three of them for a total of 16,000 maravedis. It looks as though we are witnessing real estate speculation.

On June 4, 1508, Carminatis undertook to equip a ship for fishing. His partner this time was a Spanish "vecino" from Grand Canary Island. They owned the boat and were busy equipping it and providing it with supplies for four months. The fisherman Sebastian Ruiz would fish by day in the

[18] *Ibid.,* p. 214, no. 997 (November 13, 1508).

[19] *Ibid.,* p. 168, no. 813. On p. 221, there is a deed (no. 1015) of the same date in which Carminatis similarly sells for 24,000 maravedis a house "received" from a Spaniard and adjoining the house of Bartolomeo of Milan, together with a garden which is also the property of Carminatis, who declares he has received payment for it. Now we know, from deed no. 813, that he gave credit for one year. Therefore I think deed no. 813 must be earlier than deed no. 1015 and that, in the meantime, Carminatis had granted a period of payment of a year to the Spaniard who was buying, thus nullifying the first deed. Here is an obvious example of the disadvantage of publishing a collection of notarial deeds without taking into account the chronological order.

[20] *Ibid.,* p. 213, no. 994; p. 241, no. 1075; p. 291, no. 1230.

vicinity of Tenerife, and every evening he had to bring his catch to land for salting; naturally he had a share in the profits which were distributed at the end of the fishing season in proportion to his partners' quotas. The work of Ruiz was considered that of a captain of a ship, at the head of a crew of three fishermen whose wages were paid by the three partners. In any case there were 2,000 maravedis coming to Ruiz.[21]

This seems to have been a modest enterprise since the fishing was done with rod and line *(anzuelo)* and the three partners themselves evidently took care of the stall *(tendejon)* where the fish must have been sold. Even so, it is interesting to take note of the great variety of commercial interests of our Carminatis. His primary business, however, was of a different nature. We have seen that he bought sugar and sold textiles. We shall see that he also traded in grain.

On November 26, 1508, Pedro Párraga, "vecino," undertook to pay 2,142 maravedis for cloth acquired at Carminatis' store. The payment would be made in May of 1509 in cash or in sugar, at a rate of 300 maravedis to one arroba of sugar.[22] At the same time but on no precise date, Párraga agreed to pay a similar sum for some clothes and six fanegas of barley. The payment would be made on the feast of St. John the Baptist.[23] The editors provide no link between the two deeds, although these seem to be exactly parallel to the case described earlier; [24] moreover the November 26 document must have been written at a later date. In any case it is incomplete in the manuscript. Carminatis must have known that the credit he extended to Párraga no longer had the necessary guarantees, and he had somewhat shortened the period of payment and specified the terms.

On the other hand, Párraga already had another debt with

[21] *Ibid.*, p. 213, no. 995. [22] *Ibid.*, p. 132, no. 643.
[23] *Ibid.*, p. 132, no. 641.
[24] See note 19, above. The edition, moreover, lacks notes and the introduction contains only general information.

Carminatis and it is this, no doubt, which explains the Italian's mistrust of him. On November 8, 1508, the Spaniard had in fact undertaken to pay Carminatis 10,000 maravedis for some cloth and fifty fanegas of barley. The payment was to have been made by the middle of May 1509, either in cash or in white sugar, at the rate of 300 maravedis to one arroba, which must have been the current price, given the frequent reference to such a sum.[25] Carminatis must have had barley for sale at that time, for on November 17, 1508, the "vecino" Gregorio Tabordo undertook to pay the Lombard 10,800 maravedis for 108 fanegas of barley which Fernando de Llerena had consigned to him on behalf of Carminatis. The payment would be made in March 1509 in cash or in white sugar.[26]

Where could the barley have come from? Since it was consigned by a Spaniard to a fellow countryman the suspicion occurs at first glance that Carminatis was speculating, that he was buying from certain producers a grain that was still rare on the island and selling it again to other tenant farmers who could not do without it. This would be classified under the sort of corner practiced quite frequently in the commercial methods of the time. I shall return shortly to this particular point. Sometimes the barley was exchanged for sugar, another commercial practice to which we shall return.[27]

A deed dated December 7, 1508, while giving information on similar transactions, also furnishes some further details of the type of materials sold by Carminatis. In this document Alonso Sanchez de las Islas pledges to pay the Lombard 9,566 maravedis for sixty fanegas of grain and four and a third varas of London cloth. Payment was to be made in May 1509 in cash or sugar at the rate of 300 maravedis to an arroba. A

[25] *Protocolos del escribano Hernan Guerra,* p. 130, no. 632.

[26] *Ibid.,* p. 130, no. 635. It is interesting to note that Tabordo "mortgages" a slave and an ox bearing the poetical name of Tristan. This no doubt signifies that Carminatis has the right to sell in the case of default of payment.

[27] *Ibid.,* p. 132, no. 642.

Negro slave and a roan mare were guarantee for payment of the debt.[28] On December 9, 1508, London cloth appears again, still in small quantities—two and a half varas—together with a quart of oil, a vara of other material (English), eighteen fanegas of barley, and a vara of linen (*presilla*), all for the sum of 4,000 maravedis. The buyer had no cash, so he mortgaged his land and the sugar cane planted on it.[29] On that occasion our good Carminatis looked like an owner of one of those bazaars where everything could be found, which were always very common in the colonies.

A business affair similar to this was concluded in 1509 (February 11).[30] On this occasion Carminatis sold cloth and a little linen—in other words, two kinds of material—some coral, and a tool made of iron. The client's wife already had a debt of 1,604 maravedis. The whole account amounted to 6,206 maravedis to be paid in six months, in cash, sugar, or wheat; moreover the debtor gave Carminatis a mortgage on two plots of arable land. Once again the Lombard appeared in the role of storekeeper who gave credit even to housewives. But one must be careful to note that this did not put him into a lower economic category. This is proved in a deed drawn up on August 17, 1509.[31] Giacomo de Caçaña guaranteed to provide Carminatis with no less than 200 arrobas of sugar as definitive payment of an account for merchandise and a cash loan; or the payment could be made in cash and would then be 60,000 maravedis, which indicates that the price of sugar did not vary. The extension of time was till March 1510.

There were many business deals involving the exchange of material for sugar or wheat, for example those contained in the deeds dated June 5, 1508,[32] December 1, 1508,[33] Febru-

---

[28] *Ibid.*, p. 139, no. 677.   [29] *Ibid.*, p. 140, no. 680.
[30] *Ibid.*, p. 141, no. 687.   [31] *Ibid.*, p. 147, no. 719.
[32] *Ibid.*, p. 162, no. 785.

[33] *Ibid.*, p. 138, no. 671; on this occasion there were also four varas of London cloth sold for 3,335 maravedis.

ary 13, 1509,[34] June 5, 1508,[35] and June 14, 1508.[36] On June 15, 1508, some materials were exchanged for nine arrobas of wheat and nine of barley; on June 26, 1508, the exchange was for wheat.[37] On October 26, 1508, a "vecino" called Sancho de Salazar had bought for 8,630 maravedis three and three-quarters varas of London cloth, three and a half varas of "anabta" (perhaps he meant to say "anacosta," which was cloth from Hondschote in Flanders), a vara of linen, a pair of low boots, two and a half varas of English cloth, four and two-thirds varas of red cloth from London, a halter, a harness, and a peaked cap. The trade was truly that of a dealer in materials of the latest fashion, but payment was in sugar, at 300 maravedis the arroba.[38] At an uncertain date twenty varas of linen and a pair of spurs were exchanged for sugar; on July 22, 1508, a Portuguese bought materials and a slave and payment was made in sugar.[39] On November 5, 1509, Carminatis sold six and three-quarters varas of material "media Hollanda," twelve varas of Vitry, seven varas of linen, and a cap: payment in cash or sugar. By June 26, 1510, the debt had not yet been paid and the Spanish debtor, resident on the island of Gomera, guaranteed to pay within fifteen days. The period of time granted previously had been three months.[40] The danger of selling on credit becomes obvious.

The sales of cloth made by Carminatis have been examined by now in a great many documents, so that we can have an exact idea of the type of trade practiced by the Lombard. It always dealt with the retail sale of clothes and linen, sales which evidently took place in Carminatis' store. Where did the material come from? Wherever the source is known, the material was imported. Cloth came from England or Flanders

[34] *Ibid.*, p. 144, no. 705; 5½ varas of London cloth, 40 varas of linen, and an advance of 15 doubloons for 15,400 maravedis' worth of white sugar "from one single cooking" at 300 maravedis the arroba.

[35] *Ibid.*, p. 162, no. 784; payable "in white sugar at the going rate."

[36] *Ibid.*, p. 163, no. 789.   [37] *Ibid.*, p. 163, no. 791; p. 165, no. 800.
[38] *Ibid.*, p. 168, no. 814.   [39] *Ibid.*, p. 270, no. 1161; p. 169, no. 819.
[40] *Ibid.*, p. 370, no. 1547.

(Hondschote?), linen from Holland or from France (Vitry). How did it come to the Canaries? The documents do not mention this, but the method is not difficult to imagine. At the beginning of the sixteenth century there were regular sailings of Italian convoys for Antwerp and the ports of the southern coast of England. On the return trip as well as on the way out these convoys stopped in Spain, frequently in the ports at the mouth of the Guadalquivir. The most important commercial center in that zone was Seville, where numerous Italians resided. The materials of northwestern Europe could easily slip to the Canaries through the interest of residents who were compatriots. The same thing took place with the Italians resident in the secondary centers of Lower Andalusia, such as Jerez, Cádiz, Puerto Santa María, Sanlúcar de Barrameda. It was equally possible for materials from northwestern Europe to reach northern Italy, overland, since that was common in the later Middle Ages and throughout the sixteenth century. In that case the materials were probably shipped from Italy, especially from Genoa, in Italian ships, and sent to the Canary Islands either directly or via Seville and the ports at the mouth of the Guadalquivir. In any case it is clear that Italian shipping must have had a part in the transport of materials and that the Canary Islands was one of the destinations of this traffic.

We must not omit, while making hypotheses, that, upon departure from Seville, the materials sold by Carminatis could have been transported sometimes by direct shipment to Central America, the only area of the New World at that time occupied by Spaniards. Some of these ships must have put in at the Canary Islands, as had happened on Columbus' first voyage, about twenty years earlier. In this way our Lombard's bazaar functioned as a minute nerve center on the roads of world trade, uniting, by land and sea, England and Flanders with Spain and Italy, and, in the Atlantic, Spain with its possessions in the Antilles.

Since we were able to gather the materials sold in the Lombard's shop in the Canaries into such a vast framework, we should now examine what happened to the sugar which he received in payment. It is very likely that this sugar did not find buyers in the Canary Islands themselves, since the planters produced it, and the consumers would not find it necessary to obtain provisions except from the producers. Carminatis, as we shall see, must have made arrangements for the export of this product so in demand in Europe. That he was, in fact, equipped to export sugar is suggested in a deed of 1510, which notes that the Lombard received in exchange for money advanced to a carpenter, for cloth and for wheat bought by him, twenty-five large crates of beechwood and laurel, each having the exact capacity of ten arrobas of sugar.[41] This had nothing to do with retail trade but concerned wholesale export.

Before proceeding along the road now open to us, let us continue to examine some notary deeds in which sugar figures as the contractual object. On June 5, 1509, a deed was drawn up in La Caleta, in the house of a rich Genoese landowner settled in the Canary Islands, Cristóforo da Ponte. He and his Spanish wife, Ana de Vergara, both "vecinos"— that is, citizens and not "estantes" like Carminatis, who had not given up the idea of returning to his country—agreed to pay the Lombard 82,377 maravedis for various goods bought from him. Half the payment would be made in January 1510, an extension period of six months. It could be made either in cash or in sugar at 300 maravedis the arroba, which meant that no less than 274 arrobas would be necessary to free the de Pontes of their debt. The sugar would be raw and not refined.[42]

On October 21, 1509, Pedro de Lugo, son of the man who had begun the colonization of the Canaries, Governor Alonso de Lugo, together with Cosimo de Riberol, a Genoese merchant, guaranteed to pay the Genoese Matteo Vigna, another important man to whom we shall return, 600 arrobas of white

[41] *Ibid.*, p. 352, no. 1485.   [42] *Ibid.*, p. 294, no. 1241.

sugar which the latter would supply to Carminatis in fulfillment of a debt of the governor's. The sugar was to be consigned in Cádiz which proves that it was meant for export. Previously, on September 1, 1509, Pedro Rodriguez guaranteed to pay, at the end of March 1510, white sugar for 200 fanegas of wheat and 100 of barley which he had bought from the Lombard. Similar exchanges were concluded in 1510: on January 31, sugar in exchange for wheat; on March 16, sugar to the value of 13,500 maravedis in exchange for a black slave sold by Carminatis.[43]

From the acquisition of large sums of money which we have mentioned, from the consignment in Cádiz, and in general from the large shipments of sugar, it is clear that Carminatis, who carried on the retail trade in imported cloth, dealt also in the wholesale export of sugar. We know that, at that time, very large quantities of sugar were commonly exported from Madeira to Italy.[44] Carminatis' sugar no doubt took the same road, or, when one thinks of the connection with Seville and the ports of the Guadalquivir, it may even have been exported to northwestern Europe, especially to Antwerp, where an important refining industry was developing. We have seen that on more than one occasion the sugar consigned to Carminatis was not refined. This was mentioned specifically in the contract with the de Pontes of 1510, examined earlier, but there are also other examples.

Before finishing the study of contracts in which our Lombard figures, it is well to notice again how often grain is mentioned. Apart from the deeds already cited, Carminatis sold fifty fanegas of barley for 5,000 maravedis on March 18, 1509, and on March 15, he obtained twenty-four fanegas of wheat for thirty-two fanegas of barley and eight of wheat.[45]

[43] *Ibid.*, p. 197, no. 951; p. 245, no. 1089; p. 306, no. 1281; p. 318, no. 1331.

[44] D. Giofré, "Le relazioni fra Genova e Madera nel primo decennio del secolo XVI," *Studi colombiani*, III (1952), 435–483.

[45] *Protocolos del escribano Hernan Guerra*, p. 122, no. 596; p. 121, no. 590.

In addition, let us point out two deeds in which Carminatis is dealing with trade in slaves. On February 27, 1510, Juan de Ervaes, "vecino," undertook to pay Carminatis 26,100 maravedis for a black woman slave called Francisca, whose price was 15,500 maravedis, plus various goods. The payment would be made, as usual, in sugar at 300 maravedis the arroba. On March 15 a Negro called Fernando was worth forty-three and one-third "arrobas" of sugar.[46] We should note that Carminatis carried on his business in other islands of the archipelago, as well as on Tenerife. For confirmation of this it is sufficient to cite a general mandate given on July 1, 1508, by Carminatis to the Genoese Lorenzo Borlengo for Grand Canary Island.[47] We can end with a deed in which Carminatis took part in a purely financial business deal. On October 26, 1508, Giacomo Catano, no doubt a Genoese merchant, engaged Carminatis to obtain 6,000 maravedis for him.[48]

Such is the outline of the activities of the Lombard Carminatis as it emerges from the deeds we have examined. Storekeeper in the Canaries; importer of material which he sold retail; exporter of sugar; given to real estate speculation. He was concerned in fishing and the sale of fish; he even happened to receive money in deposit to the account of a fellow countryman. He was involved in the grain and slave trade. But at this point, in order to throw light on his activity, it is necessary to put his profile into a much vaster framework, and to assign him a position in the complex of Italian activity in the Canary Islands at the beginning of Spanish colonization. The ideal method for this purpose would be to stick to the sources, that is to the notary deeds, as far as they concern the other members of the Italian colony. It is not within the limits of this chapter to do so, since, if an examination of the sole figure of Carminatis, who was not even a big merchant, required the analysis of more than forty deeds, we

[46] *Ibid.*, p. 316, no. 1321; p. 330, no. 1382.
[47] *Ibid.*, p. 85, no. 364.   [48] *Ibid.*, p. 94, no. 446.

would have to look at hundreds more to fix with any precision the activity of the whole Italian colony.

We must content ourselves with putting into a total framework what has thus far been examined, together with what has emerged from the research of the scholars of the Canary Islands. Thus we will try not to lose sight of the general perspectives of the economic situation at the beginning of the sixteenth century.

Let us begin with an article by E. Gonzalez Yañes, entitled "Importación y exportación en Tenerife durante los primeros años de la conquista (1497–1503)".[49] It deals with a period slightly earlier than that of the notary deeds so far mentioned, and it, like other articles we shall consider, has been little noted by non-Spanish economic historians.

Gonzalez first recalls that, long before the conquest of Tenerife by the Spaniards in 1494–1496, the Norman companions of Jean de Béthencourt who colonized the Canary Islands at the beginning of the fifteenth century thought of transporting, for the purpose of selling in Castile, whose king was their sovereign, the natural products of the Canary Islands, such as leather, tallow, orchil, dates, resin. Many of these products were still important in the export trade from Tenerife at the end of the fifteenth century and even in the following century. At the beginning of colonization, the municipality of Tenerife was occupied primarily with importing, as can be seen from the *acuerdos* or ordinances of its common council, for the period 1497–1507 which have been published by E. Serra Rafols.[50] Some of the measures taken by that common council were of a general character, such as the one which allowed the inhabitants of the island to pay for merchandise with natural products. This explains why we have come across so many payments in kind in the notary acts examined. The kinds of materials imported also become clear. Most important are "lienços," or linens, among which

[49] *Revista de historia,* nos. 101–104 (1953), pp. 70–91.
[50] Fontes rerum Canariarum, IV (La Laguna, 1949).

figure "presillas," often mentioned in Carminatis' deeds of sale. The source of this cloth is not mentioned. It would be useful at this point to draw attention to an unedited deed of the notary Sebastian Paez, from which we learn that a free-man laborer "estante," called Gavriel Carresco, owed Bartolomé Gayardo, Genoese and also "estante," twelve fanegas of good dry barley "que se ha de tomar medida por media fanega derecha," i.e. for half a fanega (about fifty-five litres) without fraud.[51] This grain was equivalent in value to eight varas of "lienço ginovisco." Linen also came, then, from Genoa, and not just from Holland as had been previously verified. Cloth from Vitry, already mentioned among the goods sold by Carminatis, was listed in the ordinance as "cañamazo" (canvas). London cloth was listed together with silks and brocades as precious materials, which never appeared for sale in the store of our Lombard.

One ordinance said that there was no need to import foot-wear since the island produced enough leather. However we have seen that Carminatis sold low boots. We also saw in a deed of 1508 that Carminatis sold oil by the quart; in this he was acting in accordance with an ordinance which fixed the sale of oil by whole measures, half measures and quarts," and not in bottles. We encountered a transport of 20 barrels of wine. Trade and particularly export were forbidden, how-ever, at the beginning of colonization, whereas later, with the decline in sugar production, the export of wine must have become for some time the predominant trade. Pitch was produced in great quantities, and was, even before sugar, the chief article of export. We have seen how the Genoese Antonio, who organized transports, shipped it to Madeira. The activity of foreigners, particularly of Italians, in dealing with pitch must have been extensive, since in 1507 an ordinance complained that too many pine trees were being felled on the island to make pitch.

[51] No. 3 (1507), fol. 25r (December 8, 1505); the explanation of this detail was kindly given me by Prof. E. Serra Rafols.

Onc itcm we have not yet come across but which provided an export business for some Italians was "orcellino," a lichen used for dyeing. This had been mentioned as a natural product of the Canary Islands before the Spanish conquest, especially in the accounts of Bontier and Le Verrier, chaplains to Jean de Béthencourt and Gadifer de la Salle, at the beginning of the fifteenth century, as well as in the *Navigazioni* of the Venetian Alvise da Cà da Mosto, sixty years later. An ordinance in 1499 stated that only the "vecinos" could gather the "oricello," at least so long as they were not too few for the work. This merchandise had to be paid for in cash, as the Riberols of Genoa had done.

Who were these Riberols? Dr. Marrero mentions them briefly in her article on the Genoese in Tenerife from 1496 to 1509. They had advanced money to Governor de Lugo, for the conquest of the island. They were settled in Spain but often traveled to Tenerife and maintained their own agents there, particularly Tommaso Giustiniano and Giacomo de Caçaña, whom we have already encountered. Some unedited notary deeds allow us to know more about them. On January 28, 1508, Fernando Suarez, merchant, declared that he owed Giacomo de Caçaña and Tommaso Giustiniano for the account of Francesco and Cosimo de Riberol twenty gold doubloons, the price of a slave. Payment would be made at the end of May. On the same day the first two named, this time described as agents, acknowledged in the name of the two Riberols a debt of sixteen gold doubloons for a female slave; the period of payment was the same. Two days later a slave is worth nine doubloons; all of which proves that the Riberols were engaged in the slave trade.[52]

A business of a totally different nature emerges from a deed of March 30 of the same year. Cristóbal de Ponte, Genoese, "vecino" of Tenerife, owed money, sugar, and other things to Francesco de Riberol, Genoese "estante" at Seville. Since he could not pay off the debt, Cosimo de Riberol, Francesco's

[52] Not. S. Paez, no. 5, fols. 2r, 3r, 10r.

brother, made de Ponte give up half the plantation he owned in the realm of Dabte (Daute) in Tenerife. He joined in partnership subsequently with de Ponte for the organization of the plantation and freed him of the debt. This is declared in a deed by which Francesco gave a mandate to his brother and asked him, by means of the squire Francisco de Vergara, to receipt it.[53] We know through a deed of April 4 that de Ponte already owed 200 arrobas of sugar a year as interest to Francesco de Riberol.[54]

Although Francesco resided at Seville, Cosimo lived most of the time in Cádiz. This we gather from a deed of June 19 by which a certain Blaz de Leon of Jerez de la Frontera, "estante" in Tenerife, gave a third person a mandate to obtain payment from Cosimo de Riberol in Cádiz of 9 ducats, by means of a bill of exchange of Tommaso Giustiniano with a draft on Cosimo.[55] The endorsement, of course, was not legal tender in the Canary Islands, and the bill of exchange was actually a promissory note to order. We have kept till last a deed of July 29, 1507, which shows that the Riberols were very important merchants. In it we read that they had lent no less than 1,546,500 maravedis to the Governor of the Canary Islands, Don Alonso de Lugo. This money was to be reimbursed in eleven years. When one thinks that such a sum of money represented some 50 or 60 tons of sugar at the normal price recorded in the deeds, we can get an idea of the importance of the credit granted.[56]

Now let us return to an examination of the article of E. Gonzalez Yañes. We see that other goods important to the export trade were leather and wood. The Italians we have encountered did not deal in them, whereas they did deal in grain as we have seen.

Since 1498 it had been legal to pay merchants in barley and wheat. Moreover, in 1502 the export of grain was forbidden.

---

[53] Not. S. Paez, no. 2, fol. 325r.   [54] *Ibid.*, fol. 271r.
[55] *Ibid.*, fol. 262r.
[56] *Ibid.*, fol. 465r. 1,546,500 ÷ 300 = 5,155 arrobas.

It is true that the Governor himself set a bad example, and, as we have seen, the Genoese squire Antonio was transporting it to Madeira in 1510. As for sugar, an ordinance of 1504 fixed the minimum price at 300 maravedis the arroba for white sugar, and we have come across this price many times in the notary deeds. Moreover the merchants were forbidden to resell the sugar within the island. They had, therefore, to export the sugar they received as payment. In 1506 it was established that the sugar exported had to be checked by a municipal inspector. In 1507 merchants were forbidden to export money. Naturally this must have taken place, and frequently; but the export of sugar provided one means of accumulating foreign reserves, a fact that was particularly welcome precisely because of the prohibition.

Let us now study an article of M. L. Fabrellas on "La producción de azúcar en Tenerife." [57] Sugar production was carried on from the very beginning in the Canary Islands with the collaboration of foreigners. On Grand Canary Island Italian merchants, the Soberanis, were the first to create plantations, and we shall see that in Tenerife the role of Italians was equally conspicuous. Other foreigners associated with the sugar industry in the Canaries were the Portuguese, and this is certainly not surprising, since sugar cane was brought in from Madeira. The head planters and the carpenters who built the mills were originally from Portugal. The new crop spread rapidly in the north of Tenerife; but we already know that the Romans Blasino and Giovanni Filippo, men of considerable capital, were settled in a less fertile region on the south coast, at Güimar. Some Spaniards wanted to copy them, but had no success because they lacked money.

The Genoese Tommaso Giustiniano, already known as the agent of the Riberols, owned a plantation at Taoro. At Los Realejos and Icod there were four plantations from the earliest times. Three of these were the property of Governor

[57] *Revista de historia,* no. 100 (1952) pp. 455–475.

de Lugo. Production was entrusted for a certain period to Rafael Fonte, a Catalan merchant, evidently as reimbursement for debts the Governor had contracted. On December 16, 1507, de Lugo, for his part, sold to the Genoese Cosimo de Riberol the whole of the second extract (*remiel*) of the sugar cane of Realejos and of Icod for a period of five years.[58] The first plantation in the zone of Daute, where the Genoese de Ponte also owned a plantation, was begun by another Genoese, Matteo Vigna, an associate of Gonzalo Suarez de Quemada, agent of the duke of Medina-Sidonia. Vigna had transported on a caravel the tools and the slaves necessary to build the irrigation plant. Once the plantation was organized, he had left its administration to Quemada, who had undertaken to deliver to him part of the production.[59]

We know of a contract concerning the plantation of Tommaso Giustiniano from the year 1506 by which Pedro de Uncella, native of Biscay, agreed to build an *ingenio* (sugar mill) in wood, 130 feet long, and a "purifying house" of 200 feet. The latter would doubtless be used in the refining process. No doubt these wooden buildings were very narrow since the contract simply speaks of a "sufficient" breadth. The two buildings were to cost only 21,000 maravedis—the salary of the carpenter—since the wood was taken from the surrounding land.

From the will of a Spanish plantation owner, drawn up in 1527, we also know that huts were built for the slaves and

[58] Notary deed quoted in *ibid.*, p. 460 n. 10.

[59] De la Rosa Olivera and Serra Rafols, *El adelantado D. Alonso de Lugo*, p. 78; taken from the *residencia* of the *adelantado*. One witness declares: "that I saw unload in the bay of Dabte a caravel with supplies, tools and slaves, all of which was brought by the said Mateo Viña to extract the water of Dabte and make a canal, and that then I heard this witness say that the said Mateo Viña had handed over the said enterprise to Xuares de Quemada, agent of the Duke of Medina-Sidonia, with all that had been brought in, slaves, supplies and tools in a certain sum of money for which the said Xuares de Quemada would give the said Mateo Viña a certain quantity of sugar."

for the skilled free workers. This document indicates that there were twenty-three male slaves on that plantation, of which twenty were Negro, and two female slaves whose job was probably to prepare the food. Skilled workmen must have been for the most part the refiners. In the beginning each plantation seemed to have had a *lealdador,* a technician whose job was to inspect the quality of the sugar. We know that this function later became public. If, as we have seen, the carpenter who built the huts on the plantation of the Genoese Giustiniano, was from Biscay, those who built the so-called mill—"the wheel, axle, press, rests and all other things that go with the said mill and the mill-races," as one contract says in 1506—were usually Portuguese "Maestros de hacer ingenios" (masters of sugar mills). The actual production was originally also in the hands of the Portuguese. The slaves were kept for transporting and for the purely mechanical necessities. For the most part they were African; however, especially in the beginning, there were Berbers and Guanches of the Canaries.

Fabrellas' article lists among the sugar exporters some Spaniards, such as the Catalans Miguel and Rafael Fonte, the Valencian Miron, as well as the Riberols, whom we know, and Stefano Mentón, also Genoese, whom we shall meet again in certain unedited notary deeds. He refers also to two deeds of 1506 and 1509 in which our Carminatis hired boats for transporting sugar to Cádiz, which gives us a very different idea of the sphere of action of his export traffic than that suggested elsewhere by his activity as a retail shopkeeper.

Here now are some unedited deeds referring to Cristóbal de Ponte, Matteo Vigna, and Stefano Mentón, all of them Genoese. On January 18, 1507, Cristóbal de Ponte and Tommaso Giustiniano, together with Antón Gonzalez Nájara, his son, Pedro Gonzalez, and Bartolomeo Benitez made an agreement by which the two Nájaras undertook to equip one of their ships for fishing on the coast of Río de

Oro, and for the salting of the fish which had to be consigned to other contractors in the ports of Santa Cruz, Garachico, or Orotava, at the price of three and a half maravedis per piece.[60] The two sugar-plantation owners, like their countryman the storekeeper-exporter Carminatis, did not despise the profit to be derived from the sale of salted fish. On June 12 of the same year we see, moreover, that de Ponte was at least equally busy with sugar production, since in this case it was a question of 3,000 baskets of sugar canes, with all the sugar and dregs they would produce.[61] On January 26, 1508, de Ponte declared that he owed 36,000 maravedis for the "inn of the village of Garachico," where he resided.[62] It would seem that he also directed a hotel or bar. Everything is good that brings in a profit! And to complete the picture of his varied activity, on May 2, 1508, he bought from Jacomo de Cataña, also a Genoese, a Berber slave with her son and paid 60,000 maravedis for them.[63]

Matteo Vigna, on July 17, 1506, appeared as the partner of the Genoese Gaspar Despyndola (Spinola), resident of Cádiz, to collect 126,000 maravedis owed them by Governor de Lugo and, among other things, to deliver two female slaves. The payment could be made by a bill of exchange payable in Cádiz, or else in sugar; it had to include both interest and the expenses of the exchange.[64] Some months later, on October 24, a Portuguese received from Giovanni Vigna, Matteo's nephew, twenty fanegas of barley seed. Giovanni Vigna would pay half the rent for the land and half the cost of threshing by mule; the Portuguese had to provide for two ploughings and bear the other expenses. The harvest would be divided into two parts and the cultivator would receive 1,300 maravedis for his labor.[65] This is a sort

---

[60] Not. S. Paez, no. 2, fol. 259r.

[61] Archives of Tenerife, Notary Juan Ruiz de Berlanga, no. 12, fol. 39r.

[62] Not. S. Paez, no. 12, fol. 39r.   [63] *Ibid.*, no. 5, fol. 61r.

[64] *Ibid.*, no. 2, fol. 399r.   [65] *Ibid.*, fol. 171r.

of plantation agricultural contract in which the Genoese was involved, and perhaps he had imported the seed.

On February 14, 1508, Matteo Vigna extended his activity to money exchange, by means of a real bill of exchange this time.[66] He drew on "Niculoso y Gaspar Espindola y Compaño" for the sum of 100 doubloons which would be redeemed in Cádiz by Pedro Gomez of São Tomé, who had sold five female slaves to Francisco Ximénez of Tenerife.[67] But in addition to similar commercial operations, Matteo received a delivery of 120 pigs on February 21, 1508.[68] Perhaps he had them salted to provide food for the workers on his plantation. As can be seen, there was always variety in Italian economic activity in the Canaries.

Stefano Mentón, another Genoese, sold cloth for which he was paid in cash, in wheat, or in barley; he also sold a cloak (*manta*), and on May 11, 1506, he bought a house from a parish priest.[69] Nothing indicates that he was a sugar exporter but Dr. Fabrellas recorded him as such in his article, without, however, giving proof of it.

One series of notary deeds concerns the sale of slaves. Dr. Marrero examined the slave trade in an article entitled "De la esclavitud en Tenerife."[70] She refers particularly to an agreement between Alonso de Lugo and the Genoese Matteo Vigna, who received a third of the slaves to be found in Tenerife, La Palma, and Gomera as compensation for the troubles he had taken and for the money he had spent during the conquest of the first of the islands.[71]

Even before the end of the conquest of the archipelago, some Italians were engaged in the slave trade in the Canaries, as Dr. Vicenta Cortes has shown in her article "La con-

---

[66] See also p. 150, where promissory notes to order are mentioned.

[67] Not. S. Paez, no. 2, fol. 224r.   [68] *Ibid.*, no. 5, fol. 32r.

[69] *Ibid.*, no. 3, fols. 136r (April 20, 1506); 134r (the same date); 185r.

[70] *Revista de historia*, no. 100 (1952), pp. 428–441.

[71] Seville, March 29, 1497; De la Rosa Olivera and Serra Rafols, *El adelantado D. Alonso de Lugo*, p. 155.

quista de las Islas Canarias a través de las ventas de esclavos en Valencia." [72] Non-Italian dealers were far more numerous in Valencia, but Italians occasionally carried sizeable cargoes of slaves: thus a Genoese arrived on August 12, 1494, with a cargo of 65 natives of Tenerife.[73] On April 26, 1494, Césaro de Barchi, a Florentine merchant, had transported no fewer than 136 prisoners, but among these, 134 were Negro and only two were from the Canary Islands.[74]

Among the Italians who were foremost in the economic activities of the Canaries and especially in Tenerife, the Genoese were the most numerous. Among these were to be found owners of sugar-cane plantations, even though Romans were among the pioneers of that industry which would dominate the economy of the Canaries during the whole of the sixteenth century. Matteo Vigna took part in the conquest, owned a plantation, and was involved in the most varied activity. Like the Romans he brought with him considerable capital. All the Italians invested capital in the new Spanish colony, aided and hastened its development. They also exported capital, however, especially in the form of sugar, but, on the whole, they had shown themselves to be the most dynamic and competent economic element in the life of the islands.

The reason for this is that the Italians not only possessed more liquid currency than most of the Spaniards, but they also inherited a long commercial tradition which guaranteed them an obvious technical superiority. They arrived with equipment, often loaded on their own ships, to organize the sugar production, and they also used bills of exchange. Some of them, like the Riberols, without settling in the new colonial lands, made them become profitable while operating out

[72] *Anuario de estudios atlanticos*, I (1955), 479–547.

[73] *Ibid.*, pp. 496 and 532 (no. 90). The name of the Genoese is Johanot Otobo de Mor, evidently in a corrupt form. See the transcription of the deed no. 90, *ibid.*, p. 513.

[74] *Ibid.*, p. 531, no. 83.

of the Andalusian ports. Moreover an acute business sense, inherited from an ancient economic education, born in the medieval colonial economy of the Levant and developed in all the markets of the Mediterranean and western Europe enabled the Italians in the Canary Islands to take part in every conceivable enterprise, large or small. Thus it was possible for a retail storekeeper, like the Lombard Carminatis, to be at the same time a large sugar exporter, who rented boats to transport his cargoes to Cádiz, from where they were dispersed to all parts of the Western world.

Mediterranean by tradition and origin, these Italians, colonists under a foreign flag, contributed powerfully to the realization and securing of the passage of civilization from the Mediterranean to the Atlantic world, first in the Canaries, then, almost contemporarily, in the Antilles, and later, on the whole American continent from Spanish Mexico to Portuguese Brazil. For this extraordinary expansion of the Italians, the economic aspects of which are still too little known, the Canary Islands provided one of the launching areas, and from there they conquered a position in the new West of which the Atlantic became the center.

PART III

Early Western European Colonization

8. Antonio da Noli and the Colonization of the Cape Verde Islands*

On the map of 1488–1493, once considered by Charles de la Roncière to have been inspired by Christopher Columbus, the Cape Verde Islands are accompanied by the following caption: "These islands are called in the Italian language Cavo Verde, in Latin *promontorium viride,* which were discovered by a certain Genoese whose name was Antonio de Noli, from whom these islands were named and whose name they still retain." [1]

Antonio da Noli was a Ligurian navigator who lived in the Cape Verde archipelago as a chief colonist for some forty years. In order to understand why his name remained linked for so long to these islands it is first necessary to examine his part in the discovery of the archipelago.[2]

Antonio da Noli, accompanied by his brother Bartolomeo and his nephew Raffaele, had come to Portugal with three ships, two *naus* and a *barinel.* He obtained a permit from Henry the Navigator and undertook a voyage in the course of which, according to Barros, he discovered several of the

---

* Translated from "Antonio da Noli et la colonisation des Iles du Cap Vert," *Miscellanea storica ligure,* III (1963), 129–144.

[1] This map is reproduced in C. de la Roncière, *La découverte de l'Afrique au Moyen Age* (Cairo, 1925), II, 72–73. See too the map of the world by the Spaniard Juan de la Cosa, dated 1500, which shows the "Yslas de Antonio o del Cavo Verde," in A. E. Nordenskiöld, *Periplus,* plate XLIII.

[2] See my article "Navigateurs, marchands et colons italiens au service de la découverte et de la colonisation portugaises sous Henri le Navigateur," *Le Moyen Age,* LXIV (1958), 476–497.

Cape Verde Islands.³ Which islands were these? From a decree dated September 19, 1462, we learn that Alfonso V gave to his brother Ferdinand twelve islands, discovered "five by Antonio de Noli, during the life of the Infante Dom Anrique, my uncle, God save him, which are called the island of Santiago and the island of Sam Felipe and the island das Mayas and the island of Sam Christovam and the island Sall which are in the region of Guinea." The other seven, discovered after the death of Henry the Navigator on November 13, 1460, were "the island Brava and the island of Sam Nycollao and the island of Sam Vicente and the island Rasa and the island Bramca and the island of Santa Luzia and the island of Sant Antonio, which are opposite Cape Verde." ⁴

If we compare the nomenclature of all the Cape Verde Islands known in 1462 with the present nomenclature we find that there have been some changes. The following are the current names: the northwest group comprises São Antão, São, Vicente, São Nicolau, Santa Luzia, Sal, and Boa Vista, as well as the small islands Branca and Raza; the southwest group comprises Brava, Fogo, São Tiago or Santiago, Maio, and three islets. If we compare these twelve names with the twelve names of 1462 we do not find Boa Vista and Fogo. Of these Boa Vista corresponds to Sam Christovam and Fogo to Sam Felipe in the 1462 document. Antonio da Noli, then, had discovered Sal and Boa Vista in the northwest group and Fogo, Santiago, and Maio in the southwest group. These islands belonged to Henry the Navigator. We know this from the royal decrees of 1460 ⁵ and 1462, the last of

³ João de Barros, *Asia* (1552), 1st decade, book II, ch. 1.

⁴ J. Ramos Coelho, *Alguns documentos do archivo nacional da Torre do Tombo* (Lisbon, 1892), p. 31.

⁵ "The island of Sam Jacobo e Fellipe, and the island of the Mayaes and the island of Sam Christovam and the island of Lana [Sal], with all their income, rights and jurisdictions which are now ours and by right ought to be, as well as those which the Infante Dom Amrique, our uncle, now dead, had from us" (*Ibid.*, p. 27).

which is partially quoted above, and also because they appear in one of the six decrees by which Henry the Navigator disposed of his island possessions at the end of his life. By one of these the Infante returned to the King the temporal rule of the Cape Verde Islands—the five islands of Antonio da Noli—as well as that of São Luis, São Dinis, São Jorge, São Thomas, and Santa Iria in the Azores while reserving spiritual control for the Order of Christ.[6]

When did Antonio da Noli discover the Cape Verde Islands? This has been a much discussed subject, for two other navigators who left records, the Venetian Cà da Mosto and the Portuguese Diogo Gomes, each claimed to have discovered them and it was felt the honor should go to one only. In Italy, a Venetian discovery (Cà da Mosto's) competed with a Genoese discovery (Antonio da Noli's). Later an attempt was made to secure general agreement to attributing the discovery to the Portuguese Diogo Gomes. But such attempts overemphasized the significance of nationalism and parochialism, for all of these men were in the employ of the same country, Portugal. Moreover, the example of the Canary Islands and the Azores is clear enough proof that the discovery of fairly extensive archipelagoes was usually gradual.[7] Instead of believing that the information found in Cà da Mosto's records precludes that found in Antonio da Noli's

[6] *Ibid.*, pp. 26–27, and J. Martins da Silva Marques, *Descobrimentos portugueses* (Lisbon, 1944), I, 598, no. 461 (Henry the Navigator's will, dated October 28, 1460).

[7] See my article "Lanzarotto Malocello et la découverte portugaise des Canaries," *Revue belge de philologie et d'histoire,* XXXVI (1958), 1173–1209. For the polemics alluded to above see especially P. Peragallo, *Cenni intorno alla colonia italiana in Portogallo nei secoli XIV, XV, e XVI* (Genoa, 1907), v° Noli (Antonio), and H. Major, *The Life of Prince Henry of Portugal* (London, 1877). The more recent works of D. Leite, A. Cortesão, O. Boleo, and D. Peres are mentioned in V. Magalhães Godinho, *Documentos sobre a expansão portuguesa* (Lisbon, 1956), III, 298.

or Gomes' and vice versa, there would be everything to be gained from a closer examination of the texts and dates. This is what we now propose to do.

In the account of his second voyage in 1456 Cà da Mosto told of a storm which surprised him a little beyond Cape Blanco, when he had left the coast behind, and that after two nights and three days he discovered two unknown islands. A boat was sent into one of them, which was uninhabited, and from there three other islands were spotted. The men who took part in the reconnaissance thought they could see several islands more to the west. "But," Cà da Mosto added,

it was not possible to see clearly because of the distance: I did not bother to go to them, both because I did not want to lose any more time in getting on with my voyage, and because I thought they were probably uninhabited and wild like the others: but later when they heard of the four islands I had seen, others turned up there, and it was they who discovered them; and they found that there were ten islands, big and small, uninhabited, with nothing there other than doves, and strange kinds of birds and great catches of fish.

This, therefore, was written after 1460, since until that year there were only five known islands, as we know from the decree of Sept. 19, 1462. That decree, which mentions twelve islands, may have been more or less contemporary with the writing of Cà da Mosto's second account, or at least with the chapter we have discussed. We know, in fact, from the last sentence of his account, that Cà da Mosto left Portugal on February 1, 1463.[8]

Cà da Mosto ended his chapter concerning the Cape Verde Islands in the following way:

I note that, to the first island where we disembarked, we gave the name Isola di Buona Vista, because it had been the first sight of

_____
[8] R. Caddeo, *Le navigazioni atlantiche di Alvise da Cà da Mosto, Antoniotto Usodimare e Niccoloso da Recco* (Milan, 1928), p. 293.

land in these parts; and to that other island which seemed larger than all four, we gave the name Isola di San Jacobo, because we dropped anchor there on the feast of San Filippo Jacobo.[9]

It is curious that the name Boa Vista does not appear in either the decree of 1460 or that of 1462, where it is called Sam Christovam, but after 1462 the name Boa Vista prevailed. Be that as it may, the four islands seen by Cà da Mosto must have been Santiago, Maio, Boa Vista, and Sal as they are nearest the continent and are situated in this order from south to north. The Venetian noted correctly that Santiago was the largest of the islands. Moreover, going from Boa Vista to Santiago, he came across another island which was obviously Maio. From Boa Vista an island was seen leeward, to the north; this could only have been Sal. Toward the southwest there were two other islands [10] (Maio and Santiago). All this is geographically exact and proves that Cà da Mosto had certainly been to the Cape Verde Islands.

The Venetian, however, was primarily a merchant and not an explorer. He was not thinking about colonizing and had no mandate for doing so. Nevertheless, his passage of the Cape Verde Islands gives a *terminus a quo* for determining the date of Antonio da Noli's voyage, which occurred sometime between the spring of 1456 and October 1460, when Henry the Navigator's will bequeathed the temporal control of the islands to the King. Since there were rights to be transferred it would seem certain that they had been created in 1460 at the latest. Occupation in the name of Portugal had taken place about that time, and we know from the royal charter of 1460 that Antonio da Noli carried out the occupation during the lifetime of Henry the Navigator. Thus the latter had sent the Genoese on a mission to take possession of the four islands that Cà da Mosto had seen. The Venetian had mentioned only two of them by name: Santiago and Boa Vista. In the royal decree of 1460 we find "ylha de Sam

Jacobo e Fellipe, ylha dellas Mayaes, ylha de Sam Christovam, ylha Lana," in other words there were still only four known islands, as at the time of Cà da Mosto's discovery. No mention was made in this decree of Antonio da Noli's voyage.

Antonio da Noli was in the service of Henry the Navigator and not of the King. It is possible that he had already returned when the charter of December 3, 1460, was drawn up, and that the first news of his voyage, though not an official report, was already in the possession of the King's chancellery. This would explain the new nomenclature of the islands, only one of which, Sam Christovam (Boa Vista), had been named at the time of Cà da Mosto's voyage. But this also proves that it was not yet known that Antonio da Noli had taken possession of another island. In 1462 (September 19) the possessions of the Infante Ferdinand, brother of King Alfonso V, had to be enumerated exactly. It was only then that the islands "found" (*achadas*) by Antonio da Noli in the lifetime of Henry the Navigator—that is, before November 13, 1460—were precisely listed. These islands bore the same names as in 1460, except for Santiago, which was split into the island of that name and Sam Felipe. As a matter of fact, instead of "ylha de Sam Jacopo e Fellipe," there was now "a ilha de Santiago e a ilha de Sam Felipe." But we have already seen that Sam Felipe is actually the present island of Fogo. Consequently the whole arc of five islands closest to the continent had been recognized and named by Antonio da Noli. Three of these islands—Sal, Maio, and Fogo—had not been visited by Cà da Mosto.

That the object of Antonio da Noli's voyage had been to take possession of them in the name of Henry the Navigator is proved by Henry's will of October 28, 1460, by which he left to the King the temporal rights over the Cape Verde Islands, without, however, identifying the different islands. This detail only appeared in the royal decree of December 3. It is certainly not rash to conclude that Antonio da Noli's return can be placed somewhere between the dates of these two documents and fairly close to the second. Henry the Navigator died before learning what his Genoese envoy had done on his behalf. The King had no exact knowledge as yet. This would seem to be sufficient reason to date the Genoese's return closer to the royal decree than to Henry's charter. On the other hand, it would seem certain that Antonio da Noli was given the task not only of taking symbolic possession of these islands, but also of occupying (*povoar*) them. This is implied by the Infante's will of October 28, 1460, which was concerned with their temporal and spiritual control, as well as that of Madeira and Porto Santo. No doubt this would also explain why the Genoese had used the three vessels he had brought with him from Italy, at least two of which were probably larger and heavier than the Portuguese sailing ships.

The royal privilege granted in 1462 was the first document to provide information on the form of colonial activity in the Cape Verde Islands. Thus indirectly it can enlighten us on any contribution Antonio da Noli may have made. The rights of the Infante Ferdinand are described as follows:

And we order that he should freely have the said islands and their rule and their inhabitants in the same manner and as fully as we ourselves would be entitled to by any means whatsoever, with all rivers, harbors, woods, fisheries, coral, dyes, mines, fish ponds, fishes, and with all other rights which in any way could be ours . . . and he can establish any privileges, rights, and levies in the said islands.[11]

Several islands, therefore, had now been settled, and it was anticipated that the colonists would exploit the woods, fisheries, coral, dyes, and mines. But the prince who was lord of the islands would establish what regime would rule there and dictate the necessary ordinances. This doubtless would explain why we do not possess the deed conferring the captaincy on Antonio da Noli. Such a document, if it existed,

[11] Ramos Coelho, *op. cit.*, p. 31.

would be found elsewhere and not in the royal chancellery, from which the majority of published documents have been taken.

In any case we know by a royal decree of 1466 that the colonization of Santiago was well underway by that year.[12] This privilege is worth a closer study, in order to understand its consequences.

On June 12, 1466, King Alfonso V granted a privilege to the colonists of Santiago,[13] whose captain we know was Antonio da Noli.[14] It was the King's brother, Dom Ferdinand, lord of the archipelago, who pointed out to his sovereign that he had begun to colonize (*povorar*) his island four years ago, which corresponds to 1462, the date of the decree examined above. Because the island was a long way from Portugal the colonists were willing to settle there only if they were given "great liberties and franchises." These were then enumerated. First there was the question of appellate jurisdiction in both civil and criminal matters. This was granted to the Infante over all the Moors, Negroes and white men, freemen and slaves, provided they were Christian. The colonists could, whenever they wished, trade in any part of Guinea, except Arguim, on condition they did not sell weapons, ships, or gear there. They were not required to have any special

[12] C. J. de Senna Barcellos, *Subsidios para a história de Cabo Verde e Guiné* (Lisbon, 1899), p. 14.

[13] A. J. Dias Dinis, *Estudos henriquinos* (Coimbre, 1960), I, 483.

[14] T. Monod, A. Teixeira da Mota, and R. Mauny, eds., *Description de la côte occidentale d'Afrique (Sénégal au Cap de Monte, Archipels) par Valentim Fernandes (1505–1510)*, (Bissau, 1951), 113. See too p. 181, n. 221. The chronology used in this note does not seem correct. If there were two *capitanias* in Santiago, the one in the south belonging to Antonio da Noli and the other in the north to Diogo Afonso (the Portuguese discoverer of the seven islands of the Cape Verde archipelago that Antonio da Noli had not found), nothing indicates that both of them had been granted in 1462. On the contrary, according to Fernandes (p. 114), it seems likely that the concession granted to Antonio da Noli was earlier than that by which Diogo Afonso benefited; see C. Verlinden, "Navigateurs, marchands et colons," p. 492.

license, nor be accompanied by royal functionaries, but they owed their monarch a quarter of the value of their purchase, which would be collected by a royal tax collector or *almoxarife,* or, if one had not yet been appointed, by the captain of the island. There would be a bookkeeper aboard every ship appointed by the *almoxarife* or, in his absence, by the captain. After the king's fourth had been levied on the black slaves and merchandise, the rest could be sold freely in the island, in the Portuguese possessions, in the metropolis, and even elsewhere. The buyers who imported merchandise from Cape Verde to Portugal did not have to pay the tithe. These restrictions would remain in force even if the king granted a monopoly for the trade in Guinea in return for an annual rent. There was no tithe for the export trade from Santiago either in the Portuguese possessions or in the metropolis. Similarly all imports to Santiago from the Canaries, Madeira, Porto Santo, the Azores, and all other Portuguese islands in the Atlantic were exempt from the tithe on condition that the importer possessed a certificate of residence issued by the captain.

This preferential regime, the control of which, as we have seen, was in the hands of the captain, came to an end in 1472. The Infante Ferdinand had died shortly before, and the King now restricted the privileges granted to the colonists of Santiago and, especially, to their captain.[15]

The sovereign had learned that "the captain of the said island had sent a caravel toward the Guynea which we have leased to Fernam Gomez, merchant." This refers to the famous agreement concluded in 1469 by Alfonso V with Fernão Gomez for a duration of five years [16] and which, apart from developing trade, also led to further discovery, thanks to the successive voyages of Soeiro da Costa, João de Santarem, Pedro de Escobar, Fernão do Po, Lopo Gon-

---

[15] Dias Dinis, *op. cit.,* pp. 495–499 (February 8, 1472).

[16] C. Verlinden, "Portugiesische und spanische Entdeckungs- und Eroberungsfahrten," *Historia mundi,* VIII (1959), 288.

çalves, and Ruy de Sequeira; the latter reached Cape St. Catherine, two degrees south of the Equator. The captain of Santiago and Fernão Gomez obviously regarded each other as rivals. The text of the royal decree leaves no doubt in this matter.[17]

Henceforth the captain and colonists of Santiago were restricted to trading in those parts of Guinea discovered prior to the contract made in 1469 with Fernão Gomez,[18] because "it was not our intention that the said privilege [of 1466] was to be understood to apply to such lands and places where later exchange activity appeared nor to such places as were found later and are still found everyday." [19] It was clear from this provision that the lands discovered by Fernão Gomez' captains during the duration of his contract were reserved for him. Moreover the captain and colonists of Santiago could no longer arm their ships except in Santiago itself. This measure was aimed directly at the captain, since the decree which said, in the passage quoted above, that the captain of Santiago had sent a caravel into a part of Guinea over which Fernão Gomez' contract gave him power,

----

[17] "And because the said captain was and is accused by the said Fernam Gomez; and since the said captain of the said island of Santiago as well as any other inhabitant of said island, by following our letter, clauses, and words where most explicitly contained, could send several caravels or other vessels to the said Guynea . . . ; and by so doing these things or any of them, could incur labors, and expenses, hardships either on the part of our leaseholders or contractors of the said Guinea or on the part of our *procurador* or anyone else to whom we would give the said vessels or goods as salvage, from which the said captain and inhabitants would receive great loss and harm" (Dias Dinis, *op. cit.,* p. 496). Obviously what was involved was no less than the eventual confiscation of the ships of the captain or of the colonists of Santiago who used to go to Guinea. This is a long way from the quasi monopoly of 1466.

[18] "That the said captain and inhabitants of the said island do not send nor go to any other parts to do business except to those which were already then [1466] known and discovered" (*ibid.,* p. 497).

[19] *Ibid.*

went on to say that the caravel "was armed and equipped in the island of Madeira." [20] It will be remembered that the decree of 1466 gave the colonists of Santiago the franchise for importing and exporting in Madeira. This obviously gave them an advantage over the vessels of Fernão Gomez, armed and loaded in Portugal, and it is this advantage which the decree of 1472 was meant to suppress by aiming particularly at the captain of Santiago.

Another provision of the new decree continued along the same lines. The only goods which the captain and colonists of Santiago could send to Guinea in the future were those produced on the island. They would suffice for the acquisition in Guinea of "slaves, male and female, for their service." [21] It is very clear from this what the King, and through him Fernão Gomez, wanted: that the people of Santiago should not take part in the Guinea gold trade; they had to limit themselves to the slave trade necessary for the colonization of their island. In fact the new decree expressly stated that their activity had to be confined to the area west of Sierra Leone ("Serra Lyoa").[22] Now the Gold Coast, reached in 1471 by João de Santarem and Pero de Escobar on behalf of Fernão Gomez, is east of Sierra Leone.[23] It must have been known in Santiago, whose captain would have wanted to have a share in the gold trade, and Fernão Gomez had reacted immediately: hence the decree of February 8, 1472.

Before we study the final provisions of that decree, it would seem appropriate to go into the question of the *capitania* of Santiago, in order to determine exactly who

[20] *Ibid.,* p. 496.   [21] *Ibid.,* p. 498.

[22] "And so that there be no doubt hereafter as to where . . . the said lands were discovered in which exchanges had their beginning, it is hereby declared that it was up to Serra Lyoa, and those which later were found and discovered by caravels we sent recently to search and discover more lands and products" (*ibid.,* p. 497). It is obvious that other or more lands as well as other and more products (*mercadorias*) are meant.

[23] C. Verlinden, "Portugiesische und spanische Entdeckungs- und Eroberungsfahrten," p. 288.

was the captain at the time of the decree of 1472. The privilege of 1466 referred sometimes to the captain of Santiago and sometimes to the captains.[24] At any rate, the document contained provisions concerning the future and, therefore, the whole series of captains of Santiago. In 1472 just one captain is mentioned, except in the phrases of general significance where the word is accompanied by another plural.[25] Whenever concrete facts are mentioned, the document speaks of "the captain," in the singular.

Fontoura da Costa once believed that Antonio da Noli became captain of the southern part of Santiago in 1460 and that Diogo Afonso received the *capitania* of the northern part in 1462.[26] We have every reason to accept the first date for Antonio da Noli, since he had been charged by Henry the Navigator in that year to take possession in his name. Obviously he could not do so except as the representative of the Infante, that is as captain, since all the colonists employed by Henry the Navigator held that title at that time.[27] When Henry died, on November 13, 1460, the Genoese found himself without a title. Doubtless he set out again a little later on behalf of Dom Ferdinand, who inherited from the Navigator. I am tempted to believe that Diogo Afonso, a squire of the Infante's also participated in this new expedition. This was probably when he discovered the seven islands untouched by Antonio da Noli during his previous voyage. The mission of the Genoese was not to discover but to strengthen the occupation and further the colonization. The Portuguese, on the other hand, must have returned to

[24] "O que tever carrego da governamça e capitania da dita ylha," "o dito governador ou capitam" (Dias Dinis, *op. cit.*, p. 484); "per carta dos capitaes da dita ylha" (p. 485).

[25] "Por serviço de Deus e nosso e bem e proll dos ditos capitaes e moradores da dita ylha" (*ibid.*, p. 496); "ditos capitaes e moradores" (p. 498).

[26] A. Fontoura da Costa, *Cartas das Ilhas de Cabo Verde de Valentim Fernandes, 1506–1508* (Lisbon, 1939), pp. 48 ff.

[27] See Chapter 11.

Portugal and furnished the information which made possible
the listing of the seven new islands in the decree of September 19, 1462. That this is what actually happened is confirmed
by the length of time attributed, in the decree of 1466, to
the colonial undertaking of the Infante Ferdinand in
Santiago. This was four years. Diogo Afonso must have returned to Portugal in the autumn of 1462, and perhaps even
between September 19 and October 28, the date of another
decree which specifies that the new islands were discovered
by the squire Diogo Afonso.[28]

In 1466 there was only one captain at Santiago; this must
have been Antonio da Noli, who had been there at least
four years on Ferdinand's behalf. In 1472 there was still only
one captain, and it was still the Genoese. This is clear from
the decree of that year, especially as the last provision of
that decree, to which we may now return, gives us every
reason to believe that da Noli was indeed the target of its
prohibitions. This provision is concerned with seeing that
the limitations imposed henceforth on the commercial activities of the colonists of Santiago in Guinea were not circumvented by association with nonresidents of the island,
whether nationals or foreigners.[29] The allusion is transparent,

[28] Ramos Coelho, *op. cit.*, pp. 31–32.
[29] "And because they could perchance believe that we granted them
a special favor by our said letter with the limitations and declarations
therein contained they, the said captains and inhabitants, could so act
or carry out through any of their partners with whom they have formed
a company, or by themselves and for their own profit only, by the present letter we declare that it was not our intention that any other
person whatsoever could use its privileges and permissions either wholly
or in part, except only the said captain and inhabitants. And if they, or
any of them, form partnership with anyone who is not really an inhabitant of the said island, be he our subject or a foreigner, we will and
order that if it can be proved that anyone with the aid of any of the
inhabitants of the said island had a part or a share against our order,
that everything be confiscated as our share, vessel, goods, and deposits,
since it was done against our prohibition and our orders, and that
everything be ours if in the said ports we do not have leaseholders or

especially as the man whose action had provoked the promulgation of the decree of 1472 was, precisely, the captain.[30]

It could be objected that Diogo Afonso must have been captain of the northern part of Santiago before April 9, 1473, for at that date his nephew and successor Rodrigo Afonso bore the title.[31] I am tempted to think, however, that the offensive against Antonio da Noli's commercial privileges was accompanied by another that attempted to deprive him of some of his administrative powers. If this was the case, Diogo Afonso must have been named captain of the northern part of Santiago between February 8, 1472, the date of the decree directed against captain Antonio da Noli, and April 9, 1473, the date on which Afonso's nephew Rodrigo received the title of the northern captaincy.

In any case, we know from the decree issued by Manuel I on April 8, 1497, that Antonio da Noli was captain only of the southern part of Santiago at the end of his career as colonial entrepreneur. This decree, which legalized his succession, dealt with "myce Antonio, genoez, capitan da ilha de Santiago na parte da Ribeira Grande" (the southern part of the island). Moreover, it specified that Antonio da Noli was the first to begin the colonization of the island.[32]

---

that it go to those who are our merchants and leaseholders there at the time that happens" (Dias Dinis, *op. cit.,* p. 498). Thus Fernão Gomez would profit from the confiscation.

[30] "We have been told and know for certain that by virtue of this privilege the captain of the said island sent a caravel to Guynee" (*ibid.,* p. 496).

[31] Fontoura da Costa, *op. cit.,* p. 49. But Rodrigo did not receive the letter conferring on him the captaincy until 1485. We know this through King Manuel the Fortunate's confirmation on October 29, 1496.

[32] "We have the information that the said miçer Antonio was the first to discover the said island and begin to colonize" (E. de Bettencourt, *Descobrimentos, guerras e conquistas dos Portugueses* [Lisbon, 1881], p. 67).

Examples of *capitanias,* which originally belonged to one man and were later divided as colonization developed, are not hard to find. There were such *capitanias* on Madeira, Terceira, and São Tomé.[33] But, if our interpretation is correct, Antonio da Noli must have considered himself wronged, inasmuch as his commercial privileges were also curtailed. This no doubt explained his later behavior.

The late Jaime Cortesão indicated some curious facts in this connection in his little book *A politica de sigilo nos descobrimentos.*[34] In 1474, after the death of Henry IV of Castile, fighting broke out between Alfonso V of Portugal and the new sovereigns of Castile, Ferdinand and Isabella. Alfonso V invaded Castile, and the Spaniards responded by taking the offensive against Portugal's African domains. On August 19, 1475, Isabella made claim to Africa and Guinea and fixed the dues which were owing her for trade with these regions. She claimed a fifth, that is 20 per cent, or 5 per cent less than the quarter Alfonso had claimed under the decree of 1466.[35]

[33] See Chapter 11, pp. 215, 233, 234.

[34] (Lisbon, 1960), pp. 25 ff. We have only used the data in his account based on the royal Spanish decrees we are about to examine. Some of the connections established by Cortesão between the data contained in them and in Portuguese narrative or legislative texts (especially a decision of the Cortes held at Evora in 1481) seem to us too general to throw light with any certainty on the colonial career of Antonio da Noli.

[35] "You know well and should know that the kings of glorious memory, my ancestors, from whom I come, always possessed the conquest of the parts of Africa and of Guinea, and levied the fifth of the merchandise which is received from the said areas, until our adversary of Portugal undertook to interfere, as he has interfered and interferes, in the said conquest, and levies the fifth [*sic*] of the merchandise by the consent of the Lord king Don Henry, my brother, may God give him glory in heaven; and this has done great damage and harm in my said realms and to my rents from them. And since I intend to provide and remedy this, and to take and reduce the said conquest and the lands of the said adversary of Portugal, and to make and order

In 1476 a Spanish expedition attacked Santiago.[36] Negotiations ensued with Antonio da Noli, and finally King Ferdinand took him under his protection and even kept him as captain, despite the fact that he had promised the captaincy to Anton Martin Neto, the commander of the 1476 expedition.[37] Ferdinand's decree of June 6, 1477, is so important for the history of Antonio da Noli that we shall quote it in its entirety.

Don Fernando, by the grace of God king of Castilla, León, etc. to my Grand Admiral of the sea and my chief justice of Castilla and to the princes, dukes, prelates, counts, marquises, noblemen, Grand Masters of the Orders, priors, commanders and subcommanders, and castellans of the castles and of the fortified and unfortified places, and to the councils, judges, governors and mayors, knights, squires, officers and respectable citizens, of all the cities, villages, and hamlets of all my kingdoms and dominions, and to my Grand Captain of the sea and his lieutenant, and to all captains, skippers and masters and constables whomsoever, who are now or may be on the fleet or in any other manner upon the seas, or in my ports or havens of all my kingdoms and dominions, or any other places whatsoever, any or any one of you to whom this letter be shown, or its copy signed by a notary public, greetings. Be it known to you that I have taken for myself and for the most

---

that war be made and all harm and damage, as adversary, in every way and manner possible, and in the same way to apply the said fifth to my rents; and for the great profit and use which is hoped will follow for my said realms and the subjects of them, it is my wish and intention to send and place receivers in the most noble and loyal city of Seville" (A. de la Torre and L. Suarez Fernandez, *Documentos referentes a las relaciones con Portugal durante el reinado de los Reyes Catolicos* [Valladolid, 1958], I, 92 ff., no. 30).

[36] On March 28, 1476, Anton Martin Neto received the command to arm ships for "seizing . . . whatsoever places from the said adversary of Portugal especially the island of San Antonio, which is called the island of Santiago" (*ibid.*, p. 106, no. 39). The "San" before "Antonio" is obviously superfluous; it is a reference to the island of Antonio (da Noli) as on the map of Juan de la Cosa. See note 1, above.

[37] See de la Torre and Suarez Fernandez, *op. cit.*, p. 106.

serene queen, my beloved wife, and for our royal crown, the island of Cabo Verde, of which miçer Antonio de Noli, Genoese, is
now captain; and my permission and wish are that it and its citizens and inhabitants and the said miçer Antonio be considered as
vassals and lands of my royal crown, and that neither by you the
above-mentioned, nor by any person whomsoever, any hurt or
harm or wrong whatsoever, be inflicted to them in their persons,
nor their goods, nor in any other thing whatsoever which may be
in the said island. For I command you, all and each one of you,
that henceforth you are to regard the said island of Cabo Verde
as my own and the said miçer Antonio as its captain, and the
other citizens and inhabitants of the said island as my vassals, by
homage and by nature, and you should regard them, and keep
and treat, and help and favor as my very own vassals, and do not
do nor allow any harm whatsoever to them either in their persons, nor their goods, nor in anything to them belonging; for I,
by this my letter, take and receive the said island and the said
miçer Antonio and its citizens and inhabitants and all their goods
and chattels which may be in the said island, and place them
under my royal assistance and defense, so that no one, jointly or
severally, seize, plunder, nor kill, nor cripple, nor do them any
harm or hurt whatsoever in their persons nor in their goods nor
in anything belonging to them, for any present or future cause.
And so that the aforementioned may be known unto all and no
one may pretend ignorance of the above, I order that this letter
be proclaimed publicly in the town squares, market places, and
the other customary places of the said cities, towns, and hamlets;
and the said proclamation having been made public, if any person tried or went against it, I order that you the said justices in-
dict and proceed against them with the severest civil and criminal
punishments that you find either by privilege or by law, as being
against those who violate sanctuary instituted by letter and order
of their king and rightful lord. And neither some nor any do anything else. Given in the town of Medyna del Campo, the sixth
day of June, in the year of the birth of Our Lord Jesus Christ of
one thousand and four hundred and seventy and seven years. I
the King. I Gaspar de Aryno, secretary to the king, our lord, had
it written by his order.[38]

[38] *Ibid.,* p. 127, no. 57.

Thus it is obvious that Antonio da Noli went over to the Spanish side and that he was clever enough to keep his captaincy. But it is also obvious that King Ferdinand was granting the Genoese protection against his own subjects. In fact Anton Martin Neto, who conquered the island and to whom the captaincy had been promised, could hardly be expected to be sympathetic toward the man whose intrigues had stolen from him his reward. It is interesting to note, however, that the Spanish King also spoke of only one Portuguese captain at Santiago. Doubtless one must conclude that neither Diogo nor Rodrigo Afonso had taken possession of the captaincy of the northern part of the island before the arrival of the Spaniards, and that Antonio da Noli was still the only captain at that time.

How had he been able to make the transition from enemy and prisoner to protégé of Ferdinand and a captain in the employ of Spain? He must have bargained "donnant, donnant." What did he have to offer?

Certainly the knowledge he had gained of the Guinea trade, as evident in the Portuguese decrees of 1466 and 1472, enabled him to furnish the Spaniards with precious information. Some weeks prior to the date of Ferdinand's privilege which confirmed Antonio da Noli in his captaincy, the Catholic Monarchs had granted to a Florentine merchant, Francisco Bonaguisa, and to a Barcelonian, Berenguer Granell, the right of trading with Guinea and the "mina d'Oro" (Gold Coast), the whereabouts of which they may well have learned from Antonio da Noli.[39] We know, in fact, from the Portuguese decree of 1472, that the latter had been there and that indeed it was that which had earned him the hostility of the grantee, Fernão Gomez, whose captains had been the first to reach the Gold Coast.[40] Bonaguisa and Granell were to

[39] De la Torre and Suarez Fernandez, *op. cit.,* p. 123, no. 53 (April 17, 1477).

[40] It is interesting to note that there exists a certain analogy between the Portuguese royal control over the trade in Guinea as described in

sail with the fleet that the Catholic Monarchs sent to Guinea in 1478, and they would be charged with the direction of commercial relations with the natives.[41]

In September 1479 the treaty of Alcáçovas was concluded between Spain and Portugal. Among its provisions was the recognition by Spain of Portugal's possession of the Cape Verde archipelago and exclusive right to trade with Guinea.[42] Antonio da Noli's intrigues with Spain had thus to come to an end if he wished to return to grace and above all retain his captaincy. This double aim was successfully achieved by the astute Genoese.

There can be no doubt that his situation remained quite difficult for some time. Was he restored to grace immediately? We do not know. But from the already quoted decree of Manuel the Fortunate, dated April 8, 1497, we learn that Antonio, captain of the southern zone of the island, died recently. The Genoese must have enjoyed royal favor at the time of his death since the succession went to his daughter, whose husband, chosen by the king, would be given the title of captain. Yet this provision is contrary to the *Lei Mental,* which excluded daughters. Although there are several examples of similar exceptions in distant islands, they were, nevertheless, the mark of distinct favor.[43]

Perhaps it would not be rash to suppose that Antonio da Noli's situation had been regularized in 1485, since that was the year that Rodrigo Afonso received his letter granting him the captaincy of the northern half of the island,[44] making a reality of the rights he had already been enjoying. In any case

the decree of 1466 and the control involved in the licence granted by the Catholic Kings to Bonaguisa and Granell in 1477. This analogy concerns the role of the accountants (*escrivanos*) who should accompany the caravels. See above, p. 169 and de la Torre and Suarez Fernandez, *op. cit.,* p. 126.

[41] *Ibid.,* p. 145, no. 87 (February 6, 1478).
[42] *Ibid.,* pp. 245 ff. and 277 ff.
[43] See Chapters 9 and 11, pp. 183–184, 233–235.
[44] See note 31 above.

it is certain that the Genoese was once more in the grace of the Portuguese court and that, about 1497, he was able to end, in peace and in the service of Portugal, his forty-year career as colonial entrepreneur on the Cape Verde Islands.

9. A Precursor of Columbus: The Fleming Ferdinand van Olmen (1487)*

Ferdinand van Olmen was in the service of Portugal and set out on his voyage from the Azores. These islands had been known for several decades as the Flemish Isles, not because they were discovered by Flemings, but because Flemings had played an important role in the early colonization of that archipelago.[1] Van Olmen had been active as a colonist in these islands, so it would seem appropriate to begin with a brief survey of the activity of the first Flemish colonists in the Azores.

Flemings were present in the Azores almost from the beginning of colonization. I will give a brief summary of their history in the archipelago, drawing exclusively from diplomatic sources and not from narratives, which too often misrepresent actual facts. This history began in the era of Henry the Navigator, who in 1439 received from his nephew, King Alfonso V, permission to colonize the Azores.[2] In 1443 there

---

* Translated from "Un précurseur de Colomb: Le Flamand Ferdinand van Olmen (1487)," *Revista portuguesa de história,* X (1962), 453–466.

[1] See J. Mees, *Histoire de la découverte des îles Açores et de l'origine de leur dénomination d'îles flamandes* (Ghent, 1901). Mees agrees that Ferdinand van Olmen (Portuguese, Fernão d'Ulmo was a Fleming (p. 94), but he translates his name "van den Olm." I prefer "van Olmen," a more common form in Flanders and moreover the closest both to the Portuguese transcription and to the Spanish transcription de Olmos."

[2] J. Martins da Silva Marques, *Descobrimentos portugueses* (Lisbon, 1944), I, 401, no. 315.

were already Portuguese colonists established on several islands of the archipelago, though exactly which islands we
do not know.[3] In 1447 the first concrete measures were taken
concerning the colonization of a clearly determined island:
São Miguel,[4] and only three years later, in 1450, the first
Fleming appeared, who was also the first to receive an extended charter permitting him to colonize one of the
Azores. The document granting this, dated March 2, 1450,
is of extraordinary interest. It consisted of a deed of gift of
"a ilha de Jesu Christo" (the present island of Terceira) to
"Jacome [Jacques] de Bruges, born in the country of Flanders."[5] The giver was Henry the Navigator. He called
Jacques "meu servidor." The island at the time was uninhabited, and Jacques offered to begin to colonize it. In this
charter the Infante declared that the citizen of Bruges had
made his request to him as lord of the islands. The Fleming
was given permission to colonize the island with the help of
colonists of his choice, provided they were Catholic. The
Portuguese obviously knew their fellow countrymen were
Catholic, so it is clear that this provision was meant for foreigners, and, since the colonist was a Fleming, he would most
likely have chosen other Flemings.

As the first colonist of Terceira, Jacques would receive a
tenth of all the tithes of the Order of Christ levied on the
island. Henry the Navigator, in his role as administrator of
the Order, could easily grant such a favor. The descendants
of the grantee who would reside in Terceira and help to
colonize it would enjoy a similar privilege. Jacques also was
granted the captaincy of the island—that is, the hereditary
office of governor. At that time Henry the Navigator had in
his service and under the same conditions two Portuguese at
Madeira, a Portuguese son of an Italian immigrant at Porto
Santo, and our Fleming on Terceira. The first three were
knights of the Infante; the Fleming was his servant (*servidor*).

[3] *Ibid.*, p. 425, no. 334.   [4] *Ibid.*, p. 452, no. 335.
[5] *Ibid.*, p. 470, no. 373.

The Prince granted the citizen of Bruges all judiciary powers except appellate jurisdiction in the case of the death penalty and legal mutilation, which he reserved for himself. Jacques had two daughters from his marriage with a Portuguese woman, Sancha Rodrigues; thus he had already settled in Portugal before beginning his career in the Azores. The eldest of his daughters was to inherit the captaincy if Jacques had no sons from his marriage. If she, in turn, had no son, her sister would then inherit. The Infante stated in the charter that this was a special favor and justified it as follows: "because it seems to me it should be so for the service of God and the increase of the Holy Catholic faith and equally because the aforesaid Jacques of Bruges came to settle this island, so far from the continent, as much as two hundred leagues out in the Ocean, which had never before been settled by anyone in the world." [6]

The Infante then requested the Masters and Governors of the Order of Christ who would succeed him to pay the aforesaid tenth to Jacques and his inheritors from the tithes which he himself had granted the Order. The prince similarly requested his nephew, King Alfonso V, to see that the Order continued to pay this tithe in the future.

This deed of 1450 was scrutinized in 1901 by Jules Mees, who believed that the charter in Jacques' favor was a forgery because of the provision that the captaincy might be inherited by daughters.[7] This argument does not hold, since similar provisions were made for other Portuguese islands, provisions unknown to Mees.[8] In such cases, the husband of the daughter would hold the captaincy.

Mees offered as further evidence that the 1450 charter was

[6] *Ibid.*   [7] *Op. cit.,* pp. 86 ff.

[8] For example, in 1486 for São Tomé (J. Ramos Coelho, *Alguns documentos do archivo nacional da Torre do Tombo* [Lisbon, 1892], p. 56) and in 1497 for Santiago in the Cape Verde archipelago (E. de Bettencourt, *Descobrimentos, guerras e conquistas dos Portugueses* [Lisbon, 1881], p. 67).

a forgery the fact that Jacques had a son called Gabriel, which would prove that the deed had been drawn up for the purpose of validating the rights of the descendants of the daughters of Jacques. But if that were the case, those descendants, or the people who drew up the document for them, would have been extremely shortsighted, since the 1450 charter expressly provided that inheritance by the daughters was only valid if Jacques had no son from his marriage. Moreover, Mees offered no proof that Gabriel was born before 1450. Actually he died before his father and therefore had no place in the line of succession.[9]

Jacques had left Terceira before April 2, 1474, the date on which his succession was legalized by the Infanta Dona Brites, widow of the Infante Ferdinand, who had succeeded Henry the Navigator as lord of the islands.[10] The subsequent division of the captaincy presented Mees with further difficulties. If he had been familiar with the history of this institution in Madeira and elsewhere, outside the Azores, he would have known that there were many examples of division of captaincy. Even in Terceira the captaincy continued to be divided as colonization developed. Ferdinand van Olmen, Columbus' forerunner, whose role as explorer we will attempt to follow more closely, became, after the act of May 18, 1487, captain of that part of Terceira which was called Quatro Ribeyras [11] and where, even today, there can be seen on maps a river named Ribeira dos Flamengos.

Another Flemish colonist who played an important role in the Azores was Joost de Hurtere. He came from a noble family in the area around Bruges. He settled in the Azores at the request of the Infante Ferdinand [12] between the years

[9] See Mees, *op. cit.,* p. 91, n. 2.

[10] Charter published by Drummond in *Annaes da ilha Terceira,* I, 493; similarly in *Archivo dos Açores,* IV, 159.

[11] *Archivo dos Açores,* VIII, 394.

[12] According to a request presented in 1571 to the king of Portugal by Jeronimo Dutra Cortereal, a descendant of Joost de Hurtere (*Archivo dos Açores,* I, 409).

1460 and 1470. Joost de Hurtere received from Ferdinand the captaincy of the islands Fayal and Pico. We do not know the date precisely, because as yet the certificate of appointment has not been discovered. The Flemish captain must have died around 1495, since the will of his Portuguese wife, Brites de Macedo, dated 1527, mentioned that her husband had died thirty-two years earlier.[13] Joost de Hurtere's eldest son, who had the same first name as his father, was designated hereditary captain of the islands of Fayal and Pico on May 31, 1509.[14] He married a daughter of João Cortereal, one of the captains of Terceira after Jacques of Bruges. His son, Manuel de Hutra Cortereal—whose name indicated that he had become completely Portuguese—succeeded him; but after his son, who also governed Fayal and Pico, the name of de Hurtere is found no more. Among Joost de Hurtere's companions on Fayal were the following Flemings, whose names were somewhat distorted: Willem Bersmacher, Tristan Vernes—who must have come from Bruges—Antonio Brum, and Joz da Terra or Joost van Aartryke;[15] the two latter are ancestors of Azorean families. None of these Flemings had captaincies, nor did Diogo Flamengo, who was in Terceira in 1486.[16]

A decree of King Sebastian of Portugal in 1578 referred to yet another Fleming who had played an important role in the Azores: Willem van der Haegen.[17] He is first mentioned as having been in São Jorge, and then in Fayal. After encountering difficulties in these islands with his compatriot, the captain Joost de Hurtere, he settled in Terceira, where he cultivated corn and woad, a dye much used in the textile industry, which he exported to Flanders. Since he was an adventurous man, he soon seized the opportunity to acquire

---

[13] *Ibid.*, p. 164.   [14] *Ibid.*, p. 158.   [15] Mees, *op. cit.*, p. 109.
[16] *Archivo dos Açores*, VIII, 394.

[17] J. Cunha da Silveira, "Apport à l'étude de la contribution flamande au peuplement des Açores," *Communications de l'Académie de Marine de Belgique*, X (1956–57), 71.

the captaincy of the island of Flores, which belonged to a noble Portuguese lady, Dona Maria de Vilhena.[18] On Flores he continued to devote himself to agriculture but without much success, and after several years he returned to São Jorge. From his eight children originated the different branches of a noble family still in existence in the Azores, the da Silveiras, a name which is the translation of the Flemish van der Haegen.[19]

The importance of the part played in the Azores by the Flemish is evident from the fact that a series of Flemings were captains there: Jacques of Bruges on Terceira under Henry the Navigator, Joost de Hurtere on Pico and Fayal under the Infante Ferdinand and his successors, Willem van der Haegen on Flores, and, finally, Ferdinand van Olmen in the part of Terceira called Quatro Ribeyras.

We learn more about Ferdinand van Olmen from a royal decree of July 24, 1486, by which John II of Portugal ratified a contract agreed to on June 12 by the Fleming and a certain Joham Afomso do Estreito.[20] The Fleming is described in it as "knight of the royal court and captain in the island of Terceira," not captain of Terceira, which means that he was only captain of a part of the island, as we already know. According to the decree, van Olmen would set out on a voyage "per capitam a descobrir a ilha das Sete Cidades per

---

[18] *Ibid.*, p. 75. The deed of gift has not come to light.

[19] J. Cunha da Silveira, "Willem van der Haegen, tronco dos Silveiras dos Açores," *Revista Insulana,* 1949. In this matter, too, Mees tends to be hypercritical: he supposes that Willem van der Haegen's various stays on different islands of the Azores could only be accounted for by the presence of his descendants in these islands. However there is universal agreement in the historiography of the Azores that the career of Willem van der Haegen in the sixteenth and seventeenth centuries occurred as we have sketched it here, and a careful reading of the "Saudades da Terra" (ms. in the public library at Ponta Delgada) by Gaspar Frutuoso (1586–1590) shows that this author had at his disposal documents which are lost today.

[20] Ramos Coelho, *op. cit.*, p. 58.

mandado del Rey nosso senhor." What was the significance, to van Olmen and the King, of this Island of the Seven Cities which the Fleming was supposed to discover for Portugal?

For some twenty years the Portuguese had been making a series of voyages into the middle of the Atlantic, to the west of the three archipelagoes of the Canaries, the Madeiras, and the Azores, the most western group of islands, where the Flemings had settled. As early as 1462 Alfonso V of Portugal had granted a knight of his court, Joham Voguado, extensive rights over two islands to be found in this direction.[21] Similarly, in 1474, Fernão Telles, a member of the Portuguese royal council, would be able to enjoy considerable rights over the islands that he would discover "nas partes do Mar Ouciano." [22] The following year a decree of November 10 added that if he were able to find the Island of the Seven Cities, or another already populated island, the inhabitants would be subject to his authority.[23]

The Island of the Seven Cities, also called Antilia, was one of those legendary islands which appeared on the maps of the later Middle Ages.[24] It played an important part in Columbus' geographic conceptions. In 1476 the famous Genoese had arrived in Portugal after being shipwrecked and had settled there in the spring of 1477, after a short voyage to England, Ireland, and perhaps Iceland. His brother, Bartolomeo, who in the meantime had become a cartographer, joined him there. About this time Christopher Columbus became the friend of a canon of Lisbon cathedral, Fernão Martins, who had been on a diplomatic mission to Rome and had made the acquaintance in Italy of the Florentine doctor and humanist Paolo del Pozzo Toscanelli. Toscanelli was extremely interested in determining the earth's dimensions and particularly the distance separating the east coast

[21] *Ibid.*, p. 28. [22] *Ibid.*, p. 38. [23] *Ibid.*, p. 40.
[24] W. H. Babcock, *Legendary Islands of the Atlantic* (New York, 1922), pp. 68 ff.

of Asia from the west coast of Europe. When Canon Martins consulted him in the name of the king of Portugal concerning the route to India, China, and Japan, Toscanelli had answered that it was easier to reach these countries from Portugal by sailing west than by following the African coast, as the Portuguese had been doing until then—without yet knowing whether they would really be able to reach Asia by this route.

Columbus obtained a copy of Toscanelli's letter and soon began a direct correspondence with him. We possess two of the letters written by the Florentine to Columbus, from which it appears that Toscanelli calculated the distance between the Iberian coast and China at some 5,000 sea miles, while Japan would have been about 1,500 miles from the Asiatic coast, and Antilia, the Island of the Seven Cities, would be found about halfway between the Iberian Peninsula and Japan. These estimates we know were wrong; they were much lower than the actual figures, but Columbus thought them too high. Relying on an inexact calculation from the degree of longitude to the equator, he believed that the distance between the Canaries and Japan could not be more than 2,400 miles, which in reality corresponded to the distance between the Canaries and the Virgin Islands in the Caribbean Sea, the existence of which Columbus obviously did not even suspect.

Starting with this false notion, Columbus asked King John II of Portugal for ships in order to reach Cipangu (Japan), by the western route. The King had a technical commission examine the project. This commission, which included among others José Vizinho, the great Jewish astronomer, was of course also ignorant of the actual distances; nevertheless they were competent enough to persuade the King to refuse Columbus' project. All this is well known; but not enough attention has been given to the fact that from then on the King continued to be interested in learning the exact distance separating the most western Atlantic archipelago then known —the Azores—from Antilia, the first important stage on the western sea route to Asia according to Toscanelli.[25] The man charged with the task of solving this problem, however, was not Columbus, but one of the captains representing Portugal in the Azores: the Fleming Ferdinand van Olmen.

According to the royal decree of July 24, 1486, Ferdinand van Olmen had declared to the King that he "hoped to find for him a large island, or islands, or the coast of a continent situated where it was thought the Island of the Seven Cities was to be found, and that he would undertake this at his own expense." [26] The very fact that van Olmen was uncertain about the nature of the land to be discovered—a large island? several islands? the coast of a continent?—proves that Portuguese expeditions had already been made toward Central America at that time and that coasts had been sighted, but that there had been no landing or taking possession. Could van Olmen have drawn these possibilities from the earlier attempt of Fernão Telles, mentioned in the decree of November 10, 1475, to discover this island? We do not know. What is certain is that in 1486 the talk was no longer of one Island of the Seven Cities, but of the possibility of an archipelago or even a continent. Clearly, then, the period of the hypothetical or legendary island had passed. It was known that something existed, and the "what" and "where" were precisely what van Olmen promised to discover for the King.

He himself assumed the expenses of the expedition but in return requested the gift of the island or islands or continent that he would find or that someone under his command might find, whether the land were inhabited or not. He ac-

[25] For the influence of Toscanelli's ideas see A. Altolaguirre y Duvale, *Cristóbal Colon y Pablo del Pozzo Toscanelli: Estudio critico del proyecto formulado por Toscanelli y seguido por Colón para arribar a Extremo Oriente de Asia navegando la via del Oeste* (Madrid, 1903).
[26] Coelho, *op. cit.,* p. 40.

quired complete jurisdictional powers, including appeal in the case of major criminal offenses, as well as all revenues and rights. His successor would be his eldest son or, if there were no living son, his eldest daughter or even, lastly, the nearest relative, male or female. The King would have the tithe of all the rights and revenues in the lands to be discovered. If the inhabitants refused to submit, the King would send a navy with Ferdinand van Olmen as "capitam moor," and the Fleming would always recognize the King as his lord, as befitting a good vassal. However, since the expenses of the expedition were very heavy, van Olmen gave half of the captaincy of the lands to be discovered to Estreito, a rich Portuguese colonist from Madeira, whom we have already mentioned. This Portuguese would enjoy the same privileges as the King had granted to the Fleming. The halves would be drawn by lot and Estreito could give his half to whomever he wished. In return he had to arm two good caravels equipped with all necessities, but the Fleming was to choose these caravels and provide good pilots and sailors for them, which proved that he was the nautical expert, since he could judge the values of ships and crews.[27]

Van Olmen was to pay the crew and Estreito undertook to pay the shipowner for renting the ships. Everything had to be ready and in Terceira, the island where the Fleming was captain, by March 1487. This is a clear indication that they really intended to reach the first stage on the western route to Asia by setting sail from the most westerly Portuguese archipelago; in other words, they wanted to corroborate the first part of Toscanelli's and Columbus' project as it had been presented to the king of Portugal.

Van Olmen and Estreito would each have command of one ship. A German knight was to have accompanied them on the ship of his preference; he was Martin Behaim, the famous cartographer from Nuremberg, who was living at that time on the island of Fayal in the Azores. In actual fact, and

[27] *Ibid.*

fortunately for him, he did not accompany the expedition.[28]

Van Olmen would sail for forty days to the west and Estreito would follow him, obeying his written instructions. This again proves that the Fleming was the real leader and nautical technician of the expedition. After forty days Estreito would assume command, and van Olmen would follow him until they were back in Portugal. Neither man could issue orders in the lands they discovered without the consent of the other. In case of disagreement the King would intervene as judge, and Portuguese law would prevail. Estreito put 6,000 white reals at the immediate disposal of van Olmen. All these provisions figure in the contract signed by the two associates on June 12, 1486, and confirmed by King John II in his decree of July 24, 1486.

A second royal decree, dated August 4, 1486, granted Estreito the territories he would be able to discover in the course of the second part of the voyage, that is, after the forty days during which van Olmen would have command of the expedition.[29] He obtained this privilege in return for fitting out the ships for a period of six months and because, after the forty days during which he would be under the orders of the Fleming, he wanted to continue exploring until the six months were up. However, the territories to be discovered had to be discovered within two years. The latter clause would surely indicate that what the King was really interested in, and what he really was waiting for, was the discovery within forty days of the island, islands, or continent of the Seven Cities, i.e. the discovery with which van Olmen was charged. What would perhaps happen later had a much more hypothetical aspect.

It is particularly striking that the Fleming had predicted a

[28] Moreover, he does not mention it on his terrestrial globe preserved in the Germanisches Museum of Nuremberg; see S. E. Morison, *Portuguese Voyages to America in the Fifteenth Century* (Cambridge, Mass., 1940) p. 46, n. 78.

[29] Ramos Coelho, *op. cit.*, p. 62.

voyage of forty days to reach Antilia. Obviously he really
hoped to find within that period the lands for which he had
been given special rights by the King, who also expected, or
at least hoped, that the discovery would be made within that
time. This requires a brief explanation. In no other Portuguese concession of lands to be discovered—and there were
many—is any such time limitation found. This, then, could
only have been based on information brought back from previous Portuguese voyages, those which had first questioned
whether the Seven Cities was an island, an archipelago, or a
continent. For this question to have been raised, a coast line
must have been sighted without having been reached, and
the mention of forty days means that its distance from the
Azores must have been estimated. When, moreover, we recall
that in the late summer and early fall of 1492 Columbus
would reach the island of San Salvador in the Bahamas
thirty-six days after sailing from the Canaries, then we realize
that van Olmen and the king of Portugal knew what they
were talking about when they spoke of forty days in 1486.

Now we must raise the following question: Why had Columbus been overlooked by the king of Portugal at the time
van Olmen was given permission to explore and all the
privileges?

The answer is simple. Van Olmen obtained the permission
because he offered to finance the expedition himself, as did
all the Portuguese who undertook voyages to the west about
this time. It was still the same for the brothers Corte Real in
1500, 1502, and 1506.[30] Columbus never suggested such a
thing, not even later in Spain. The king of Portugal did not
wish to invest funds in trans-Atlantic expeditions which he
rightly considered much more dangerous than those undertaken by Diogo Cão and Bartolomeu Dias about the same
time along the coast of South Africa.

Van Olmen himself furnished proof of how great was the

[30] *Ibid.,* pp. 123, 131, 150.

risk. It is certain that he tried to carry out his plan. We know this from a passage in the *Historia de Indias* of Las Casas, the famous defender of the indigenous people of America against the greed of Spanish colonists. Las Casas relates that a Galician sailor informed Columbus in Murcia concerning a land that had been seen to the west of Ireland, and he adds that those who had seen it said it was the land Hernan de Olmos, i.e. Ferdinand van Olmen, had tried to reach.[31] Las Casas says that he will come back to the question later. Then he forgot to do so, as often happens in his *Historia* and in his other writings, where the polemic against the evils inflicted on the Indians often made him lose the chronological thread. But what else could he have added, except for the account of the Fleming's voyage? If this had never progressed beyond the planning, there would have been nothing more to say.

There are two reasons for Ferdinand van Olmen's failure. First, John II's decree of July 24, 1486, stated that the expedition had to be ready to leave Terceira by March 1487. It seems clear that the voyage actually got underway toward the end of the winter of 1486–1487, and our evidence for this is its failure. That period of the year is extremely bad for crossing the Atlantic Ocean, especially in a westerly direction and in small caravels which generally displaced no more than fifty or sixty tons. In addition, the Azores were much too southerly a point of departure at this season. Van Olmen was not able to make use of the trade winds which, at the end of summer and during the first three weeks of the autumn of 1492, carried Columbus so calmly and peacefully from the archipelago of the Canaries, situated much further south, to the Bahamas.

Moreover, van Olmen must have set out to sea in a northwesterly direction as was the tradition among the navigators of the Azores, from Diogo de Teive before him, to João

[31] B. Las Casas, *Historia de Indias,* ed. Millares Carlo (Mexico City, 1951), I, 69.

Fernandes and the brothers Cortereal later.[32] All of them reached the waters of Newfoundland and Labrador, where several of them met death. This must have happened to Ferdinand van Olmen. The passage from Las Casas proves that van Olmen actually set out in this direction, since the land that van Olmen wanted to reach was "to the west of Ireland." The beginning of the year is an extremely difficult time for such a voyage, particularly with such small ships.

In any case, it is certain that John II had given his Flemish captain an imposing task. In fact, 1487, when he sent van Olmen west, is the year of that king's reign during which the greatest efforts were made in the area of discovery. Such efforts were required of the best men everywhere. Pero da Covilham, the little-known predecessor of Vasco da Gama, followed the whole eastern coast of Africa and reached Calicut in India on an Arab boat ten years before the first Portuguese expedition by sea.[33] Afonso da Paiva cemented relations with the Negus of Abyssinia, the legendary Prester John, who was to help Portugal against Islam along the route to the Indies. Bartolomeu Dias followed the west coast of Africa and discovered the Cape of Good Hope. All these expeditions set out from Portugal in 1487, the same year that van Olmen left the Azores in a westerly direction. John II wanted to know at that time which was the best road to the Indies, to the south and east in the wake of numerous Portuguese expeditions along the African coast starting with Henry the Navigator, or to the west as foreseen by Toscanelli and Columbus. That the African route was good was proved by Covilham and Dias. But the fact that the Fleming van Olmen had been sent to make the western attempt proves, despite

[32] See, for example, B. Penrose, *Travel and Discovery in the Renaissance, 1420–1620* (Cambridge, Mass., 1952), pp. 142–146.

[33] See C. Verlinden, "Vasco da Gama in het licht van zijn Portugese en Arabische voorgangers," Mededelingen van de Koninklijke Vlaamse Academie voor Wetenschappen, Letteren, en Schone Kunsten van België, no. 4, (Brussels, 1957).

his failure, what a great sailor and man he was. If he had succeeded and if he had reached the Caribbean area, the Portuguese language would have been spoken not only in Brazil but throughout the whole of Latin America. Thus the fate of a whole continent sometimes depends on that of one man!

The voyage of van Olmen and the other Portuguese expeditions of 1487 bore an influence on the career of Columbus, and, as a result, on the discovery of America on behalf of Spain. In mid-1485, the Genoese went to Spain and made the same proposals as he had made to Portugal with equally little success. At the beginning of 1488 he wrote to John II from Seville, once more offering him his services, and this time the king invited him to come to Lisbon. What had happened? Why had the Portuguese sovereign seemingly renounced his earlier opposition? Van Olmen had set out ten months earlier and he had provisions for only six months. It seemed certain therefore that his expedition had perished, men and ships. Columbus must have learned of it in Seville, for there was active communication between the Italian colony of Lisbon and that of the great Andalusian port. The Genoese must have thought the moment had come to try his luck once more in Portugal; but during his stay in Lisbon, in December 1488, Bartolomeu Dias entered the mouth of the Tagus after discovering the Cape of Good Hope. Columbus' chance in Portugal had gone. The king of Portugal now knew that the route to the Indies was open. The western route no longer interested him. When he once more became interested, Columbus had already discovered the New World, but under the flag of Spain. The man who could have prevented this from happening and who could have given the whole of Latin America to Portugal was the Fleming Ferdinand van Olmen, Portuguese captain in the Azores. The sea and fate would not have it.[34]

[34] For this interpretation of the importance of the voyage of van Olmen, see also C. Verlinden, *Kolumbus: Vision und Ausdauer* (Göttingen, 1962).

10. Medieval Influences in the Rights and Privileges of Columbus*

On April 17, 1492, in the Santa Fé camp during the final stages of the siege of Granada, the Catholic Kings granted Columbus a contract that set out the limits of his authority, thus accomplishing something that was far more important than the personalities involved: they half opened a door through which the legacy of the European Middle Ages would enter America. What Columbus had demanded and obtained from Ferdinand and Isabella was, on the one hand, rights of an ancient and feudal nature, and on the other, advantages which were mainly economic but were nonetheless of an essentially traditional character.

The Spanish sovereigns had already encountered similar cases. Nor was it the first time they had been persuaded to grant special powers to explorers and conquerors of new lands. In 1480 a pact had been made with Alonso de Quintanilla and Pedro Fernández Cabrón providing for the conquest of Grand Canary Island. In signing it, however, the Catholic Kings did not give up any truly seigneurial rights, as for example John II of Castile had done in 1420 so that Alfonso de las Casas could occupy a great part of the archipelago of the Canaries. In 1480, Ferdinand and Isabella kept their monarchical authority intact and left the way open for political centralization.

Then, in 1492, Columbus brought about a historical re-

* Translated from "Influencias medievales en los titulos colombinos," ch. 5 of *Cristóbal Colón y el descubrimiento de América*, by C. Verlinden and F. Perez Embid (Madrid, 1967), pp. 51–57.

gression. Relying on clearly medieval precedents he obtained double powers as Admiral of the Ocean and Viceroy of the Indies. These powers were modelled respectively on those of the Admiral of Castile and on those of the viceroys in the Aragonese territories of both Spain and Italy.

It is necessary to stress the clearly traditional character of the concessions that Columbus was granted. At the time of the signing of the Santa Fé agreement, a list was drawn up, at the request of the Genoese, of all the rights and powers belonging to the Admiral of Castile, and Columbus succeeded in obtaining these for himself. Some years later, in 1497, at the time of his third voyage, Columbus even requested copies of all the privileges granted the admirals of Castile in the past. The oldest among these privileges dated from 1405. The list of medieval precedents of Columbus' privileges, then, takes us back to an epoch when the powers of lords and high dignitaries of the Crown of Castile were much wider than at the time of the discovery of America. Thus Columbus' bourgeois origins did not prevent him from consciously linking himself to feudal traditions! So conscious was the link, in fact, that when he realized he had not been granted all the concessions granted to the Admiral of Castile, he hastened to have these gaps filled, this time going back as far as the fourteenth century. His actions indicate how vividly aware this founder of the modern world was of medieval precedents.

I do not wish at this time to elaborate on the office of Admiral of Castile, the point of departure and model for that of Admiral of the Ocean. It is enough to remember that in 1492, when Columbus became Admiral of the Ocean, he was merely continuing a tradition to which other Genoese had previously belonged, such as Benedetto Zaccaria and the two Boccanegras who had been Castilian admirals or the six Pessagnos who had served Portugal since 1317. It is obvious that the heritage of the Middle Ages was strong. Columbus also contributed to this heritage when, in seeing that his

office was modelled on that of the admirals of Castile, he continued the tradition of the Enriquez family, hereditary
admirals and members of the highest Castilian nobility. Like
them, Don Christopher Columbus—who bore the title of
Admiral as of April 30, 1492—considered that the rights and
contracts concerning the sea and ports were part of his
jurisdiction and seigneury, as stated in a privilege granted to
the Admiral of Castile in 1399. This term "seigneury"
clearly emphasized the feudal character of the methods used
by the admirals of Castile, profiting from the weakening of
royal power, to strengthen their office. The discoverer intended to maintain this feudal tradition in America.

Naturally Columbus did not remain petrified in the
medieval past, which he had endeavored to continue; nor
did the Catholic Kings, as is seen clearly from the following
example. The Admiral of Castile had the right to a third
share of the cargo of ships leaving ports of the kingdom and
levied the same percentage on profits of all kinds acquired
by the fleet. Columbus, on the contrary, was allowed no
more than an eighth share in the cargoes and a tenth of the
profits. It seemed a small share to a man who had hitherto
obtained so many advantages, and he proposed a solution
befitting a businessman who was accustomed to the subtleties
of joint commerce and who had previously collaborated with
the Centurionis, the Spinolas and the di Negros. Columbus
claimed the eighth and tenth he had been granted, plus
the third due to the Admiral of Castile, a total of more than
55 per cent. From a strictly realistic point of view, this was
a beautiful example of ruthlessness.

But no doubt Columbus, considering his own convenience
and following medieval precedents, had forgotten that the
Castilian monarchy at the end of the fifteenth century was
advancing firmly toward centralization and absolute power.
Certainly the sovereigns may have hesitated to make full use
of this power, and proof of this is the advantages they
granted to Columbus. However they were well able to obtain

compensation and in this case Columbus' appetite seemed excessive, so that in reality he received 10 per cent less than his Castilian colleague. Medieval tradition had spoken through the mouth of Columbus, in the area of administrative practice as well as in that of commercial usage. The sovereigns, on the contrary, tried to break loose from it whenever possible.

The struggle between medieval tradition and the monarchy's efforts at centralization continued in America during the whole period of settlement of the Spanish empire. And when, finally, the central power triumphed over the centrifugal forces inherited from the Middle Ages, there was no alternative but to incorporate them as part of its legacy.

Let us go back again to our point of departure, the terms of the Santa Fé agreement. Columbus may have acquired prestige and distinction as an admiral, but as viceroy he was much less successful. No doubt the lack of precise and characteristic medieval precedents, at least in the Castilian political system, was of benefit in this case to the monarchy, which from the beginning limited Columbus' function as viceroy to certain times and places, thus depriving this position of the feudal and hereditary elements inherent in the office of Admiral of the Ocean. In the brief period of thirty days which separated the terms of the agreement from the appointment, however, a spectacular event took place. On April 30 not only was the office of admiral hereditary but those of viceroy and governor also became so. The hereditary advantages of the offices of admiral, viceroy, and governor were consolidated even further in the hands of Columbus some years later. In 1497 he was given the permission to constitute a first-born or primogeniture fief for his property, vassals, inheritances, and permanent offices. The formula by which the royal chancery fulfilled this was the same as served to recognize the rights of a lord over the property he held from the king. Nothing could be more medieval or more feudal.

Strengthened by this privilege, Columbus regulated his succession by will. He disposed of his offices as if he held them in fief. This process was essentially the same as the way in which the great seigneurial families in other times had freed themselves from royal power insofar as conceptions of feudal vassalage permitted them to do so. Columbus, the bourgeois who had been ennobled five years earlier, intended to "feudalize" himself to the fullest possible extent in order to broaden his rights and powers and those of his inheritors. And the peculiar character that Columbus strove to give to his hereditary possessions was also underlined by his express stipulation that they could not be forfeited as a result of civil-law crimes but only by crimes of lese majesty. This was an agreement between the king and himself as between sovereign and vassal.

Obviously the Castilian sovereigns had relinquished to Columbus much more power than they had wished in 1492. One might say that at certain times Columbus exercised a sort of hypnotic influence around him to which even the Kings succumbed. But once the charm was dispelled by absence, what an awakening! and what a reversal of the situation!

Whenever the occasion arose, the Crown employed its usual procedure for prosecuting vassals: it appointed an investigating judge, equipped with special powers, and entrusted him with the defense of its rights. That which it had so often done in Europe the Crown now did in America too. But—let us make good note of it—there was nothing exceptional about this. It was the normal reaction of a centralizing power against a high official with feudal rights and autonomist tendencies. Since the beginning of colonization the course of history has been identical on both sides of the Atlantic, and this course has been determined by their common point of departure: the European Middle Ages.

That Columbus was responsible for introducing the Middle Ages into America, at least as far as he himself was concerned and in whatever had bearing on the function of institutions in which he personally played a part, has been made clear by the preceding considerations. But, in their turn the functionaries who surrounded him were provided with honors of similarly medieval origin, transferred to America in the form they were given during the later Middle Ages: for example, his brother, the governor (*adelantado*) Bartolomeo Columbus, and subsequent governors, direct successors of the Castilian and Leonese functionaries whose offices were created during the Iberian Reconquest in the thirteenth century; and the judge (*alcalde*) Francisco Roldán, the rebel of 1499, and his successors.

At this point we enter the particularly strange world of the officials of secondary importance, who were to be decisive in helping the central power to repress the autonomist tendencies of the feudalizing Columbus family. These men, of whom the majority belonged to the lesser nobility, did not behave according to feudal principles. Columbus behaved like a medieval lord and intended to broaden his autonomy at the expense of the Crown. His subordinates, on the other hand, considered themselves faithful representatives of the centralized monarchy, and for them maintaining this role was the best way of increasing their own authority to the detriment of that of their chief. During the struggle which followed whoever strove to gain every possible advantage lost and, when the reckoning was made, it was the monarchy that had benefited.

It is important to stress that these events took place against the traditional background of the late medieval conflicts between royal authority and particular powers. Medieval evolution continued on the other side of the ocean; the course of history from its origins was identical in the Ancient World and in the New.

This was already evident in the epoch of Columbus. It became even more valid with respect to many colonial institutions during the succeeding centuries. It was true not only of the Spanish empire in America but also of all the colonies founded on that continent by the various colonizing powers. The seigneurial form which clothed many of the land concessions in America—whether in Portuguese Brazil, British Virginia, French Canada, or the Dutch Antilles—was such a widespread phenomenon that one can speak of a colonial acceptance of feudal law, just as one can speak of European acceptance of Roman law.

But to speak of acceptance is to speak of evolution, constant and living adaptation. Whatever medieval institutional elements Columbus, and with him the Castilian government, had introduced into America were progressively adapted and transformed. The same process occurred in institutions introduced by the other colonial powers. This evolution would be incomprehensible but for its relationship to the European and medieval points of departure. Columbus is one of the figures who appear most clearly as a living and human link between the metropolitan and colonizing Middle Ages in Europe on the one hand and the new colonial world of America on the other.

11. Feudal and Demesnial Forms of Portuguese Colonization in the Atlantic Zone in the Fourteenth and Fifteenth Centuries, Especially under Henry the Navigator*

The first appearance of feudal forms of colonization at the beginning of the Crusades was in the Western nations' possessions in Palestine. Thereafter they were found in the Levant, especially in the French and Italian settlements in the Byzantine Empire and on the Aegean islands. The juridical forms of possession went hand in hand with demesnial patterns of exploitation and cannot be disassociated from them. These feudal and demesnial patterns of French and Italian colonization along the eastern shores of the Mediterranean are the precedents of the Portuguese colonial patterns with which we are now concerned.[1]

* Translated, with revisions, from "Formes féodales et domaniales de la colonisation portugaise dans la zone atlantique aux XIVᵉ et XVᵉ siècles et spécialement sous Henri le Navigateur," *Revista portuguesa de história*, IX (1960), 1–11.

[1] For a general view of these precedents see Chapter 1. For feudal and demesnial forms of colonization in Palestine see J. Prawer's studies: "Colonization Activities in the Latin Kingdom of Jerusalem," *Revue belge de philologie et d'histoire*, XXIX (1951), 1063–1118; "The *Assise de teneure* and *Assise de Vente*: A Study of Landed Property in the Latin Kingdom," *Economic History Review*, 2d ser., IV, no. 1 (1951) 77–87; "The Settlement of the Latins in Jerusalem," *Speculum*, XXVII (1952), 490–503; "Etude de quelques problèmes agraires et sociaux

The Italian precedents in particular provide a link between the patterns of medieval colonial organization in the eastern Mediterranean and the most ancient analogous phenomena in the Atlantic zone, especially since the first colony there was established by Italians.

The oldest example in the Atlantic zone is the Genoese Lanzarotto Malocello in the archipelago of the Canaries.[2] This Genoese in the service of Portugal had discovered some of the Canary Islands around 1336, one of which is still known today as Lanzarote. A little later he served in the French fleet, and then once again entered the service of Portugal. For this reason, when he appears in Portuguese documents he bears the name of Lanzarote de Framqua (France). At the beginning of the second phase of his career in the service of Portugal he discovered the island of Gomera in the most western part of the Canary archipelago. On June 29, 1370, King Ferdinand of Portugal made him a gift of the islands of Lanzarote and Gomera and named him "nosso vassalo," thus rewarding his Genoese collaborator for discovering these islands and for conquering them in the name of Portugal.[3] The objective was for Lanzarotto to colonize them and secure them for Portugal.[4] The gift was made as a "free and pure gift between the living, valid for ever . . . for him and all his heirs and successors." It was therefore hereditary and involved all legal (*reaaes e corporaaes*) rights, "with

---

d'une seigneurie croisée au XIIIᵉ siècle," *Byzantion*, XXII (1952), 5–61; XXIII (1953), 143–170.

[2] For a fuller account of his career see C. Verlinden, "Lanzarotto Malocello et la découverte portugaise des Canaries," *Revue belge de philologie et d'histoire*, XXXVI (1958), 1173–1209.

[3] "As yllas que trobou e nos gaanou" (the islands he found and won for us); J. Martins da Silva Marques, *Descobrimentos portugueses* (Lisbon, 1944), I, 127, no. 115.

[4] Indicated in the charter of 1370 by the term "pobrar" (to populate), which means not that the islands were uninhabited but that as yet no white colonists had settled there; see C. Verlinden, "Lanzarotto Malocello," p. 1197.

every jurisdiction, criminal and civil, with simple and mixed dominion and vassalage for both persons and possessions except for appeal of penal crimes which is reserved for us." [5] The beneficiary's jurisdiction was, therefore, extensive, but also limited by appeal to the royal tribunal in penal cases. Thus not only was the conquest made in the name of the king, and not only were the islands held from him, but he was also the supreme justice. This was a feudal situation.

A deed of ratification dated 1376 mentioned Lanzarotto's "senoria" over the islands.[6] The Genoese then appealed to the king to re-establish his duties as "capitom moor" of the islands, a title which he had lost as a result of attacks by the natives—the Guanches—and by rivals coming from Europe, i.e. Castilians. This title would seem to imply two things: first that Lanzarotto already held his colonial fief in *capitania*, an institution we shall learn more about from later deeds of gift concerning other islands or territories, and secondly that he could divide his "capitania" into subfiefs and grant them to other "capitãos," in relation to whom he was the "capitom moor," captain-in-chief, direct vassal of the king. At that time, however, the king was not able to restore his vassal to possession of his colonial fief, and he granted him in compensation one of Portugal's purse fiefs, namely the revenues from the soap-works of Tavira, Castro Marim, Alcoutim and Aldeia de Martim Longo in Algarve.[7]

In 1385 a decree of King John I of Avis informs us that Lanzarotto had recently been killed in the island of Lanzarote as "capitam moor of the islands in war and navigation." [8] His son Lopo Afonso "cavaleyro, nosso vasallo" (knight, our vassal), received his father's endowment. The son had Portuguese first names, so it is very likely that his father had married a Portuguese woman and thus gained entry into Portuguese nobility. This is certain as far as the son was concerned since he was called "cavaleyro." Lanzarotto him-

[5] Silva Marques, *loc. cit.*   [6] *Ibid.*, p. 155, no. 137.   [7] *Ibid.*
[8] *Ibid.*, p. 186, no. 162.

self did not appear as such during his lifetime in any royal decrees, although he bore the title of admiral. He came originally of a Genoese family of large merchants.[9]

In order to have a better understanding of the Portuguese institution of *capitania* we should refer to the history of the Madeira Islands during the fifteenth century.

This group of uninhabited islands known already in the fourteenth century to the Genoese in the service of Portugal,[10] was rediscovered in 1425 by the Portuguese João Gonçalves Zarco and Tristão Vaz Teixeira, two gentlemen in the service of Prince Henry the Navigator.[11] For this reason King Duarte, who ascended the throne in 1433, gave the islands in fief to his brother the Infante. This was done in a decree dated the first year of his reign (September 26, 1433) at a time when there was a boom in colonization.[12] The King decided that the Infante "should have and hold from us in all the days of his life these our islands, i.e. the islands of Madeira, and of Porto Santo, and of Deserta." The Infante would hold his fief with all the rights and revenues attached to it, as the King himself would have exercised and levied them, and he would have civil and penal jurisdiction except in cases of death and legal mutilation. However the King

[9] Numerous Malocelli are found in R. Doehaerd, *Les relations commerciales entre Gênes, la Belgique et l'Outremont d'après les archives notariales génoises des XIIIᵉ et XIVᵉ siècles* (3 vols.; Brussels, 1941); cf. the table in vol. III.

[10] See my study mentioned in note 2.

[11] F. Machado in A. Baião, H. Cidade, and M. Múrias, eds., *História da expansão portuguesa no mundo* (Lisbon, 1937), I, 276–280.

[12] J. Ramos Coelho, *Alguns documentos do archivo nacional da Torre do Tombo* (Lisbon, 1892), p. 2; Silva Marques, *op. cit.*, p. 272, no. 256. We know that colonization began at that time from a passage in a decree of the same date in which the King gives the "spiritual das nossas ilhas" to the Order of Christ, of which Henry was the governor. The King said that "now the Infante is colonizing on our behalf" (*ibid.*, p. 273, no. 257). This document also reserves for the King "a quota and the tenth of all fish of these islands."

reserved for his Casa do Civel in Lisbon the right of appeal in judgments made by the Infante in the civil courts. Henry the Navigator could also supervise all public works; he could grant lands "in perpetuo ou a tempo ou aforar." The latter term referred to the quota concessions. All this was to be carried out "sem perjuizo da forma do foro per nos dado aas dictas ilhas," i.e. without prejudicing a general privilege which the king had granted the islands of the archipelago. This privilege established certain taxes for the King's profit which the Infante could suspend but which would be payable again after his death. Exemptions could only be granted by a personal certificate. The King also reserved for himself the right to mint money.

The analysis of relations between king and colonial vassal in this case was much more detailed than in the deeds concerning Lanzarotto Malocello. In the earlier case, there had been a right of appeal to the royal tribunal for penal cases; in this case, the vassal did not have the rights of penal jurisdiction, and the right of appeal was available even in civil cases. Moreover there existed a sort of royal constitutional privilege that applied to the whole of the archipelago. We do not possess the text of this document, but analogous *foros* or *forais* (privileges) have been preserved relating to subsequent captaincies in Brazil.[13] A complement to the *foro*

---

[13] C. Malheiro Dias, *Historia da colonização portuguesa do Brasil* (Porto, 1924), III, 312 (*foral* for the captaincy of Pernambuco). In the *História da expansão portuguesa no mundo* (I, 290) there is an extract from a decree of May 7, 1493, ratifying another decree, undated, which the editor attributes to John I, according to an eighteenth-century copy. Silva Marques, who reproduces this text in its entirety (II, 109, no. 82) goes further and dates it 1426, without giving any reasons for this. This document says that the colonists of Madeira did not owe the king a tax, but we know from Duarte's decree of 1433 that he had granted all the islands of that archipelago a privilege which provided for such taxes. In any case it is impossible for the document published in *História da expansão* to be the constitutional charter of Madeira, since it was enacted solely for the main island, whereas the decree of 1433 speaks of

of Madeira that has not been preserved was undoubtedly the privilege of June 1, 1439, by which Henry the Navigator and the inhabitants of Madeira, Porto Santo, and Deserta were exonerated for five years from tithe and portage for products exported from the islands to Lisbon and other Portuguese ports.[14]

On May 8, 1440, we find the Infante granting "Tristão, cavaleiro da minha casa," a section of Madeira whose boundaries are given.[15] This Tristão was very probably the same as the discoverer of 1425. He would hold his land from the Infante, and he would be able to hand it down to his eldest son or to his second son and to their descendants in direct line. In the case of nonage of the heir, the prince or his successor would appoint his substitute. Tristão and his heirs would dispense civil and penal justice in the name of the Infante, except in cases of capital punishment or legal mutilation. Right of appeal to the Infante was provided; this must have applied to civil affairs and ordinary penal affairs, since, by the decree of September 26, 1433, grand penal justice was reserved for the king. The process of appeal, then, appears to have been quite complicated: according to the decrees of both 1433 and 1440, one could appeal to the Infante's tribunal—and even higher, to the Casa do Civel—in the case of civil affairs; for penal cases pertaining to the lower courts of justice, appeal was made to the Infante's tribunal; higher penal cases were completely out of the hands of the Infante as well as of his vassals.

Tristão also obtained a monopoly on the mills established

---

a constitutional charter for the whole of the archipelago. The document in question also deals with several captaincies, whereas we shall see that the captaincies on Madeira date from 1440 and 1450. Therefore it would be wiser not to use this text.

[14] Silva Marques, *op. cit.*, I, 400, no. 314; ratified July 18, 1449 (*ibid.*, p. 468, no. 371).

[15] *Ibid.*, p. 404, no. 318.

in his fief. He could build the mills himself or assign the right to a third party, except for the hand mills, which could not be operated for anyone but the owner without permission of the lord. Tristão could not allow construction of an "atafona," or mill operated by animals.[16] He was permitted to build ovens "emque ouver poya," ovens for which a communal tax was to be paid, but the colonists could bake bread in their own homes for their personal use provided that they did not bake for anyone else. The lord had the right to sell salt at a fixed price by the bushel (*alqueire*); if he did not have any, then the colonists could sell salt until Tristão had refurnished his supply. The beneficiary received a tenth of the Infante's revenue in his territory. These revenues were enumerated in the basic charter (*foral*) which the Infante had drawn up. Thus there must have been one lease or charter originating from the King (as we have seen) and another (for Madeira?) issued by the Infante. This charter is not extant.

The revenues were hereditary, like the fief. As long as he respected the charter, the beneficiary could distribute lands, but they had to be cultivated within five years under penalty of forfeiture. Even if after five years of cultivation the land remained unproductive for a subsequent period of five years, it might still change hands. Thus the Infante was very desirous of making his colonial soil as profitable as possible as quickly as possible. He reserved for himself, moreover, the right of dividing up the lands which were not distributed by Tristão and his successor. The lord could not prevent the colonists from selling their lands and settling elsewhere. When someone committed, in a fief on the island, a crime whose punishment entailed whipping, and then fled to an-

[16] This proves that the first sort of mill mentioned was the windmill or water mill, since "atafona" and hand-mill are distinguished from them. Therefore there were water mills and windmills, mills driven by horses, mules, or oxen, and hand mills.

other fief, he could be deported on demand to the tribunal of the place where he had committed the crime. When debts were involved, the punishment would be meted out in the place where the debtor was apprenhended.

The inhabitants could kill cattle that had become wild, both on the fief where they were living and elsewhere. This did not apply to cattle placed in the "ilhetas" or other enclosed areas to be raised by the authorities (*senhorio*). Domestic cattle could be taken from one fief to another, but they had to be on a lead to prevent them from causing damage; if there was damage, the owner had to make amends.

We can compare the decree we have just analyzed with that of November 1, 1446, for Bartolomeo Perestrello at Porto Santo.[17] This Perestrello, whose daughter was later to marry Christopher Columbus, was the son of Filippo Pallastrelli of Piacenza, who had gone to Lisbon about 1385 to trade there. The son, born probably around 1400, took the more Portuguese name of Perestrello.[18] In 1428 he seems to have been settled for the first time at Porto Santo. At least this is what is affirmed by both Cà da Mosto who knew him personally and João de Barros in his *Asia*.[19]

Like Tristão in the charter of 1440, Bartolomeo Perestrello in that of 1446 was termed "cavalleiro da casa" of the Infante. He too had to govern the island—"minha hilha," said the Prince—for the Infante "com justiça e direito." The gift was hereditary in direct line for the eldest or second son,

[17] Silva Marques, *op. cit.*, p. 449, no. 353. This decree is also in Ramos Coelho, *op. cit.*, p. 10.

[18] R. Caddeo, *Le navigazioni atlantiche di Alvise da Cà da Mosto, Antoniotto Usodimare e Niccoloso da Recco* (Milan, 1928), p. 119; P. Peragallo, *Cenni intorno alla colonia italiana in Portogallo nei secoli XIV, XV e XVI* (Genoa, 1907), vº Pallastrelli; *idem, I Pallastrelli di Piacenza in Portogallo e la moglie di Cristoforo Colombo* (Genoa, 1898).

[19] Caddeo, *op. cit.*, p. 171; João de Barros, *Asia*, 1st decade, book I, ch. 7. F. Machado's dating (1423) is not convincing (*op. cit.*, p. 280).

provided he were old enough for the job. The beneficiary would dispense civil and penal justice, but the Infante reserved for himself death and mutilation sentences. Perestrello also held the monopoly on mills (*moynhos de pam*) except for hand mills which, however, could not be operated for a third party without his permission. Another seigneurial tax for which he levied a silver mark annually concerned the water pipes, which were made of planks and used for irrigation. Two planks a week could take the place of the annual mark. The Infante had the right to a tenth of that tax. Those who set up machinery (*engenho*) for mining iron ore or other metals had to pay one mark. The ovens which baked for third parties belonged to Perestrello. He also had the right to sell salt at a fixed price per bushel. Here too other inhabitants of the island could trade in salt so long as their lord had none, but they had to abstain as soon as he had replenished his supply. The regulations controlling land concessions and cattle were the same as in the charter of 1440.

Concerning the right of appeal the Infante seems to have taken advantage of the confusion apparent in the gift of 1440 to increase his own jurisdictional powers. In the 1440 document, immediately after the mention of the right of inflicting sentences of death and legal mutilation, there is written: "que a apelaçam venha para mym" (the appeal should come to me), but it is impossible to say precisely what the appeal concerns. The explanation of the process of appeal I have given above is based on a logical combination of the provisions of the charter of 1433 and the gift made by the Prince in 1440. In 1446 it is very clearly stated, after mention of death penalty and legal mutilation, "que esto venha perante mim" this should come before me. Appeal (*apelaçam*) is not mentioned this time; thus it would seem that the Infante denied jurisdictional powers to the royal tribunal in this domain. That he wished to profit from the fact that King Alfonso V was a minor by making his expanding island domain as autonomous as possible is a fact that becomes more evident later.[20]

One provision of the charter of 1446 yet remains to be emphasized: the gift was made because the Infante wanted to reward Perestrello "since he was the first who colonized the said island on my behalf." Perestrello therefore undertook the colonization at the Prince's order. He had been very efficient in that role. In less than twenty years grain had been produced, mills built, irrigation canals constructed, cattle systematically raised, and mining begun. It is not surprising, then, that Alvise da Cà da Mosto, the Venetian collaborator of Henry the Navigator's during his last years, who had visited Porto Santo in 1455, was of the opinion that the island had a good tenant.[21] He added that Porto Santo produced "wheat and oats for its own use" and that it was "abundant in beef, wild pigs, and countless rabbits." The "wild pigs" were surely the cattle that had gone wild, mentioned both in Madeira in 1440 and in Porto Santo in 1446. Cà da Mosto even spoke of a resinous product ("sangue di drago"), of fish—also mentioned in Madeira [22]—of wax, and of honey, which did not appear in the charter of 1446. The "sangue di drago" was exported, as we learn from Cà da Mosto.[23]

On the death of Perestrello in 1458, or a little later, his son, called Bartolomeo after his father, was seven or eight years old and too young to succeed him. Until he became of age the captaincy was filled by Pero Correa. The charter which gives us this information shows that the Infante continued to consider cattle breeding important in Porto Santo and also that the cattle had increased considerably since 1446.

---

[20] This did not prevent the decree of 1433 from being ratified without change in March 1449 by King Alfonso V (Silva Marques, *op. cit.,* p. 464, no. 366).

[21] R. Caddeo, *op. cit.,* "Prima Navigazione" (of Cà da Mosto), p. 171.
[22] See note 12 above.   [23] *Ibid.*

There were herds all over the island, and measures were taken to see that owners paid for damages wherever necessary. Beehives are mentioned, which reminds us of the wax and honey observed by Cà da Mosto. This progress was the result of the last eleven years of Perestrello's administration.[24]

As far as the legal form of the transmission of power is concerned, we have an example in a bill of sale by the minor son, Bartolomeo Perestrello II, represented by his mother and his uncle, who were his guardians. The buyer was Pero Correa, a fidalgo in the retinue of the Infante. The object was the *capitania* of Porto Santo which the charter of 1446 does not yet name by its technical name.[25] This *capitania* was legally to revert with all its rights to the son and successor of the original beneficiary. The substitute would direct and administer in his name. Since the young Bartolomeo would lose the *dominium utile* of his island until he came of age, Correa was to pay him the 10,000 reales annually which he received from the Infante as a member of his retinue. This constituted the purchase price.

Some of the provisions of the charter are interesting because they help us to gain a better understanding of certain passages in the documents examined previously. Thus we see this time that in the matter of higher penal justice the Infante had appropriated the right of appeal. The vassal or *capitão* therefore had full powers in matters of penal law, but over him there was an appeal to the Infante in matters of higher justice.

This deed was confirmed the following year by the King.[26] We learn then that the Infante had arranged the marriage of

24 Ramos Coelho, *op. cit.* pp. 23–25; Silva Marques, *op. cit.*, pp. 548–550.

25 In the charter of 1458 it was expressly stated that this *capitania* was held by Perestrello from the Infante "and that he should hold it like the other captains do in my other islands." The *capitania* was therefore presented as the normal form for the gift of an island or part of an island in the insular domain of the Infante.

26 August 17, 1459; Silva Marques, *op. cit.*, p. 557, no. 438.

Pero Correa with one of Perestrello's daughters, "who had been captain for him of his island of Porto Santo." At the Infante's request the King then ratified the preceding charter without changing or adding anything. Thus the modifications that had been gradually introduced into the judiciary powers of the Infante and his vassal were implicitly recognized.

A charter of May 3, 1447, concerning lands situated in Madeira shows how the subvassals of the King, vassals of the Infante, themselves granted lands to third parties.[27] João Gonçalves Zarco (or Zargo), one of the two discoverers of Madeira in 1425, was the benefactor in this case. He held the title of "knight of the house of the Infante dom Anrique and regent for the said lord in the island of Madeira, in Funchal and its district." Thus he was not "capitão," but "regedor" instead. This did not prevent him from being lord of Funchal and of the surrounding domain. The beneficiary is Gil Gonçalves, "inhabitant of the island." He received "for all time" a land "to use," therefore with the obligation of cultivating it. The boundaries of this land in relation to others already distributed are described in detail. It could be sold, given, and inherited by the beneficiary and his heirs in direct line. The beneficiary would continue to hold the rights provided the land was cultivated within three years, which constituted a shorter period than the five years provided for in the charter of 1440 for the same island. The same land had been previously granted to someone who had let it lie fallow for seven or eight years, which no doubt explains the severity of the clause concerning the period of time. The desire to make the soil yield was so great that the beneficiary was forbidden to lay out a road across his land to be used by his neighbors. Finally, it is worth adding that the document was drawn up by a notary of the island appointed by the Infante.

A charter of March 9, 1448, intended for the *almoxarife* of Madeira, i.e. the officer appointed to collect the seigneurial revenues for the Infante, indicates the degree to which the

[27] Silva Marques, *op. cit.,* p. 453, no. 356.

fiscal administration was already productive.[28] Maciot de Béthencourt, who played an important part in the Canary Islands, had given up to the Infante his revenues and seigneurial rights (*remda e senhorio*) on the island of Lanzarote in the archipelago of the Canaries.[29] In exchange he received 20,000 white reales a year of hereditary rent on the revenues of Madeira. Thus Lanzarote was being sold to the Infante. If Castilians, French, or someone else were to become masters of Lanzarote, the Infante would still be compelled to pay the rent on Madeira. The clerk of the *almoxarife* of Madeira had to register this charter, and payment could be made in silver or in kind as the seller wished.

It was not until November 1, 1450, that João Gonçalves Zarco, regent of Funchal on Madeira, received an extensive fief on the island.[30] This was the part of the island which had not been granted to Tristão ten years earlier. Here again, as in 1440 for Tristão and in 1446 for Perestrello, the term *capitania* did not occur. It will be remembered that the word has only been found in 1458 in Porto Santo.[31] This does not mean, however, in the cases where the term is lacking, that a *capitania* was not involved, since, as far as the beneficiary's powers were concerned, the document of 1458 was a ratification of that of 1446 which does not use the word. The decree of 1450 said that the gift was made to reward Zarco, "since he was the first who colonized the said island on my behalf," as the 1446 charter had done for Perestrello. All the other provisions are in exact agreement with those of the gift of 1440 to Tristão.

King Alfonso V's decree of ratification, dated November 25, 1451, is interesting because it put an end to the usurpa-

---

[28] Silva Marques, *op. cit.*, p. 457, no. 359.

[29] I have taken up this question in an article that has been printed in the proceedings of the Congresso luso-espanhol de estudos medievais (Porto, 1968).

[30] Silva Marques, *op. cit.*, pp. 483 ff., no. 385.

[31] See note 24 above.

tion of powers which Henry the Navigator had achieved at
the expense of royal power.[32] The decree expressly says
"where it is said in the charter of my said uncle that appeal
from death penalty or mutilation should come before him,
we wish that it come before us as provided in the mentioned
privilege of the King, my lord and father." In fact this decree
of 1451 also ratified the decree by which King Duarte granted
the Madeiras in fief to Henry in 1433, and even that of
Alfonso in 1449 which seemed to accept the situation created
in the meantime by the Infante.[33] The crisis provoked by the
minority of the King from which the Infante had tried to
profit belonged now to the past. A decree of January 18,
1452, re-established royal authority in all its breadth over the
other *capitania* of Madeira, i.e. that of Tristão.[34] It is curious
that nothing similar happened in Porto Santo!

João Gonçalves Zarco, whom we have already seen granting
land in 1447, did it again in 1452.[35] This time the gift was
made to a couple. The land had to be cultivated within five
years, and they were permitted to make roads for their neighbors. Otherwise the conditions were the same as in 1447.

In 1452 Henry the Navigator concluded a contract himself
which had real economic importance.[36] The Infante made
known to João Gonçalves Zarco, "my knight and my captain
in my island of Madeira," that he had given Diogo de Teyve,
his "escudeiro" (squire), the right to construct a water-
powered mill for making sugar. The prince himself called the
agreement a contract. Teyve had to yield a third of his produce to the Infante. The former would provide the mill
(*engenho*), and the latter a press (*lagar*). The sugar-cane fields
(*canaveaaes*) would be laid out by Teyve and completely harvested. If Teyve were successful he would enjoy a monopoly;

[32] Silva Marques, *op. cit.*, p. 488, no. 389.
[33] See note 20 above.
[34] Silva Marques, *op. cit.*, p. 499, no. 391.
[35] Silva Marques, *op. cit.*, p. 499, no. 397.
[36] *Ibid.*, II, p. 343, no. 222.

if not, the Infante could grant another contractor the right to construct a mill. This probably means, therefore, that sugar producers had to allow mills and presses to work to full output. If there were an overproduction of sugar cane, another contractor would be allowed to process it in his own mill. The Infante's *almoxarife* would collect the third owed to the Prince; Teyve had to provide the latter with sugar lumps which came from the mould and powdered sugar, purified in tubs. Zarco received the order to have Teyve construct the *engenho*.

This contract had no trace of feudal or demesnial form. It started a sort of partnership between the Infante and his squire for the production of sugar on Madeira. Moreover it was the official deed of birth of sugar production on the island. Perhaps it was sugar from Teyve's enterprise that was shown in 1454 to the Venetian Cà da Mosto, before he became associated with the Infante in trading in Guinea.[37]

In 1454, on February 14, João Gonçalves Zarco took for himself, his wife, and his heirs, four lands whose boundaries are marked with great detail.[38] These lands were taken in accordance with the "regimento" of the Infante, that is to say they would be cultivated within the required time. The Infante's notary registered this appropriation and declared that everything had been carried out according to the rules. Zarco takes on here the title "knight of the house of the Lord Infante dom Anrique and captain for him in his islands of Madeira on the side of Funchal and its district."

On May 3 of the same year, Diogo de Teyve sold a land which had been given him by a charter of Captain Zarco. Its

[37] "Some sugar samples of the Madeira Island" (Caddeo, *op. cit.*, p. 167). See C. Verlinden, "Navigateurs, marchands et colons italiens au service de la découverte et de la colonisation portugaises sous Henri le Navigateur," *Le Moyen Age,* LXIV (1958) p. 476.

[38] Silva Marques, *op. cit.,* I, 514, no. 403. Mention was made among others of a house which belonged to a certain Joham de Frolença (Florença or Florence), perhaps an Italian colonist. We also learn that the Infante himself was exploiting lands.

price was 2,000 white reales. The land was exempt from ecclesiastical tithe (*dizimo a Deus*). The deed was drawn up by
the clerk of the Infante's notary, who was absent from the
island.[39]

A document dated April 29, 1457, is interesting because
it showed how the Infante attracted strangers to his islands
in order to participate in the colonization, in this case a German.[40] The charter was sent to Zarco as captain and member
of the Infante's Council. It is interesting to emphasize that
reference is made here to a council such as has not appeared
in the documents and of which there is no mention in the
literature concerning Henry the Navigator. Since Zarco was
a member of it, there is reason to believe that it was a council
of government for the insular domain which the Infante
held in fief from the King, a domain whose autonomy we
have seen him try to increase at the expense of the Crown
whenever he had the opportunity. The German was called
Henry and was a "Knight of Santa Caterina." He obtained a
deed from Zarco by which he received land. With the help of
seven or eight cultivators (*lavradores*)—perhaps also Germans
—he was to plant vines and sugar cane, cultivate vegetable
gardens, and build houses and a chapel. Another German,
Andrea Allemam, possessed land in the neighborhood of the
concession of the Knight of St. Catherine. He assured the
Infante that he had put his land to good use and requested a
deed of ratification, which the Infante sent to Zarco. If there
should be an interruption in the cultivation of the land, the
captain had to give up the uncultivated land in *sesmaria*.
Here we have the first mention of this Portuguese institution
on Madeira. We will return to it later. Let us simply note
for the time being that such distribution in *sesmaria* of lands
not cultivated within five years was ordained by a decree of
Henry's for Madeira, mentioned but not reproduced in the
deed of April 29, 1457. The threat of being transformed into
sesmaria did not apply to the pasture lands belonging to the

[39] *Ibid.*, p. 515, no. 404.   [40] *Ibid.*, p. 541, no. 423.

concession granted to Henry of the Order of St. Catherine.
The latter owed a tithe of the produce of his lands, except
for yew trees, sugar cane, dyes, and gum, the entire production of which was reserved for the Infante. Perhaps the gum
was resin, like the "sangue di drago" already mentioned on
Porto Santo. The German was not allowed to establish on his
lands ovens, mills, or water mills for pressing the sugar cane
(*engenho dagoa*), except for kitchen ovens and hand-mills
for his own personal use. The Infante's charter of ratification
was in turn validated by the King on May 18.[41]

With this decree the series of documents concerning land
concessions on Madeira under Henry the Navigator is complete. No other privileges for this period are as yet known. A
general view of the evolution of colonial land concessions by
the Portuguese can only be achieved after other Portuguese
possessions in the Atlantic region have been examined.

It is now necessary to consider for a moment the anteced-
ents in Portugal of the *sesmaria,* mentioned in the deed for
Madeira of 1457 and elsewhere. Virginia Rau, of the University of Lisbon, has dealt with this subject in her book *Sesmarias medievais portuguesas.*[42] Without trying to trace the
history of the institution in its entirety we shall examine
briefly here the form it took in the metropolis in the fourteenth and fifteenth centuries. King Ferdinand, the last prince
of the Burgundian dynasty before the accession to the throne
of John I of Avis, promulgated in 1375 a law concerning
sesmaria. It was meant as a reaction to the decrease in cultivated land caused by the demographic recession following the
Black Death as well as by the development of cattle raising at
the expense of agriculture. The law compelled landowners
to cultivate their land under penalty of expropriation. It also
contained numerous other provisions which need not concern
us here. The curious thing is that the term *sesmaria* was not
used, even though the law was known under this name.[43]

41 *Ibid.,* p. 543, no. 424.   42 Lisbon, 1946.
43 Rau, *Sesmarias medievais portuguesas,* p. 76.

However in the application of this law John I granted lands in *sesmaria*. For example, a decree of 1413 concerned lands which had not been put to use by their owners and which were granted in full ownership by a royal commissioner (*sesmeiro*) to persons who agreed to cultivate them within a set time. This commissioner determined the extent of the parcels; in addition to the King, numerous lords also granted land in *sesmaria*.[44]

Henrique da Gama Barros in his classic *Historia da administração publica em Portugal nos seculos XII a XV*, dealt at some length with *sesmaria*.[45] He showed that in the later middle ages the obligatory cultivation imposed by *sesmaria* was found quite frequently in the metropolis. It is not surprising, then, that this system was transmitted to the colonies. Although the institution only appeared by name on Madeira in 1457, it is obvious—judging from what we have seen—that even in 1447 when Zarco granted "for all time" to an inhabitant of the island land which another had let lie fallow, this was a case where *sesmaria* was applied. The captain in this case interceded in the name of the lord, i.e. the Infante, as *sesmeiro* (commissioner), but he did not go on to a further apportionment. Even in 1440 it was already a question of lands which had to be cultivated within five years under penalty of concession to others. This too was the result of an application of the system of *sesmaria*. The "regimento" of the Infante in the charter of 1454 was probably an application of the system on Madeira, and in the charter of 1457 for Henry the German an ordinance of the same kind is mentioned.

Now let us examine a series of deeds concerning the Azores, beginning with a brief decree of Alfonso V, dated July 2, 1439, by which Henry the Navigator received permission to colonize (*pobrar*) seven islands of the archipelago

[44] *Ibid.*, pp. 81, 85.
[45] Ed. T. de Souza Soares (2d ed.; Lisbon, 1950), VIII, 322–354.

on which he had already landed sheep.[46] This procedure of first landing livestock before commencing the actual colonization of a largely uninhabited territory is found quite frequently.

In 1443 (April 5) the King, at the Infante's request, granted Gonçalo Velho, "commander of the islands of the Azores" and the colonists a five-year exemption from paying tithe and portage on the products they exported from the islands to Portugal.[47] This measure corresponds to those taken for the Madeira islands in 1439.

It seems that in 1447 Henry the Navigator was not the only one interested in the Azores. His brother Pedro, regent of the kingdom, owned the island of São Miguel at that time.[48] The colonists were exonerated from the tithe on bread (or grain), wine, fish, wood, and vegetables produced on the island or sent to Portugal. The aim was to encourage settlement of the Prince's island (*sua ilha*), but Pedro died in the battle of Alfarrobeira in 1449 and disappeared as a rival of the Navigator's in the Azores.

Of particular interest is the charter of March 2, 1450, by which Henry the Navigator made a gift of the island of Terceira in the Azores to Jacques of Bruges.[49] On January 8, 1453, the King gave the island of Corvo to the Duke of Braganza.[50] He did it "of his own free will and absolute power, without the duke asking for it, nor anybody else on his behalf." This bizarre formula would seem to show that the King did not wish to take into consideration the older rights of Henry the Navigator on the archipelago. Moreover, it was about this time, in 1451 and 1452, that the King's rights in the matter of appeal to the higher courts of justice were re-established on Madeira. Among the advisors to the

[46] Silva Marques, *op. cit.*, p. 401, no. 316, and Ramos Coelho, *op. cit.*, p. 6.
[47] Silva Marques, *op. cit.*, p. 425, no. 334.   [48] *Ibid.*, p. 452, no. 355.
[49] This charter is discussed in detail in Chapter 9, pp. 182–184.
[50] Silva Marques, *op. cit.*, p. 500, no. 398.

King, the Duke of Braganza, head of the bastard line, was hardly one to love the sons of John I, whose place he took as political advisor at the same time as his son, the Count of Arraiolos, after the death of the regent Dom Pedro in the battle of Alfarrobeira (1449).[51] The Duke received Corvo without paying any tithe, "be it uninhabited as it is, or even if it became colonized." There was no provision for appeal to the royal tribunal. The King merely reserved the right to declare war and conclude peace. The island could not be given to anyone except to a Portuguese subject. The currency had to be the King's. Thus this was a hereditary gift, but it had a feudal aspect in the King's supreme right with regard to currency, war, and peace, as well as the transfer of territory.

A document of March 12, 1453, informs us that the Portuguese intended to colonize the Azores with exiles.[52] A certain Joham Vaaz from Montemor o Novo had been condemned for murder to exile on São Miguel under the regency of Dom Pedro, who had wanted to populate the island. The banishment was later commuted to a similar penalty at Ceuta.

An analogous case is reported in a text of 1454 (May 18).[53] A certain Afomso do Porto was sent to the Azores about 1448 by the governor (*corregedor*) of Entre Douro e Minho, who was carrying out, according to the document, an order of the regent's, Dom Pedro, "to send all the exiles he could to colonize the said islands which should now begin to be inhabited." Perhaps colonization by exiles was again applied to São Miguel which in 1447 belonged to Dom Pedro. Afomso do Porto, in any case, obtained his release from banishment and was able to return to Portugal.

That this banishment was actually meant for São Miguel would seem even more likely from a document of 1455 (April 10) by which the King remitted the penalty of a

[51] H. Livermore, *A New History of Portugal* (Cambridge, 1966), p. 116.

[52] Silva Marques, *op. cit.*, II, 344, no. 223.   [53] *Ibid.*, I, 517, no. 406.

woman from Lisbon who had been banished to São Miguel; she had been accused of the murder of a child who had actually been the victim of Moorish slaves. This banishment too had been decreed by Dom Pedro. The woman had married in the Azores and her husband wanted to return alone to Portugal. Her mother in Lisbon requested and obtained annulment of the penalty imposed ten years earlier. If this chronological fact is accurate, Dom Pedro must have been in possession of São Miguel since 1445.[54]

On May 19, 1460, by an order issued to Frey Gonçalo Velho, "my knight and captain for me in my islands of Santa Maria and São Miguel in the Azores," Henry the Navigator set out the regulations for civil and penal justice on these islands.[55] Civil jurisdiction belonged to the judges of the islands. Appeal could be made to the captain and, over him, to the Infante. There was no appeal in cases of lower penal justice; prosecution was in the hands of the captain. In cases of higher justice, the captain's judgments could be appealed to the Infante and, above him, to the King. Every higher appeal had first to be made through the Infante, which meant that direct appeal to the King was forbidden. This again was almost certainly a personal interpretation of the Infante, who attached such importance to it that he provided for a penalty of 1,000 reis to be paid to his chancery if this provision were not observed. There must have been conflict over jurisdiction between the Infante and the royal tribunal, because immediately after this, there follows a provision that if the notary made a mistake—if he drew up a case in contradiction to the Prince's orders—he would be dismissed by the captain. This provision was certainly linked with the conflict over powers of jurisdiction and appeal, as was also clear from a previous passage dealing with documents concerning damage or testimony which could only be established by the notary. The royal tribunal therefore had probably tried to make the Infante's notary an in-

[54] *Ibid.,* p. 524, no. 413.   [55] *Ibid.,* p. 569, no. 446.

strument of its own authority. Moreover, licenses for the colonization of Santa Maria and São Miguel should have been granted by the central administration, since the Infante gave the order to arrest Diogo Lopes and Rodrigo de Bayona, two prospective settlers, if they appeared on the island without a license issued by him, and to send them away as his prisoners.

In 1460, shortly before his death, Henry the Navigator took a series of measures concerning his islands, the first being on August 22, for Jesu Christo (Terceira) and Graciosa in the Azores.[56] He gave these islands to the Infante Dom Ferdinand "my most appreciated and beloved son" [57] and to his male heirs in direct line, with the exception of the *espritualidade* (spiritual rule) which was reserved for the Order of Christ, which would receive, with this object the twentieth of the revenues of the island, or half the Prince's tithe.[58] In each island a *vigario* of the Order would watch over the ecclesiastical administration. These vicars were suggested by the beneficiary and appointed by the Order. The King confirmed this charter on September 2.[59]

The ecclesiastical administration of the Madeira Islands was controlled by a charter granted by the Infante to the Order of Christ on September 18, 1460.[60] He gave these islands to the King, but he made exception for the *espritualidade,* which belonged to the Order of Christ. He declared, moreover, that he had not previously granted any charter concerning the ecclesiastical administration, but we know,

[56] *Ibid.,* p. 574, no. 450.

[57] This Ferdinand was a younger brother of King Alfonso V and the adopted son of Henry the Navigator. He bore the titles of Duke of Béja and Lord of Moura. On November 14, 1457 the King had given him the islands which his ships and crews could discover, keeping for himself the right of appeal in cases of higher penal justice (*Ibid.,* p. 453, no. 425).

[58] The passage concerning the revenues of the Order is not clear in the charter. I interpret it on the basis of the charter for the Order on Terceira and Graciosa dated September 18, 1460 (*Ibid.,* p. 582, no. 456) which is discussed below.

[59] *Ibid.,* p. 576, no. 451.   [60] *Ibid.,* p. 579, no. 454.

from the document of 1450 for Jacques of Bruges, that the Order at that time enjoyed certain rights on Madeira as well as on Terceira. Thus there was now established for the Madeiras by law what had already existed in fact. An analogous situation had existed since 1450 on Terceira, but it was ratified and somewhat modified, as far as the amount of the ecclesiastical taxes was concerned, in the gift to the Infante Ferdinand of 1460, which moreover created similar conditions on Graciosa. On Madeira, according to the charter we are examining, a *vigario* already existed. The chaplains were supposed to say a mass every Saturday for the repose of the soul of the Infante.

On September 18, 1460, the Infante granted the islands of Santa Maria and São Miguel in the Azores to the Order of Christ,[61] which seemed to be a ratification of an existing situation. The Infante declared, in fact, that "I gave several years ago my islands of São Miguel and Santa Maria to the said Order." But there had never been a charter of gift, and before the Infante became sick, he regulated the judicial situation on Santa Maria and São Miguel, doing it in a very personal way, in the charter of May 19, 1460, discussed above. He had addressed himself then to "Frey" Gonçalo Velho as captain, but the latter was also a member of the Order of Christ. Was this a means of simplifying the eventual transfer to the Order? Was it even a kind of guarantee to the Order? We cannot answer these questions. In any case, the Infante on September 18 gave the islands to the Order with a more normal judicial situation than in the charter of May 19. Henceforth the appeal in the higher courts of justice would go to the King, but "with appeal to the Order." This was infinitely more vague than the wording of the May 19 document, but it allowed for an arrangement to the advantage of the Order of Christ. Here, too, masses for the repose of the soul of the Infante were to be celebrated.

Also on September 18 the religious administration of Jesu

[61] *Ibid.*, p. 580, no. 455.

Christo (Terceira) and Graciosa, whose secular possession had been given to the Infante Ferdinand on August 22, passed to the Order of Christ [62] with a twentieth part of the revenues of these islands, which would be used to support the *vigarios* of the Order. Once again masses would be said.

On the same day, the Infante gave to the King the islands of São Luis, São Dinis, São Jorge, São Tomas and Santa Iria in the Azores.[63] He called them all "my islands"; he kept the religious administration for himself and for the Order of Christ; he granted the latter a twentieth part of the revenues of the islands and the nomination of *vigarios* at the King's suggestion.

In his will of October 28, 1460, the Infante made a gift of Madeira, Porto Santo, and "Guinea com suas ilhas" to the King and made him executor of his will: "Likewise I beg the King my lord that he would be my executor, for his is everything mentioned in this my will and I make him the heir of all that belongs to me." [64] By this document the Infante recognized the King's supreme dominion over all his possessions. It is peculiar that he should give everything to the King without taking into account the gifts he had already made to the Infante Ferdinand and to the Order of Christ where Terceira, Graciosa, Santa Maria, and São Miguel were concerned. Thus now he presented things as the King felt they should be presented: the final decision on the distribution of the islands could only belong to the sovereign and to him alone because he held the right of eminent domain. It is nonetheless striking that the Infante should give to the King islands which the latter already held under his sovereignty or suzerainty and that this gift, as far as the four islands whose useful domain had been given to the Infante Ferdinand and to the Order of Christ were concerned,

[62] *Ibid.*, p. 581, no. 456.

[63] *Ibid.*, p. 583, no. 457. Ramos Coelho, *op. cit.*, p. 27, gives only the registry of this charter but mentions by mistake the Cape Verde Islands.

[64] Silva Marques, *op. cit.*, p. 589, no. 461.

could only, at least in the mind of Henry the Navigator, have bearing on the eminent domain which the King possessed by law in his capacity of suzerain. As for the Madeiras which were given in this document to the King, the Infante had already declared in his charter of September 18 for the Order of Christ that he had given them to the sovereign. The documentary verification of this gift therefore was only made in the will.

After the death of the Infante (November 13) the King gave to the Infante Ferdinand, on December 3, 1460, all the islands concerned in the preceding charters, including the two islands of the Azores bequeathed to the Order of Christ, and, in addition, a series of Cape Verde Islands which had not been mentioned in previous documents.[65] These islands were Madeira, Porto Santo, Deserta in the Madeiras, São Luis, São Dinis, São Jorge, São Tomas, Santa Iria, Jesu Christo, Graciosa, São Miguel, and Santa Maria in the Azores, and "ylha de Sam Jacobo e Felipe, ylha de las Mayaes, ylha de San Christovam e ylha Lana" in the Cape Verde archipelago. This gift was made "with all rents, rights and jurisdiction that belong to us in them and that we should have by right, as the Infant Dom Anrique, my uncle, who is with God, held them from us.

On September 19, 1462, the King gave a series of islands to Dom Ferdinand,[66] who now held, as well as his former titles, those which previously belonged to Henry the Navigator: Duke of Viseu and Lord of Covilham. The Infante laid claim to the prior gift of 1457.[67] The new gift was made "com toda juridiçom civell, crime, reservando pera nos feitos crimes, alçada nos cassos em que caiba morte ou talhamento de membro" (with all civil and penal jurisdiction, reserving for us among criminal cases, appeal on cases of death penalty or mutilation). The Portuguese wording is not very clear, and the distinction between "crimes," over which the Infante

---

[65] *Ibid.*, p. 593, no. 464.　　　[66] Ramos Coelho, *op. cit.*, p. 31.
[67] See note 56 above.

had jurisdiction, and "feitos crimes," over which the King retained power, remains mysterious. However if we read "nos" twice before "feitos," everything becomes clear.[68] Thus one could translate: "reserving for ourselves in penal cases the appeal of suits involving the death penalty or mutilation." The islands concerned here are the five discovered by Antonio da Noli, plus an additional seven—that is, the entire Cape Verde archipelago. The nomenclature is somewhat modified in comparison with that of the decree of December 3, 1460, mentioned above.[69] The rights of the Infante over these islands were very extensive. They concerned "seigneury and colonists, with all the rivers, anchorages, woods, fisheries, coral, dyes, mines," i.e. all rights concerning shipping, fishing, coral fishing, mining, and wood used for dyes. The Infante could enforce all the "foros, direitos e trabutos," i.e. grant constitutional privileges [70] and impose taxes.

The last seven islands of the Cape Verde archipelago were discovered by Diogo Afonso, squire of the Infante Ferdinand, as we learn from a decree of October 29, 1462,[71] by which King Alfonso V gave to his brother an island which had been seen to the west-northwest of the Canaries and the Madeiras by a certain Gomçallo Fernamdes, originally from Tavira. This island had not yet been formally discovered, but the King was granting it nevertheless, "with all rents and rights, power, jurisdiction, as the Infante has the said seven islands that we gave him."

Some equally enigmatic islands were the object of a royal gift to Joham Voguado "knight of our house and clerk of our administration," on February 19, 1462.[72] They were Lono and Capraria, two islands which can be found on previous maps [73] and which are actually a part of the Azores, but un-

[68] Later the phrase appears with "nos" twice.
[69] See also Chapter 8, pp. 162–163.   [70] See above, p. 207.
[71] Ramos Coelho, *op. cit.*, p. 32.   [72] *Ibid.*, p. 28.
[73] Lono is obviously a corruption of Lovo or Luovo which appears on the maps made during the second half of the fourteenth century. Cap-

der different names. The address of the decree is characteristic:

To all those who will see this our charter: let it be known that in
the parts of the Ocean Sea whose conquest has been given to us by
privilege of the Holy Father, there were found two islands, not yet
inhabited by anybody, nor given to anybody who should colonize
them; which islands according to the sea-maps are called the one
the island Lono and the other Capraria, and since to us belongs
the right of having occupied deserted and abandoned places,
which God gave us, so that we may have the government of these
nations and seigneuries.

This is the first reference to the Pope's allocation to the
king of Portugal of islands to be conquered in the ocean.
Moreover, mention is made of the obligation imposed by God
on the king to colonize these islands. A similar obligation had
been invoked in the charter of Henry the Navigator of 1450
for Jacques of Bruges. In addition it is curious to note that
Lono and Capraria actually correspond to Santa Maria and
São Miguel of the Azores, which had been colonized long
ago.[74]

Whatever the situation, Joham Voguado received these
islands in "pure and irrevocable gift valid for living persons,
with hereditary rights, for him and all his descendents." The
king kept for himself, as was the custom, only the right of
appeal in cases of higher penal justice "for we wish and are
pleased that all the rest, criminal or civil, he have without
any appeal above him." The colonists would enjoy the same
rights as those on Madeira.[75] Joham Voguado could grant his
islands a *foral* or constitutional privilege "which *foral*, to be
given by him, we wish to be firm and valid as if it had been
given by us." Trade (*traucto*) in the products of the islands
was free "inasmuch as it is not done with infidels and does

raria dates from the same period. See K. Kretschmer, *Die italienischen
Portolane des Mittelalters* (Berlin, 1901), p. 687.

[74] Kretschmer, *loc. cit.*   [75] Ramos Coelho, *op. cit.*, p. 28.

not concern items prohibited by the Holy Church." This prohibition against trading with the infidels came from the papal
ordonnances. We shall return to it shortly when we examine
the rights granted by the Pope over the ocean domains mentioned above. Finally, the beneficiary could transfer the possession of his islands to whomever he wished "since from
now on we forego and abdicate all seigneury in rights or
profits, and place, transmit, and hand them over to the said
Joham Voguado and his successors for all time." This formula through which there was the risk that the supreme
power of the king might disappear, was obviously too broad,
especially where the law (*direito*) was concerned, since appeal in cases of higher penal justice remained the prerogative
of the royal tribunal. Actually there was very little risk that
the king would see his power diminished, for the "real"
islands of Santa Maria and São Miguel belonged to his
brother Dom Ferdinand!

The references to the Pope's intervention, in the justifi-
cation of Portuguese conquests, and of the Church where
trade with the infidels was concerned, are allusions to the
famous bull *Romanus pontifex* of January 8, 1455.[76] This
bull enlarged the right of conquest which the Pope had
acknowledged in favor of the Portuguese in the bull *Dum
diversas* of June 18, 1452.[77] In 1452, the Pope was thinking
only of the Moors of Morocco; in 1455, he was worried about
all the territories to the south of Cape Bojador and of Cape
Non. As for the prohibition of trade with the infidels, the
bull of 1455 excepted the king of Portugal, who could
engage in this commerce so long as he did not deal in
"iron, wood, gear, ships or weapons." [78] This enables us to

[76] Silva Marques, *op. cit.,* I, 503, no. 401, where it is given the erroneous date of 1454.

[77] L. M. Jordão, *Bullarium patronatus Portugalliae regum in Ecclesiis
Africae, Asiae atque Oceaniae* (Lisbon, 1868), I (1171–1600), p. 22.

[78] For the 1455 bull see my article "Navigateurs, marchands et colons
italiens," pp. 469 ff.; and for a detailed analysis of the relations between

understand what was meant by trade with the infidels mentioned in the charter of 1462 for Voguado.

The request for the concession of islands whose existence was not known for certain became a common occurrence in Portugal at that time. There seems to have been a feverish desire for discoveries. Thus in 1473 (January 12) the Infanta Dona Brites, widow of the Infante Ferdinand, asked the king for an island for her children that had been seen from Santiago in the Cape Verde archipelago and which the Infante, her husband, must have had searched for in vain. In the event that the Infanta's ships found this island, it would be granted to her children, just as the eldest son had received the other islands possessed by his father.[79] The island possessions of Henry the Navigator increased by the discoveries made under the Infante Ferdinand had therefore been passed on to his young son.

On June 21 of the same year Ruy Gonçalves da Camara, who had faithfully served the king in Africa, received any island which he would be able to discover with his ships. The gift was hereditary and another example of a very imprecise gift.[80] There was more detail in a decree of Alfonso V's for Fernão Telles in 1474 (January 28).[81] This Fernão Telles was a member of the Royal Council and governor of the house of the King's daughter. He received "whatever island he may find or that may be found by those whom he would send to colonize, provided they would not be situated in the parts of Guinea." Thus these islands were situated beyond the

---

the Pope and Portugal, see C. M. de Witte, "Les bulles pontificales et l'expansion portugaise au XVᵉ siècle," *Revue d'histoire ecclésiastique,* XLVIII (1953), XLIX (1954), LI (1956), and LIII (1958); especially concerning the Bull of 1455 in vol. LI, pp. 428–453.

[79] Ramos Coelho, *op. cit.,* p. 37.

[80] Mentioned *ibid.;* text in M. Monteiro Velho Arruda, *Colecção de documentos relativos ao descobrimento e povoamento dos Açores* (Ponta Delgada, 1932), p. 41.

[81] Ramos Coelho, *op. cit.,* p. 38.

Cape Verde archipelago. Here again it is a question of islands "in the parts of the Oceanic Sea," as in the decree of February 19, 1462, mentioned above. The reference to the "Oceanic Sea" was certainly another reflection of the ideology manifested in the bull of 1455 where the ocean is mentioned several times in connection with Portuguese expansion.[82] The gift was approved by the Crown Prince who, as we shall see, had meanwhile received the islands of the Cape Verde archipelago. The beneficiary had to acknowledge the right of appeal to the sovereign in cases of higher penal justice. Again the colonists were granted the privileges accorded the inhabitants of Madeira, and Telles could grant a *foral*. He was given freedom to trade. The King renounced his dominion (*senhorio*), but the formula is clearer than in the gift of 1462 to Voguado and it is obvious that it concerned useful dominion ("direitos como utill ou proveytoso"). In addition, Telles was given the islands "which are called Foreyras" discovered by Diogo de Teyve, whom we know as a sugar producer on Madeira, and his son Joham. The latter had inherited the islands at his father's death and had given them up to Telles on contract. The King ratified this contract.

Fernão Telles obtained a new decree on November 10, 1475.[83] It contained the provision that if the beneficiary should find the island of the "sete Cidades" or another island already inhabited, the population of these islands would come under his authority. The Island of the Seven Cities was one of the legendary islands of the Atlantic Ocean.[84] The King had formerly granted Henry the Navigator, and after him his own son, the heir apparent, the privilege that only they would be authorized to go to the islands of Guinea or be able

[82] See my article "Navigateurs, marchands et colons italiens," pp. 469 ff.

[83] Ramos Coelho, *op. cit.*, pp. 40 ff.

[84] W. H. Babcock, *Legendary islands of the Atlantic* (New York, 1922), pp. 68 ff.; Babcock, however, does not mention our document. See also Chapter 9, pp. 187–192.

to trade there without royal permission. Telles obtained a similar advantage for the inhabited islands which he or his ships could discover, on condition "that the said islands should not be in the seas close to Guinea, since I have given these to my said son, and that they should not have been given for trade and navigation to my subjects of the realms of Castile and Portugal." The heir apparent thus held an analogous privilege for the whole Guinea area—at that time as far as the islands of Fernando Po, Principe, and São Tomé at the eastern end of the Gulf of Guinea.[85] Moreover, the King now claimed Castile and, as a result, had to take into account privileges relating to colonial trade granted not only to the Portuguese but also to Castilians. This latter point naturally concerned the archipelago of the Canaries. With regard to the Portuguese commercial privileges we are immediately reminded of the type of commercial monopoly previously granted to Fernão Gomes.[86]

There was yet another island still to be discovered in a decree of June 30, 1484, by which John II gave to Fernam Dominguez do Arco, of Madeira, the captaincy of the island in question. This captaincy would be held from the King in the same tradition as that of Madeira.[87] In 1485 (September 24) the King granted the captaincy of São Tomé to João de Paiva.[88] By this decree the institution of captaincy spread as far as the Gulf of Guinea. On January 11, 1486, João de Paiva disposed of half of the island, and on March 14, 1486, it appeared that the other half would go to the future husband of his daughter.[89] These two deeds of gift have not been published by Ramos Coelho, so that it is not possible to know their purport with certainty. However it is not difficult

---

[85] Fontoura da Costa in *História da expansão portuguesa no mundo,* I, 357 ff.

[86] *Ibid.,* p. 358. As for Alfonso V's claims to Castile, it must be emphasized that the deed was drawn up in Zamora (Spain); see Livermore, *op. cit.,* pp. 119 ff.

[87] Ramos Coelho, *op. cit.,* p. 56.   [88] *Ibid.*   [89] *Ibid.,* p. 57.

to reconstruct this development hypothetically. The colonization of São Tomé began in 1485 under the leadership of João de Paiva, who kept for himself a part of the captaincy and had it ratified by the King in January 1486. Then he requested that the other half be reserved for the future husband of his daughter. This is along the same lines as the provisions made on Terceira for the daughters of Jacques of Bruges.[90]

After the concession granted to Jacques in 1450, Flemings began to play an important role in the Azores, as we have seen.[91] Jacques had left Terceira before April 2, 1474, and at that time he was thought to be dead. In fact the Infanta Dona Brites, widow of the Infante Fernando, at that time regulated Jacques' succession.[92] Examination of the decree of January 12, 1473, shows that she had this power of regulation since she administered the island domain of her minor son, the Infante Diogo.

The Infanta declared that, since Jacques' widow could provide no precise information concerning the disappearance of her husband, João Vaz Corte Real should be given the captaincy as a reward for the services he had rendered the dead Infante and their son Don Diogo. He would have the right to choose one of the two halves of Terceira: Praya or Angra. The latter had for some time—apparently since 1471—belonged to Alvaro Martins Homem. Was Jacques of Bruges already dead then? It is impossible to know; but even if he was still on Terceira in 1471, this would not raise any difficulty, since a captaincy had been similarly shared on Madeira; we have even seen a captaincy on São Tomé which was originally whole, having been later divided, and we know that in the Cape Verde archipelago, Antonio da Noli, at the end of his stay only held part of his island in captaincy.[93]

[90] See Chapter 9, pp. 183–184.   [91] See Chapter 9.
[92] Charter published by Drummond in *Annaes da ilha Terceira*, I, 493, and in *Archivo dos Açores*, IV, 159.
[93] See Chapter 8, p. 174.

Perhaps, after all, Alvaro Martins Homem had married Jacques' younger daughter and had thus been more readily recognized as captain. If he married either of the daughters it must have been the younger, since the eldest daughter had married the English nobleman Duarte Paim, as we learn from the *Saudades da Terra,* written in the sixteenth century by the Azorean Gaspar Fructuoso. Paim even claimed the captaincy, but he did not obtain it because he could not put forward the charter of 1450,[94] which proves that at the time of the court case, the provisions concerning the rights of his wife were not considered illegal, but no proof was offered. That the rights of the younger daughter should have been respected once she had married Homem should not surprise us, since the latter already possessed part of the island when Corte Real became captain. He had also rendered services in the discoveries, and moreover he was not a foreigner like Paim. Homem had anyway to give in to Corte Real who preferred the part that had originally been given to him, and was given the other half by a charter of February 12, 1474.[95]

We should add, moreover, that the hypothesis of a marriage between Homem and the younger daughter of Jacques of Bruges is not even necessary, since we have examples of divisions of captaincies in other places. Even on Terceira the captaincy had been subsequently divided, as we know from our examination of the career of Ferdinand van Olmen.

Various gifts of islands were still made before the end of the century. On May 30, 1489, John II gave to the Duke of Beja the right to trade and the "senhorio" of Guinea from Cape Ponta da Galé to the spot—six miles beyond Cape Verde—where the first commercial relations with the Joloff chief Gudumel were initiated by Lourenço Dias, inhabitant of Lagos and squire of Henry the Navigator. The gift

[94] J. Mees, *Histoire de la découverte des îles Açores et de l'origine de leur dénomination d'îles flamandes* (Ghent, 1901), p. 89.
[95] Drummond, *Annaes,* I, 490.

included all the rivers, islands, and islets. Another gift from King Manuel to João Fernandes, on October 28, 1499, granted him the captaincy over any island that he discovered. On May 11, 1500, the same prince gave Gaspar Corte Real whatever islands and territories he could discover.[96]

Before ending, I would like to examine two decrees of 1502 and 1506 concerning islands in the Atlantic Ocean. The first was a gift from King Manuel, on January 15, 1502, to Miguel Corte Real, a nobleman of the King's retinue.[97] He had invested money in an expedition his brother Gaspar made to Newfoundland, but, since his brother had not returned, Miguel requested permission to go and look for him on condition that he had royal confirmation of the renunciation promised by his brother of part of the land to be discovered. In that part he would have jurisdiction, revenues, and captaincy. In the case of his brother's death, the King would give to him all that his brother had been able to discover.

On September 17, 1506, another brother, Vasqueannes Corte Real, obtained a similar privilege.[98] The text includes the gift to Gaspar Corte Real of 1500. The latter obtained "the captaincies with civil and penal jurisdiction with all kinds of appeals for him and his heirs and successors, without permission for anybody to appeal for whatsoever case or amount to any royal court." Thus in this case there would be no appeal to the king; jurisdiction was entirely in the hands of the beneficiary. Perhaps this might be explained, as in several other cases, by the distance that separated these territories from the seat of royal power. The king reserved only the right to send a functionary into the territories of Corte Real to control his administration, but Corte Real could not be suspended. He could be punished, however, and eventually he must submit to the royal tribunal for this purpose; his domain would mean-

[96] Ramos Coelho, *op. cit.*, pp. 65, 95, 123.   [97] *Ibid.*, p. 131.
[98] *Ibid.*, p. 150.

while be governed by a person appointed by him but with the agreement of the king. The king would draw up a *foral* in which his own revenues for the territory would be determined. From these revenues Corte Real would receive one quarter. If the king traded in that area, a quarter of the revenues would return to the beneficiary. This clause would apply equally if the king leased his right of trading there or granted a license to that effect. In the case of free trade, Corte Real could only apply the normal rights which were coming to him. Mills, salt, machinery (*engenhos*), irrigation pipes, "and all that the captains of the other islands hold by virtue of our gifts"—all this would belong to him.

We are dealing, then, with a decree which describes the typical institutional content of the captaincy at the beginning of the sixteenth century. Normal succession would be through the males in a direct line, but the eldest daughter could also inherit if there were no sons, or even the nearest relative, male or female. It was expressly declared that the "ley memtall," which excluded women, did not apply. In fact, this had been the rule for a long time in the case of gifts of distant lands. Since Gaspar and Miguel Corte Real had undertaken the expedition at their own expense, since Vasqueannes had done so also, and since the first two had died, their rights, as they were described in the preceding gifts, would pass to Vasqueannes and his descendants.

Thus the grant of a captaincy was considered formally as compensation for the investments and personal risk assumed by discoverers and undertakers of colonization. This had in fact always been the case, but until the document of September 17, 1506, it had never been so apparent.[99]

[99] "And taking into account that the said Gaspar Corte Real, his brother, was the first discoverer of the said lands, at his own expense, with much trouble and risk of his person, and that finally, with many servants and men, that he had with him, he died and also that later Miguel Corte Real, his brother, who was our court janitor, going to research his said brother with ships and crews, which he equipped at his

I end here the non-American series of Portuguese concessions of colonial territories in the Atlantic zone which it was my intention to review in this chapter. Of course, in order to gain a total view of the evolution of feudal and demesnial forms of Portuguese colonization in the Atlantic zone, one would have to go on to examine captaincies in Brazil and even on the continent of Africa. I intend to do both in a future book, but I would like, as a sort of provisionary conclusion, to recall here, some of the most important facts we have established.

The oldest colonial tenure we have studied is the one granted by King Ferdinand to the Genoese Lanzarotto Malocello. It permits us to see that the Portuguese system of colonial tenures was established in the fourteenth century, during what I have called the first phase of Portuguese colonial expansion, and did not begin in the fifteenth century, as is generally believed.

The history of colonial concessions in the Madeiras during the time of Henry the Navigator has been examined in detail. We have established that demesnial and feudal forms of colonization had by then developed much more than in the fourteenth century and in a constantly reciprocal relationship. It is apparent that Henry wanted to profit

---

own expense, which cost him much of his fortune, to research and find his said brother and also to serve us by discovering the said lands, for which he took as much trouble as he could, and, after his said brother, he died likewise and with him many servants of his and his father's and of the said Vasqueannes, whom he had taken with him, and considering that in this whole feat the said Vasqueannes with his own fortune, servants and men always helped his said brothers, and even today pays from his own the debts and bonds that for this cause his said brother left, therefore it is but reasonable that the praise and merit of the service in which his said brothers ended their lives be perpetuated in the said Vasqueannes Corte Real and in those who from him are descended; we by the present charter declare successor to our said gift the said Vasqueannes Corte Real and all his heirs and successors" (*Ibid.*, p. 152).

personally from the minority of Alfonso V to secure the judicial autonomy of his insular domain by reserving the right of appeal for the royal tribunal. This attempt was doomed to failure in the Madeiras, but it persisted in the Azores, and traces of its effects may be seen in the will of the Navigator in 1460. In the same way a particular council of Henry's for the administration of Madeira appeared in a deed of 1457. It would be valuable to examine these tendencies toward autonomy with regard to the insular possessions of the Portuguese princes, not only in Henry the Navigator's time, but also in the last decades of the fifteenth century.

Although we only have express evidence of *sesmaria* for the first time on Madeira in 1457, the practice goes back at least to 1440, as we have seen in this chapter. But here again it is necessary to take into account the evolution after the epoch we have examined in order to trace a picture of the whole. As far as the Azores are concerned, I have tried to estimate the role of the Flemings who held positions from the Portuguese Crown during their colonization of these islands in the fifteenth century.

Finally, I believe that examining as a whole the concessions of islands and lands yet to be discovered in the western Atlantic during the last decades of the fifteenth century opens up new perspectives, not only on the evolution of colonial tenure in keeping with the spirit of the institutions of the period, but also on the actual importance of Portuguese voyages to the West about this time. In this aspect, as in several others, the examination of specific examples must by necessity precede the reconstruction of the institutional evolution. As far as that evolution is concerned it would seem that, since the fifteenth century, those who undertook colonization regarded the colonial concessions as a reward for their work, a reward which the most important of them tried to use effectively to increase their autonomy.

The Crown, on the other hand, tried—nearly always with success—to reduce that autonomy to proportions fitting the prestige and authority of the centralized and increasingly absolute monarchy.

Index

Cortereal (or Corte Real), João Vaz, 185, 194, 234
Cortez, 23
Corvo, Azores, 221
Covenant, 9, 10
Covilham, Pero da, 107, 194
Crete, 5, 11, 20, 31, 70, 83, 94, 97
Crimea, 5, 7
Crusade colonies, 9
Crusade principalities, 5
Crusade seigneuries, 5
Cuba, 22, 23, 25
Cyprus, 5, 9, 19, 31, 71, 89, 91, 97
kingdom, 11, 81, 83
Cyrenaica, 54

Dabte (Daute), realm of, Tenerife, 150
Democracy, 55, 59
Dias, Bartolomeu, 73, 192, 194, 195
Diogo, Portuguese prince, 234
Dominica, Lesser Antilles, 25
Duarte, king of Portugal, 206, 216

Egypt, 91, 94
Embriaci, Genoese noblemen, 12
Emperor, 62
Empoli, Giovanni da, 110, 111
Encomendero, 40
Encomienda, 40
Engenhos, 23, 109, 211, 237
England, 74, 123, 142
Enlightenment, 69
Epirus, 95
Española, 128; *see also* Haiti
Estreito, Joham Afomso do, Portuguese colonist on Madeira, 186, 190
Europe, geographic, 52-54, 69, 71
Europe, historic, 52-59, 69, 71, 75, 76
Exiles, 222

Famagusta, 89, 91
Fayal, Azores, 185, 186, 190
Fazendeiros, 15
Ferdinand, king of Portugal, 100, 204, 219, 238
Ferdinand, king of Spain, 113-131, 175, 178, 196
Ferdinand, Portuguese prince, 162, 166, 168, 172, 184, 186, 224, 226, 227
Fernandes, João, Portuguese explorer, 194, 236

Fernandez Cabrón, Pedro, Genoese colonizer, 125, 196
Fernando Po, 233
Feudalism, 63-66, 222
Fief, colonial, 16, 205, 209, 218, 238, 239
Flanders, 123, 142, 185
Flemish colonists, 181, 186, 239
Flemish Isles, 181
Florence, 102, 105, 119
Florentines, 99, 101, 121
Flores, Azores, 186
Fonduk (warehouse), 12, 80
Fonte, Miguel, Catalan merchant, 153
Fonte, Rafael, Catalan merchant, 152, 153
Foral (pl. *forais*), 207, 209, 229, 232, 237
Forbin, Jean, merchant of Marseille, 104
France, 40, 46, 54, 143
Frangoumates, 82
French, 92
Funchal, 134, 214, 217
Fundamental Orders, 10

Galgala, 18
Gallipoli, 92
Gama, Vasco da, 73, 110, 194
Garachico, Tenerife, 154
Genghis Khan, 71
Genoa, 66, 72, 80, 100, 105, 117, 119, 143
government, 93
Genoese, 5, 22, 24, 29, 70, 72, 80, 83, 88, 91, 92, 99, 103, 118, 121, 124, 129, 206
Germany, 64
Gibelet, 80
Giraldi, Luca, Florentine merchant, 110
Giustiniano, Tommaso, Genoese merchant, 137, 151, 152
Gold Coast, 171, 178
Gold trade, 171
Gomera, Canary Islands, 22, 142, 204
Gomes, Diogo, Portuguese discoverer, 163
Gomez, Fernam, Portuguese merchant, 169, 178, 233
Gonçalves, Gil, colonist of Madeira, 214

Siberia, 58

Sicily, 20, 27, 40, 54, 114, 116, 117, 119, 123, 124

Sidon, 18

Sierra Leone, 171

Siklābi, 36

Slave Coast, 30

Slave revolt, 25

Slave societies, 44

Slave trade, 23, 24, 28, 47, 48, 50, 83, 87, 88, 94, 108, 124, 146, 155

Slavery:
  colonial, 26-32, 40-51
  medieval colonial, 31, 39
  medieval European, 34-38
  penal, 43, 44

Slaves, 11, 19, 149, 152, 155, 171
  Abkhas, 85
  Albanian, 93
  Berber, 154
  Bulgarian, 86
  Caucasian, 29, 85
  Circassian, 85, 93
  domestic, 47, 81, 90, 91, 96
  freed, 40, 44, 82, 91
  Greek, 29, 31, 89, 93, 95
  Guinean, 46
  Hungarian, 86
  Indian, 22, 42, 43, 44, 45
  Jewish, 91
  Lezghian, 85
  Mongol, 79, 85
  Moslem, 37, 38, 39, 40, 85, 90
  Mozarab, 90
  Negro, 22, 24, 25, 30, 38, 39, 46, 47, 48, 79, 90, 91, 125, 141, 146, 153, 156
  Negro, in Europe, 29, 38, 39
  Russian, 86
  Serb, 90, 93
  Slav, 36
  Slavonian, 90, 93
  Sudanese, 46
  Tartar, 93
  Turk, 39
  Zyguian, 86

Smyrna, 90

Soberani, Italian merchants, 151

Social mobility, 69

Sorchati, Crimea, 84

Soviet system, 53

Spain, 27, 40, 44, 46, 48, 54, 90

Spices, 111

Spinola, Gaspar, Genoese merchant, 154

Spinola, Oberto, Genoese merchant, 119

Sudan, 29

Sugar-cane plantations, 5, 124, 135, 141, 150, 151

Sugar production, 17-26, 70, 127, 128, 137, 139, 151, 156, 217

Sugar trade, 144, 145, 153

Sulciman the Magnificent, 72

Sweden, 74

Syria, 18, 81

Tamerlane, 71

Tana, Russia, 31, 94

Tartars, 29, 31, 45, 85

Techniques, Italian, 130

Technology, 50

Teive (Teyve), Diogo de, Portuguese explorer, 193, 216, 232

Teixeira, Tristão Vaz, Portuguese colonizer, 206, 208

Telles, Fernão, Portuguese explorer, 187, 189, 231

Tenerife, 22, 125, 126, 135, 146, 147, 150, 151

Terceira, Azores, 175, 182, 184, 185, 186, 190, 193, 221, 224, 225, 226, 234

Teutonic Order, 18

Textiles production, 139

Tiberias, 18

Tortosa, Palestine, 80

Toscanelli, Paolo del Pozzo, 187, 190

Transportation, maritime, 70-72

Trebizond, 94

Tripoli, 18, 80

Turks, Ottoman, 71, 95
  Seljuk, 65, 81

Tyre, 12, 18, 70, 80

United States, 74, 76

Usselinx, Dutch merchant, 10

Valencia, 20, 115, 117, 120, 156

Van der Haegen, Willem, Flemish colonizer, 185, 186

Van Olmen, Ferdinand, Flemish discoverer, 181, 184, 186-195, 235